To the memory of Joseph B. Strum

BRANDEIS: BEYOND PROGRESSIVISM

Philippa Strum

UNIVERSITY PRESS OF KANSAS

Published by the University Press of Kansas (Lawrence, Kansas 66049), which was
organized by the Kansas Board of Regents and is operated and funded by Emporia
State University, Fort Hays State University, Kansas State University, Pittsburg State
University, the University of Kansas, and Wichita State University

Library of Congress Cataloging-in-Publication Data

Strum, Philippa.
    Brandeis : beyond progressivism / Philippa Strum.
        p.   cm. — (American political thought)
    Includes bibliographical references and index.
    ISBN 0-7006-0603-3 (hardcover) ISBN 0-7006-0687-4 (pbk.)
    1. Brandeis, Louis Dembitz, 1856–1941. 2. Judges—United States—
Biography. I. Title. II. Series.
KF8745.B67S77   1993
347.73′2634—dc20   93-18649

Printed in the United States of America
10 9 8 7 6 5 4 3 2

CONTENTS

ACKNOWLEDGMENTS

When my biography of Louis Dembitz Brandeis was published in 1984, I thought my involvement with the justice had ended. "Involvement" it was, as the research and writing had been spread over ten years, interspersed with teaching, other publications, childrearing, and all the minutiae of life. My family and friends learned more about Brandeis than they had ever wanted to know. My husband claimed I talked to Brandeis in my sleep. My daughter heard me quoting a journalist to the effect that an interview with Brandeis left the impression that the answers to all the world's problems could be found in Euripides. Her rather caustic comment across the dinner table was, "Well, to listen to you, Mom, it sounds as if all the answers can be found in Brandeis."

Perhaps not. But two decades after I first began reading Brandeis carefully, his ideas are as exciting and as relevant as ever. New scholarly works about him have been published, more of his letters have been unearthed, the attempt to assess his ideas and to apply them to current social problems has proved a never-ending process, and I have had almost ten additional years in which to read and think and regret all the things left unsaid in the biography. So I am grateful to Carey McWilliams and Lance Banning, editors of this series on American political thinkers, for giving me the opportunity to revisit and reexamine Brandeis's thought.

Five colleagues spent an extraordinary and much appreciated amount of time reading through various drafts of the manuscript, commenting on everything from substantive matters to typos and some of my worst manglings of the English language. If there are few factual errors in the book, it is because every word was subjected to the eagle-eyed scrutiny of Melvin I. Urofsky and David W. Levy, editors of the Brandeis *Letters*, whose unfailing generosity to other Brandeis scholars deserves warm acknowledgment. Vincent Blasi, whose article on Brandeis's *Whitney* opinion will no doubt remain a classic, brought his wide range of knowledge to a meticulous and thought-provoking reading of the manuscript. Jill Norgren, whose pointed questions frequently fill the margins of my manuscripts, demonstrated once again her command of scholarly literature and the eclectic point of view that makes her such an invaluable reader. Peter Rajsingh, with his solid command of political theory, taught me how much one can learn from a student and the ways in which the teacher-student role can be reversed and enriched.

David de Lorenzo, curator of manuscripts and archives at the Harvard Law School, was gracious in helping me to track down elusive references. Thanks also are due to Fred Woodward, director of the University Press of Kansas, to production editor Megan Schoeck, and to copy editor Claire Sutton, all of whom were as meticulous about keeping to our time schedule as they challenged me to be.

My father, Joseph B. Strum, began critiquing my writing when I was in elementary school and never stopped. He commented upon, annotated, and frequently proofread almost all my scholarly work. His breadth of information was stunning and his command of English impeccable. I don't believe I ever mastered the intricacies of "who" and "whom" to his satisfaction, a lapse that he bore with his usual wry good humor. He managed to read through and correct this manuscript shortly before he died. I am fortunate to have had him as a friend and an intellectual guide as well as a father, and it is with great love that I dedicate this book to his memory.

INTRODUCTION

In our Democracy, the hopeful sign would be recognition of politics & government as the first of the sciences & of the arts.[1]

Most American political scientists define politics as the struggle to obtain and use power in the public arena.[2] They emphasize process and institutions and the ways in which power is acquired or lost. Those scholars particularly interested in process and power examine phenomena such as elections, media, political consultants, direct mailings, funding and expenditures, negotiations with and among politicians and interest groups, and the relationships among congressional committees, economic interest groups, and the federal bureaucracy. Those choosing to concentrate on institutions and power analyze the formal institutions mandated by the Constitution, the alterations they have undergone during more than two centuries, and the institutions unmentioned in that secular bible but of major current consequence today: political parties, corporations, unions, pressure groups, media, political action committees, the "alphabet agencies" that constitute a major portion of the executive branch, and the White House staff. It is fashionable to stress the "science" in political science rather than the "political," which could imply choices among competing values.

Louis Dembitz Brandeis, by contrast, never specifically defined politics, although politics played a major role in his life. His political ideas are apparent in a number of sources: the political causes with which he chose to be involved; the speeches he made, both as a lawyer

1

and a statesman, during the years before he joined the United States Supreme Court; the articles he wrote about various aspects of American political and economic life, some of them collected into books; the letters he sent to innumerable correspondents; the advice he gave to Woodrow Wilson and Franklin Roosevelt before and during their presidencies; and his Supreme Court opinions. These sources suggest that Brandeis's view was less akin to much of today's American process-oriented political science than to the democratic spirit of Thomas Jefferson. Like other political thinkers and politicians, he cared about power. Unlike many, he emphasized not means but goals, and the purpose most important to him was the establishment, by the government and other institutions, of policies that would best enhance individual fulfillment. Indeed, the only justification for any political, economic, or social institution was its contribution to that overarching goal. Although he believed that the human need for emotional and intellectual interaction necessarily resulted in the creation of community, and although he pointed out the concomitant responsibility of the individual to the community and its well-being, he never forgot that the legitimacy of government — that most formal expression of community — depended upon its serving as the extension of individuals.[3]

His individualism was far from selfish. The individual had always to be treated as subject, never as object; and to whatever extent the state affected the individual, it was justified in doing so only if it extended the individual's freedom. This view, he believed, was what the Founding Fathers had in mind.[4]

Brandeis's emphasis on individual freedom did not imply approval of the self-centered capitalist of the late nineteenth and early twentieth centuries or of the worker whose only interests were private. Crucial to individual fulfillment was a participation in the political process that both contributed to the enhancement of freedom and became an element of individual fulfillment. Brandeis would have agreed with Rousseau that a human being's faculties can be fully exercised and developed only in a civil state, where citizens enjoy the freedom that comes from "obedience to the law one has prescribed for oneself."[5] Similarly, he paralleled John Stuart Mill in viewing fulfillment of "public duty" as aiding in the development of character and of a government that "can fully satisfy all the exigencies of the social state."[6]

Brandeis repeatedly emphasized that human beings had not only rights but responsibilities. The citizen who had adequate time and knowledge to participate in the political process and did not do so was reprehensible, for he or she was guilty of taking without giving. Brandeis became known as "the people's attorney" because of his devotion to public causes—a devotion for which he refused to accept remuneration and in fact spent substantial amounts of his own money as well as his time and energy. He did so out of a conviction that individuals who possessed talents that might help others had an obligation to use them and that involvement in public policymaking was one of the highest forms of civilized behavior. Leaving politics to the politicians was inexcusable. He considered it "obvious" that no democratic government could work well without citizen participation. "It is customary for people to berate politicians," he noted. "But after all, the politicians, even if their motives are not of the purest, come much nearer performing their duties as citizens than the so-called 'good' citizens who stay at home."[7] Just as Mill declared that "the contented man, or the contented family, who have no ambition . . . to promote the good of their country or their neighborhood . . . excite in us neither admiration nor approval,"[8] so Brandeis argued that "public discussion is a political duty" and a nonparticipating citizenry was the "greatest menace to freedom."[9]

His political thought, then, centered on such basic concepts as the individual, liberty, rights, responsibilities, power, justice, human possibilities, and human limitations. Most of these words have been used by a multiplicity of political theorists and politicians. Brandeis, however, combined them into a unique formulation of the ideal state that maximized individual involvement in both the political process and economic decisionmaking and that secured political and economic autonomy in the industrial age. He did not view the state as an entity that would do for others what they could not do for themselves; rather, it was to be both the expression of the cumulative will of individuals and the mechanism by which they would control their own lives.

These premises led to his opposition to bigness in both governmental and economic institutions. The basic unit of democracy is the individual; of capitalism, the dollar and the work unit. Two of the key questions with which Brandeis wrestled were how to reconcile the emphasis on individual dignity implicit in democracy with the emphasis on profits that is so central to capitalism and how to respond to the assertion that capitalism demanded the creation of ever-larger entities. He thought that overly large institutions inevitably lost their ability to think in terms of individuals and to respond to their needs. Worse, they tended to be beyond the intellectual understanding and control of any individual. This problem was as true in the political sphere as it was in the economic. A federal executive branch so big that it could not be comprehended, much less controlled, by the president was as undesirable and dangerous as a corporation whose chief executive officer did not know what the company's departments were doing. Bigness resulted not in the efficiency that often was claimed for it but in sloppiness, inattention to detail, and, ultimately, injustice either to the taxpayers who funded the public bureaucracies or to the workers within a private corporate entity. Perhaps Brandeis would not have agreed that "small is beautiful," but he would have joined Socrates in advocating moderation in all things, including institutional size.

His insistence upon institutions large enough to be efficient but small enough to be controllable was and continues to be misinterpreted by the leaders of the New Deal and their heirs as a sentimental and unsophisticated yearning for an earlier age that could and should not be replicated. Their scorn, coupled with Brandeis's preference for action and short speeches and articles rather than for political treatises, has led to his being ignored as an American political thinker with ideas well worth considering. Today's scholars remember him primarily for the opinions he wrote during his twenty-three years of service on the Supreme Court. Lawyers focus only on the opinions and on his contribution to sociological jurisprudence, which lay in his insistence that facts about society's needs were key in ascertaining whether particular legislation was constitutional.

This response is particularly unfortunate because Brandeis may have had some of the answers to the problems that continue to plague American society. It has become a commonplace for American politicians following in the footsteps of Jimmy Carter and Ronald Reagan to appeal to the electorate's inchoate sense that big government has somehow gotten out of hand; the government repeatedly expresses surprised dismay at the "necessity" to spend taxpayers' money to "bail out" huge corporations on the verge of economic collapse; General

Motors, that exemplar of "bigger is better," is rethinking and retrenching;[10] and neither big government nor big business has demonstrated the will or the knowledge to solve the problems of poverty, homelessness, inequality, individual financial insecurity, or unemployment. Perhaps it is time to revisit Brandeis.

It is conceivable that his ideas, and particularly his rejection of the popular belief that big, centrally managed corporations were not only the organic wave of the future but crucial to the nation's economic well-being, were wrong. The unwillingness of the New Deal to try them out rendered that speculation moot. Anyone who reads Brandeis, however, will find the accusation of naiveté itself naive. Brandeis understood quite well how the economy worked and the impact that his thinking, if implemented, would have on it. That fact can be demonstrated by explaining how his thought reflected his experiences and how experience was filtered through the stubborn insistence on human dignity that was a constant of his life. This book, therefore, is the story not only of his thought but also of the context in which it developed.

Brandeis was not a philosopher, nor, despite his continuous and eclectic reading, did he derive his ideas primarily from books. As a young man he had read Emerson and James, and his approach was both pragmatic and utilitarian, but he would have been puzzled if asked to what school of political thought he belonged. He had premises and first principles. He regularly addressed the question of how to make institutions work in keeping with those principles, but, consonant with both the American distaste for ideology and his view of himself as an activist, he had no interest in producing a treatise expounding his philosophy, nor did he employ the vocabulary of political theory common to the academy. "I have no rigid social philosophy. I have been too intense on concrete problems of practical justice," he maintained.[11] "As a whole, I have not got as much from books as I have from tackling concrete problems," he added. "I have generally run up against a problem, have painfully tried to think it out, with a measure of success, and have then read a book and found to my surprise that some other chap was before me."[12]

Brandeis did not use the theorist's phrase "political virtue," for example, and yet it is implicit in his discussion of civic responsibility. The focal point of his thinking, as that of William James, was the individual.[13] Brandeis had copied passages from James into the notebooks he kept while in law school, and although there is no record of his ever having used the word "pragmatism," his approach to social problems surely can be given that name. The key mechanism he employed to bring the individual and society into harmony was experience. He considered experience filtered through intelligence to be the primary source of knowledge about almost everything, including the way the good state could best be achieved. In this view he paralleled not only James[14] but John Dewey. Interestingly, John Dewey, reviewing Felix Frankfurter's *Mr. Justice Brandeis*, praised Brandeis's "strict adherence to this policy of reference to factual context" and added, "Nor can I imagine any sound social or ethical philosophy in which this idea is not fundamental."[15] Dewey's philosophy of instrumentalism was based on experimentation.[16] He had acknowledged that while there was "real uncertainty and contingency" in the universe and the world was "in some respect . . . incomplete and in the making," there was "in things a grain against which we cannot successfully go." The coexistence of uncertainty and of something immutable required experimentation if truth was to be found: "We cannot even discover what that grain is except as we make this new experiment or that fresh effort . . . in a world where discovery is genuine, error is an inevitable ingredient of reality."[17] Human beings had to use error, "to turn it to account, to make it fruitful."[18] Like Dewey, Brandeis viewed experience and experimentation as good in and of themselves because of the knowledge that could be derived from them. Certainly experience was central to his thought. He learned from it; he regarded speculation without experimentation as useless. His openness to new ideas was one aspect of an extraordinary mind and character; in this, he personified the approach to politics that he espoused. To see *how* his ideas developed may be to understand *why* they took the shape they did.

There were ways in which Brandeis's thought resembled that of late nineteenth-century English reform liberals, although there is no indication that he was familiar with their thinking. Rather, faced with similar problems, he came to many similar solutions. One historian has described the Fabian vision "of a society that was scientifically — which is to say, rationally — organized, in which all the parts were arranged, ordered, regulated, planned, so as to make for the most efficient and equitable whole;"[19] it was a vision that Brandeis shared.

He would not have agreed, however, with their desire to move power from the individual to the state or with their distrust of the average person.[20] Instead, he would have seconded John Dewey's statement that "democratic equality may be construed as individuality";[21] individualism was fostered by political equality and, eventually, by economic equality as well.

There are two additional, unusual elements in Brandeis's thought that should be noted before turning to its evolution and the role that the times in which he lived played in its formulation. The first is the relationship between traditional civil liberties and economic rights; the second is the nature of citizenship.

Americans generally use the term "civil liberties" to connote the individual's right to be free from governmental action. They employ a separate category of "civil rights" to describe equal treatment of all citizens by the government and the government's assumption of responsibility to ensure equal treatment by various private bodies such as employers, places of public accommodation, and universities. Human rights as defined by such post–World War II documents as the Universal Declaration of Human Rights and the International Covenant on Economic, Social and Cultural Rights have included a category more usually found in European polities and generally given the rubric "economic rights": the right to an assured income, to adequate medical treatment, to education.[22] American civil libertarians still are embroiled in the questions of the extent to which such economic rights should be part of national policy and the degree to which they can be subsumed under already existing sections of the Constitution.

Brandeis may have been one of the few major political figures in the twentieth century to adopt a peculiarly American approach that would reject the perceived dichotomy between civil liberties and economic rights. He did not speak of economic rights but of economic liberty, or, rather, of liberty in the economic sphere as part of an all-encompassing liberty that made life worth living. Brandeis used the words "rights" and "liberties" somewhat interchangeably, meaning both the moral demand of the individual to be free from governmental interference and the individual's claim on the government for provision of such services as education without which a citizen could not participate meaningfully in the political process. He viewed the Founding Fathers as sharing his belief that "Liberty . . . [is] the secret of happiness,"[23] and in many ways his mature thought was an attempt to outline the roles that could be played by the national and state governments, law, and economic entities in ensuring individual liberty. "Liberty" meant as much control of one's fate as is humanly possible; economic liberty meant an extensive degree of control by the individual over his or her life in the economic sphere. Brandeis saw political and economic liberty as inextricably interrelated. A person deprived of economic liberty could not be a politically free and active citizen.

Because he postulated the necessity for both economic and political liberty, Brandeis went beyond progressivism. Most Progressives viewed the proper role of government as the creation and maintenance of a relatively even economic playing field, which required government to become the regulator of big business on behalf of the citizen. Brandeis ultimately rejected the idea of government regulation of big business in favor of the conviction that, like political democracy, economic democracy can best be guarded by individuals rather than by the state. His vision of economic liberty was similar to his picture of political liberty: a society in which members of an entity, whether citizens of a democratic political system or workers in a factory, make the decisions most important to their lives. One might in fact argue that Brandeis was a republican about politics but a democrat when it came to the economy. He accepted the necessity for representative government in the sprawling United States, although he preferred the pure democracy practiced by the Jewish communities in Palestine on their kibbutzim. His goal of worker-participation, although he never described it in detail, appears to have been closer to one of pure workplace democracy. He developed an economic counterpart to Mill's belief that as people know their own interests best,[24] the only government that can be trusted to adopt policies in the people's best interest is one chosen by the people themselves; the only people who can articulate and create workplace policies that will be just are those who are most affected by them.

The second element of importance to Brandeis's thought is the nature of citizenship, or more specifically, civic duty and civic courage.[25] To him, as to the Greek philosophers, civic virtue was involvement in public life.[26] It was obvious to Brandeis that citizenship brought responsibilities as well as rights, for the whole premise of democracy is that the citizens will rule. Citizens were obliged to participate actively in the political process and not only because their failure to do so would prevent the political system from being truly democratic. Citizen responsibility was a means, but it was also a good in itself; it was a method by which human beings developed their full potential. "The development of the individual is . . . both a necessary means and the end sought," Brandeis declared. "The great developer is responsibility."[27] Human beings would grow as a result of fulfilling their democratic responsibilities in both the political system and the workplace. Here Brandeis went beyond Plato to concentrate on the beneficent effects of civic "virtue" not only on the "polis" but on the individual as well. Thus there was a psychological component to Brandeis's thought: Democracy was not only, as Winston Churchill is reputed to have said, "the worst political system ever invented except for all the others"; it was the system best designed to produce truly free, fully developed human beings.

The performance of civic duty depended upon adequate leisure. Without time to inform themselves, citizens could not participate intelligently in the political process. Here Brandeis, whose life-style and work habits tended toward the puritanical, departed from the Protestant work ethic. Puritans sought the measure of a person in his or her work. Brandeis found it, in good part, in the citizen's use of leisure time for participation in political life and other self-fulfilling activities. "Leisure does not imply idleness," according to Brandeis. "It means ability to work not less but more, ability to work at something besides breadwinning. . . . Leisure, so defined, is an essential of successful democracy."[28] Leisure was a psychological as well as a physical necessity. He could "do twelve months' work in eleven months, but not in twelve," Brandeis said, and assumed the same was true of other people.[29] The intelligent use of leisure was as good for the citizen as it was for the society. Any economic system that did not permit adequate leisure time therefore doomed both individual self-fulfillment and any hope of democracy.

To Brandeis, a major component of the free, developed person was courage. Personal courage was a theme of his life, and he demonstrated it on dozens of occasions. Perhaps one of the earliest examples occurred when his eyes gave out while he was a student at Harvard Law School and a number of doctors told him he would have to abandon his goal of becoming a lawyer. Brandeis ignored them and kept looking until he found a doctor who agreed that by minimizing his own reading and relying on fellow students to read most of the necessary material to him, he could continue in the law. The "only" requirement was that Brandeis develop a photographic memory, and so he did, going on to earn the highest grades of any student in the law school's history.[30]

Civic courage was simply that sort of personal courage extended into the public arena. To Brandeis, personal liberty and courage in the civic sphere were inextricably linked. The Founding Fathers, he would write, not only "believed liberty to be the secret of happiness," but they also "believed . . . courage to be the secret of liberty."[31] Brandeis equated moral courage and civic virtue with freedom. It was only the good citizen who could truly be free, for the willingness to face the vicissitudes of public life was a prerequisite of liberty. Brandeis learned civic courage from the adults in his abolitionist family, whose abhorrence of slavery made them highly unpopular with their Kentucky neighbors. He needed it again as a Bostonian. During his student days at Harvard and his early years as a practicing attorney, he was "taken up" by Boston Brahmins, invited to their homes and their soirees.[32] His experiences as a lawyer, however, convinced him that many of the ideas held by the welcoming Brahmins were wrong. He began to oppose their deeply held beliefs about the preponderant power employers should enjoy and their view of state legislatures as properly being little more than the instruments of the propertied classes. Brandeis came to believe in equal power for employees and employers, and he was shocked at the ability of capitalists to buy legislative votes. His popularity with many of his Brahmin acquaintances quickly disintegrated, but he was certain that as a citizen he had an obligation to speak for what was right. Repeatedly, throughout his life, in making opponents of the big banks and the money trust, Charles S. Mellen and the massive New Haven Railroad empire, J. P. Morgan and the steel trust, President Taft and the Morgan-Guggenheim syndicate in the Pinchot-Ballinger affair, Brandeis demonstrated his own civic courage.[33] He expected no less of the people around him; moreover, he made it a part of his belief system and of his political thought. Involvement in public life was a challenge, and there was nothing Brandeis relished more. "Bear in mind," he told an admirer, "that in canoeing I have enjoyed not only floating down streams. Paddling up them was also a feature."[34] He was known among his summer neighbors on Cape Cod as a man who would brave the wildest waters in his canoe. His canoeing might almost be a metaphor for his approach to the political process: "Floating down" was to be enjoyed, but "paddling up" was to be expected and was to be greeted with zest. Being a citizen in the contentious world of public policy was more than a responsibility; it was fun.

1

EARLY IDEAS: CONFORMITY AND THE SEEDS OF EVOLUTION

The brain is like the hand. It grows with using.[1]

In 1913 a reporter asked Brandeis, "How came you by your democracy? You were not bred to it?" Brandeis replied, "No; my early associations were such as to give me greater reverence than I now have for the things that are because they are. I recall that when I began to practice law I thought it awkward, stupid, and vulgar that a jury of twelve inexpert men should have the power to decide. I had the greatest respect for the Judge. I trusted only expert opinion." Later, he said, "I began to see that many things sanctioned by expert opinion and denounced by popular opinion were wrong." And he added, "Experience of life has made me democratic." By "democratic" he meant able to see the virtues of the ordinary, nonexpert individual.[2]

Brandeis was "bred" to a belief in political democracy but not to the egalitarian economic definition of democracy he had adopted by 1913 and would retain for the remainder of his life. His early thinking, like that of most young people, was quite different from his later ideas. He was unlike many thoughtful young people, however, in his tendency to adhere to established truths rather than to rebel against them. The young Brandeis was far more conservative, or at least quite different in his conservatism, from the mature Brandeis. One might describe his early economic ideas as those of a nineteenth-century laissez-faire liberal. The personal liberty he emphasized throughout his adult life initially was the liberty to vote, to participate in political affairs, and to earn one's living without governmental interference. By the second decade of the twentieth century, he was defining liberty quite differently. Brandeis learned from experience, and as his experiences accumulated his ideas changed considerably.

Louis David Brandeis was born on November 13, 1856, in Louisville, Kentucky, the youngest of four children. His father, Adolph, was a partner in a prosperous business that included a grocery and general-produce store, a wholesale grain outlet, a flour mill, a tobacco factory, an 1,100-acre farm, and a river freighter. Adolph had emigrated from Prague as a young man with limited funds, partly in the traditional search for economic success that brought so many others to the United States. Another element, however, in Adolph's move and that of the twenty-six other members of his family and two related families who later joined him was their sympathy for Austria's democratic Revolution of 1848 and their reaction to its failure.[3] The families possessed a strong sense of morality and of social responsibility as well as a commitment to public service. Brandeis's first memory was of his mother carrying food and coffee to the Union soldiers outside his family's home in Louisville. Although Adolph became sufficiently wealthy to employ servants, who in nineteenth-century Kentucky invariably were black, the family never treated them as slaves or supported the "peculiar institution."[4]

Brandeis's idol was his uncle Lewis Dembitz, whose last name Brandeis substituted for his original middle name. Dembitz was a delegate to the convention that nominated Lincoln for president in 1860, served as Louisville's assistant city attorney, drafted the first "Australian" ballot law ever to be adopted in the United States, created a local tax-collection system, translated at least part of *Uncle Tom's Cabin* into German, and translated the books of Exodus and Leviticus into English. He possessed a seemingly unquenchable thirst for knowledge, reading a dozen languages, becoming a good enough amateur astronomer to forecast the 1869 eclipse of the sun to the minute, and writing a treatise on *Kentucky Jurisprudence* that was considered definitive.[5] Brandeis remembered his uncle as "a living university."[6] His uncle's ties to the organized Jewish community and his concern for the future of Jews later helped impel Brandeis toward Zionism and the political thought that resulted from his involvement in it.

Brandeis's parents acknowledged their Judaism but were not interested in its rituals. His mother, dismissing the notion "that sins can be expiated by going to divine service and observing this or that formula," taught her children that "only goodness and truth and conduct that is humane and self-sacrificing towards those who need us can bring God nearer to us" and that "our errors can only be atoned for by acting in a more kindly spirit." She strove to imbue them with "the highest ideals as to morals and love" and insisted that the family talk about politics rather than money or other similarly "vulgar" matters at the dinner table. So Brandeis began life with a mixture of the belief in laissez-faire capitalism typical of his father's occupation, the political idealism and cultural background of sophisticated, liberal middle European Jews, and a view of public service as a moral imperative.[7]

Neither his early education in Louisville nor his years at the Annen-Realschule in Dresden (1873–1875) altered his ideas, although they added substantially to his knowledge. By the time he left Dresden for Boston he was fluent in French, Latin, German, and Greek; he had studied literature, mineralogy, geography, physics, chemistry, and mathematics; and he was knowledgeable about music and art. Most important to him, however, the Annen-Realschule had taught him to think. He was excited by his discovery there that "ideas could be evolved by reflecting on your material." He knew exactly what he wanted to do: "to go back to America and . . . study law. My uncle, the abolitionist, was a lawyer, and to me nothing else seemed really worth while."[8] Even then, it appears, he equated being an attorney with taking a moral stance.

His three years as an undergraduate and as a graduate student at the Harvard Law School (1875–1878) were spent using the newly introduced case method to study the law. His courses — contracts, property, torts, civil procedure, criminal law, evidence, equity, trusts, constitutional law, sales, real property, wills, and bills and notes — reflected a legal system predicated on the dominance of private property and designed to protect it. After a few months of practicing commercial law with a relative in St. Louis, Brandeis returned to Boston to join his wealthy socialite classmate Samuel Warren in opening a law firm representing small factory owners and merchants. At the same time, he was asked to teach a course on evidence at

Harvard; a few years later, the Massachusetts Institute of Technology hired him to teach a course on business law.[9]

There is no indication that Brandeis had any early doubts about the laissez-faire capitalism implicit in his law school studies, even after the devastating economic experiences his father underwent when Brandeis was a teenager. Adolph's business began to falter in 1872, and he realized that the country was about to experience a recession. He therefore sold the business and took his family to Europe, fully expecting to return after a year or so to reestablish himself, but for various reasons the family came back to Louisville in 1875. Adolph then established a cotton business, only to see it collapse within two years. In 1878 he and his son Alfred founded a retail store that, although ultimately successful, did not do well while Brandeis was at Harvard. The only money Brandeis's family could spare while he was in law school was a loan of a few hundred dollars from Alfred, so Brandeis maintained himself by tutoring the son of Prof. James Bradley Thayer and other young students and by proctoring examinations. He lived so frugally that by 1878 he had not only managed to repay his brother but had saved some money that, beginning a lifelong pattern, he invested in what he considered to be nonspeculative bonds. His successful law practice, his frugality, and his conservative investments would make him a millionaire twice over by the time he joined the Supreme Court in 1916. Adolph had been sufficiently disturbed by his own financial problems, however, to regret his son's having decided against a "safe" teaching career in favor of the chancier prospects of private practice.[10]

In 1897, testifying before the House Ways and Means Committee against a proposed law raising tariffs, Brandeis sounded the theme of laissez-faire. He announced, "I appear for those who want to be left alone, those who do not come to Congress and seek the aid of the sovereign powers of the government to bring them prosperity." His clients wished to be "left undisturbed in business" rather than artificially protected from competition. He lambasted reliance upon governmental involvement in the economy as destructive of "the old and worthy sturdy principle of American life which existed in the beginning when men succeeded by their own efforts."[11] There are echoes of laissez-faire individualism in his 1904 statement: "Few things in the world are worth while having that are not attained by struggle."[12]

None of his letters or speeches suggests any doubt that small-scale capitalism, presumably typified by his clients, was good and that it was only the growing "excesses" of capitalism by "the great captains of industry and of finance" that were leading to social discontent.[13] It seems fair to assume that the son of a small businessman, educated at Harvard about a legal system designed in part to protect small business and using that system on behalf of his business clients, initially held beliefs supportive of small-scale laissez-faire capitalism.

Brandeis's economics may have been traditional, but he quickly developed a novel approach to the practice of the law.[14] In his first heady years as a practitioner he simply rejoiced in the excitement of cases, particularly those involving litigation. Soon, however, he became choosier. His frugality at Harvard had taught him that minimizing his material needs brought a kind of freedom. He had no desire to work for clients whose claims he felt to be illegitimate; frugality meant he would not have to. "I would rather have clients," he said, "than be somebody's lawyer."[15] "Having clients" meant that he would pick his cases and that he would use his ability to understand, frequently better than his clients did, their legal and related problems and to decide the best way of handling them. He insisted on knowing the underlying situation that led to immediate concerns. The result was a familiarity with his clients' businesses that eventually would alter his political thinking. For the moment, however, he saw his approach as no more than a wise way to practice law.[16]

Apparently, as a younger attorney, conditioned by his early life and the dominant mores, Brandeis saw no reason to question the premises of laissez-faire capitalism. By 1905 and after more than two decades of practice, however, he had begun to wonder about the social utility of large corporations and about their impact on a society and a governmental system that had taken small-scale capitalism as a given. His earlier views may have been in part no more than those attitudes to be expected from the son of a small businessman and the lawyer for others, but an additional aspect of his thinking was his concept of the practice of law. He liked the idea of the independent attorney functioning in a laissez-faire economy as much as he disliked the trend he thought he saw among twentieth-century lawyers. He considered it immoral for lawyers to function as guns for hire, particularly when their employers were corporations attempting to affect the political process. He reminded the Harvard Ethical Society in 1905 that in the early United States, "nearly every great lawyer was then a statesman; and nearly every statesman, great or small, was a lawyer." He much regretted that lawyers no longer held "a position of independence, between the wealthy and the people, prepared to curb the excesses of either" but had turned their backs on the people in order "to become adjuncts of great corporations."[17]

The perception of public service as a duty, not only of the lawyer but of any citizen and not only of any citizen but particularly of the lawyer, was part of Brandeis's family legacy. His association with Samuel Warren made him a member of Boston society and led to his involvement in the public-oriented concerns that were among his new acquaintances' interests. He found himself speaking before Edward Everett Hale's Unitarian congregation on the obligation of citizens to pay their taxes, testifying before the state Insurance Committee about a bill designed to value policies uniformly for taxation purposes, appearing at hearings of the state legislature to argue against women's suffrage (a position he would reject within a few years), and involved in a move to limit the impact of lobbies on the state legislature.[18]

Even if his family heritage, his new position in the world of the Brahmins, and his own inclination had not led him into public life, his clients' concerns would have done so. In 1886 Warren & Brandeis represented a number of paper manufacturers who were attempting to repeal a city ordinance that, as a purported health measure, required all imported rags to be disinfected in Boston. Despite the fact that his clients had already had the rags disinfected abroad, they were forced to pay the monopolistic Boston Disinfecting Company five dollars a ton for disinfecting them again. Brandeis, satisfied that the sanitizing process abroad was sufficient for health purposes, represented the manufacturers first before Boston's Common Council, which refused to repeal the law, and again when one manufacturer unsuccessfully brought suit against the law. One of his daughters later stated that it was this fight that awakened him to the dangers of monopoly.[19]

Dealing with public bodies also showed Brandeis the corruption that was rampant in many late nineteenth- and early twentieth-century state legislatures. In 1898 George Fred Williams, an attorney and member of the Massachusetts legislature, asked Brandeis for help in exposing the routine bribery of state legislators. Brandeis agreed to look at the liquor lobby, already chafing at a law that prohibited the sale of liquor except with a meal and currently threatened with an even more restrictive temperance bill. He went about the task in his idiosyncratic, seemingly quixotic way. One of his clients was William D. Ellis, the distillers' representative in Massachusetts. Brandeis called Ellis in, handed him a list of all the members of the state legislature, and asked him to check the names of those who could be bribed. When Ellis finished the task, Brandeis asked, "Ellis, do you realize what you are doing?" and, as Brandeis remembered it, lectured him about the evils of bribery until "tears ran down the liquor agent's face." Then Brandeis decided he would represent Ellis's group, the Massachusetts Protective Liquor Dealers' Association, in its fight against the bill, on condition that Ellis be named head of its Executive Committee and that the association spend no money on the battle unless it was approved by Brandeis.[20]

He reasoned that the impetus for the liquor dealers' bribery was the passage of laws that made their business impossible. The "anti-bar" or meal-only Massachusetts statute was largely ignored, but the dealers had to resort to bribery to keep the law from being enforced and to attempt to revoke it. Brandeis drew up a less restrictive proposal. "You can remove liquor dealers from politics by a very simple device," Brandeis told the legislature; "make the liquor laws reasonable." The legislators followed his advice, the newspapers trumpeted his accomplishment, and he wrote to his fiancée, "I think I can accomplish much" in what was then his "pet reform," the liquor trade, "by making the dealers respectable." He felt he had proved the worth of his policy of "dignified publicity, eliminating lobbyists and lobbyists' practices." The association paid him $2,000 for his efforts. It was less than he could have received, he said some years later, but he wanted to demonstrate that by openly spending far less than they had spent secretly in earlier years, the dealers could achieve at least as much.[21]

A few years later Brandeis began his first long-term battle on behalf of the public, against the Boston Elevated's attempted monopoly over Boston's public transportation system.[22] His involvement stemmed partly from his anger at a policy he saw as penalizing the people and partly from his close association with merchants whose customers depended upon cheap public transportation. The fight was long but ultimately successful, and he discovered that he was good at using his legal and organizational talents on behalf of the public and that doing so was immensely satisfying. His continued work as the people's attorney led him to study a wide variety of fields and to question many of his early assumptions. He became interested in the life insurance business, for example, in 1905, when a group of Bostonians, learning of corruption in the Equitable Assurance Company that insured them, organized the New England Policy Holders' Protective Committee and asked Brandeis to represent them. He agreed to do so on condition that he be unpaid so that he could act in the interest of the public as well as that of the committee. The study he undertook of the insurance industry led to his realization that industrial workers who bought small life insurance policies from the three largest companies selling such insurance were being routinely cheated. Convinced that the companies' activity in this field was bad for the workers, he devised the system of Massachusetts savings-bank life insurance that exists to this day. He wrote in 1905 that although he considered the insurance companies overly big, "I am well aware that it is not fashionable at the present time to suggest that anything can be too large, and I am disposed to think that in regard to most businesses, it would not be wise to place any limit upon size." But his inclination not to interfere with the size of business in general was one of the many elements of his thinking that would be altered by his experiences.[23]

The Boston Elevated fight enabled him to refine his ideas about monopoly, which he came to oppose as much in the field of public utilities as he did in the area of private business. He rejected the proposal that the Elevated be permitted a monopoly under governmental regulation for the same reasons he later argued against a merger of the New York, New Haven and Hartford Railroad Company with the Boston and Maine Railroad: "This would be like surrendering liberty and substituting despotism with safeguards. There is no way in which to safeguard people from despotism except to prevent despotism. There is no way to safeguard the people from the evils of a private transportation monopoly except to prevent the monopoly. The objections to despotism and to monopoly are fundamental in human nature. They rest upon the innate and ineradicable selfishness of man. They rest upon the fact that absolute power inevitably leads to abuse. They rest upon the fact that progress flows only from struggle," i.e., from competition.[24]

He uncovered legislative corruption once again, reporting during the transportation fight that the supposedly public service corporation was buying legislators' votes with promises of jobs for the political hacks to whom they owed favors. He told an ally that he had discovered "from one to two hundred" such persons on the payroll of public corporations. He drafted two bills designed to eliminate such ties but decided not to complicate the transportation fight by raising the issue.[25] He kept his drafts, however, and in 1903 he urged Gov. John L. Bates to include mention of the proposed antibribery laws in his inaugural speech. The governor did so, but the legislature took no action.[26] Unperturbed, Brandeis addressed the Boot and Shoe Club and the Unitarian Club on the subject, citing specific instances of legislative larceny, bribery, and fraud.[27] He contrasted the secrecy by which corruption flourished with the right to know, crucial in a democratic society. The citizen's first obligation, he argued, was "to know," which required "a diffusion of knowledge on all these [public] matters." It was "dishonorable" and "a shameful breach of trust" to accept anything else."[28] When a Massachusetts legislator demonstrated some interest in the subject two years later, Brandeis sent him a copy of one of his draft bills.[29] Finally, in 1906 one of the bills, supported by the Public Franchise League, became law.[30]

Another experience with public affairs that became important to his political thought was his 1910–1911 involvement in the Pinchot-Ballinger affair, which began with the decision of William Howard Taft's secretary of the interior to sell government-owned lands in Alaska to private commercial interests and continued with Taft's participation in an attempted cover-up of the scheme, and resulted in congressional hearings about both. Brandeis was asked to be present at the hearings to represent *Collier's Weekly*, the journal that had published an incriminating report by a Land Office field agent concerned about governmental improprieties and that had been threatened with a libel suit. The immediate impact on Brandeis was total immersion in questions of land use, government ownership of land and other natural resources, and his formulation of a proposal for government ownership of land that would be leased to individuals or groups[31] and that would be under the general policy control of small-scale communal groups.[32]

Brandeis's political thought was an amalgam of his background with his experiences and the ideas they generated. His treatment of ideas

as experimental plans of action, originating in a problem, is reminiscent of John Dewey.[33] Whether he was immersing himself in workers'
life insurance, fighting corruption in the Massachusetts legislature,
or exposing the presidential cover-up in the Pinchot-Ballinger affair,
his values were being filtered through experience and emerging transformed. There was nothing in his upbringing, his formal education
in English and American law, or his partnership in a law firm most of
whose clients owned such small businesses as paper, shoe, and leather
manufacturing plants or retail establishments that would lead him
to doubt either the virtues of laissez-faire capitalism and a market
economy or its existence in the United States. Nonetheless, those
elements of his background later merged with experience to alter his
ideas.

A major part of his family's legacy was its high moral standards
and sense of public responsibility. He believed that public acclaim
was less important than acting properly and maintaining faith with
other human beings. In 1889, when Brandeis was thirty-two, his father
complimented him upon one of his successes. "I could not recall ever
having been proud of anything accomplished or to have deemed any
recognition an honor," Brandeis replied. "Indeed, I believe that the
little successes I may have had, were due wholly to the pressure from
within — proceeding from a deep sense of obligation and in no respect
to the allurement of a possible distinction." He wrote to his fiancée
that the value of "right living . . . is surely underestimated by even
the good people of the world." Character was crucial, whether or not
it produced results: "It is the effort — the attempt — that tells." So it
was not surprising that he became disgusted by the legislative corruption revealed by his work on matters such as the Boston subways,
and he fulminated against "the wickedness of people shielding wrong-
doers and passing them off . . . as honest men." Legislators were too
interested in material things. Brandeis agreed with Matthew Arnold
that "life is not a having and a getting; but a being and a becoming."
His openness to "becoming," to learning and changing, to considering
new ideas was reflected in the emphasis on facts and their importance
so similar to his uncle Dembitz's insistent quest for knowledge.[34] It
was an emphasis on the lessons of experience that also paralleled the
developing school of pragmatism typified by William James and John
Dewey.[35]

Brandeis's thinking always included an emphasis on individualism and equality of opportunity. The specifics of both goals, however, developed over time. He began with the traditional capitalist's stress on the individual as an economic entity best able to function without governmental intervention, sharing the apparent belief of his class and era in the minimalization of government. In fact, as he found, hidden behind a formal assertion of laissez-faire individualism was the use of the government's right of eminent domain to buy and turn over valuable land to private entities, grants of public land to railroads, the government-created doctrine that corporations must be treated legally as individuals and accorded all the rights recognized by the Constitution as belonging to people,[36] the use of law to "protect" employers from employees' attempts at unionization, or the creation of policies that enhanced the growth of the trusts he came to abhor.

Many people — clergy, economists, reformers, philosophers, academicians, even state officials — shared Brandeis's discovery that laissez-faire capitalism, assuming it had ever existed in a pure form in the United States, had become a facade; similarly, a chorus of voices, however small initially, was calling for government regulation to undo the concentrations of power and wealth created by society.[37] Theorists concerned with liberty and equality made up part of the chorus. John Dewey, for example, had argued in 1888 that political democracy requires economic democracy, had identified the social element in the accumulation of wealth at least as early as 1889, and was soon criticizing laissez-faire economics and calling for government regulation.[38] Brandeis, however, relied on experience as his teacher. His individualism emphasized human dignity and educability. He agreed with Jefferson that all people were equal in their possession of at least a modicum of reason and the capacity to use it, however different their levels of intelligence might be. Education was crucial not only for citizenship but to enable people to live the well-rounded lives that constituted human fulfillment. Brandeis relied upon experience to educate him in political economy.

Thus nothing in Brandeis's early values necessarily doomed his faith in capitalism; when his values were juxtaposed with circumstances, however, that was the result. Yet the most important alteration in his thought did not follow from his discovery of new phenomena: government corruption, public utilities, the insurance industry. He took for granted an understanding of the relationship between labor and capital. It was only when he reexamined his basic assumptions about relationships in the economic world that his thought was transformed into a coherent, highly creative philosophy. A major element in the process may have been the shocking discovery, to him, that some "respectable" people did not share his regard for individualism, as he defined it, or for the tenets he assumed were embodied in democracy.

2

FROM LAISSEZ-FAIRE CAPITALISM TO WORKER-MANAGEMENT

Industrial democracy should ultimately attend political democracy.[1]

In 1892 Brandeis was confronted with dramatic proof that capitalists could be less than altruistic or even humane. He was preparing to teach a course on business law at the Massachusetts Institute of Technology. The notes he had nearly finished writing for his lectures were designed to demonstrate how the common law had evolved in tandem with industry and commerce. The congruence between law and society had become part of Brandeis's thought. He assumed that law invariably reflected all relevant aspects of the community from which it had emerged. Seen as organic, law could not but be good in responding to the needs of the people.

One morning before the semester began, he picked up his newspaper and learned of the violence that had erupted at the Carnegie steel works in Homestead, Pennsylvania, when the company decided not to renew its contract with the steelworkers and refused to deal with a union. Brandeis had been friendly for some years with Mary Kenney, a labor organizer, and the man she eventually married, John F. O'Sullivan, a union official. A few days earlier Kenney had told Brandeis about her trip to Homestead during the contract's last weeks. The company clearly expected violence when the contract ran out, for it had erected walls with apertures for guns around the steel-mill grounds. The violence started when the contract expired, wages were slashed, and the workers went out on strike. Henry Clay Frick, Carnegie's manager, hired Pinkerton guards to protect strikebreakers and sailed them up the Ohio River. The Pinkertons arrived at Homestead on boats, realized that the strikers, dug in on the bank of the river, would not permit them to land, and began to fire their Winchesters. The steelworkers suffered most of the casualties in the ensuing battle. Brandeis later remembered his reaction: "I saw at once that the common law, built up under simpler conditions of living, gave an inadequate basis for the adjustment of the complex relations of the modern factory system. I threw away my notes and approached my theme from new angles. Those talks at Tech marked an epoch in my own career."[2]

Brandeis realized that nothing in the formal legal institutions explained "human affairs in their manifold relations" as they existed in Homestead. He was appalled at "that battle, where organized capital hired a private army to shoot at organized labor for resisting an arbitrary cut in wages" and began to think seriously for the first time about "the relations of labor to industry." He set about revising his notes to cover the "Legal Relation of Labor and Capital," convinced that if law was both a dynamic entity that reflected changing social conditions and an embodiment of morality, the law of the twentieth century would have to keep pace with the new phenomenon of highly concentrated capital. Brandeis quickly learned that the law was neither necessarily moral nor egalitarian, there being no meaningful equality between Carnegie and his workers.[3]

Ten years later he faced directly the difficulties inherent in the capital-labor relationship. His client William H. McElwain, a major shoe manufacturer, called Brandeis in when the business began to experience difficulties. The employees had refused to accept the pay cut McElwain considered to be reasonable and necessary under the circumstances. Brandeis went to the plant and found that the employees were paid well when they worked, but their work was seasonal and they earned nothing out of season. He was amazed to learn that McElwain had no idea how much his workers earned each year rather than each working day. Seeking more information, Brandeis turned to John Tobin, head of the International Boot and Shoe Workers' Union, who was acting as the striking workers' representative, and heard the same story of high but seasonal wages. McElwain sought to end the impasse by suggesting that the workers be paid on a piecework basis; Tobin wanted wages calculated on the basis of hours. Brandeis rejected both ideas and instead proposed a detailed system that would enable labor to be spread out during the year to prevent irregularity of employment. The two sides agreed, the system was put into effect, and it worked.[4]

Brandeis learned three major lessons from the McElwain experience. First he saw that irregularity of employment was disastrous for workers, so much so that thereafter he considered it the major problem for labor and insisted, "Unemployment is as unnecessary as disease epidemics."[5] He saw regularization as helpful to employers as well as to employees because it would enable them to recoup their initial investment in machinery quickly by running it throughout the year, to increase volume and subsequently to lower prices with the result of increasing volume even further, and to find employees who might be willing to accept lower wages in return for guaranteed regular employment. Second, he learned that, given sufficient information about the facts of the situation, labor and capital could behave reasonably, as he believed McElwain and Tobin had done. He remained in contact with Tobin, having discovered that union leaders — or at least one of them — were as reasonable as employers and that he could speak with the former as easily as with the latter. Although he had socialized with labor-movement figures such as Kenney and O'Sullivan, this was the first time he had negotiated with a labor leader in the workplace. Brandeis was referring to the McElwain experience when he said that "many things sanctioned by expert opinion and denounced by popular opinion were wrong." In Brandeis's world, one opinion ensconced in popular belief was that unionization was an evil. The third and related lesson was, as he had earlier seen in the Homestead strike, that inequality of power resulted in human misery; in the absence of unions, employees were at the mercy of employers. The priority he placed on the dignity of individuals made that situation unacceptable, for he was not so naive as to think that employers automatically would interest themselves in the dignity of others rather than in profits.[6]

One of Brandeis's basic premises was that human beings had the right to govern themselves in the economic as well as in the political sphere. He had now learned that such self-government, or at least something as basic as a modicum of control over their wages, was impossible for workers unless they were organized. Brandeis had become convinced that unions were a necessity. John Stuart Mill had asserted that in the public sphere, "the rights and interests of every or any person are only secure from being disregarded when the person interested is himself able, and habitually disposed, to stand up for them."[7] Brandeis took this idea into the workplace, viewing unions as enabling workers to stand up for their interests.

Speaking to an organization of employers in 1904 he said, "Some way must be worked out by which employer and employee, each recognizing the proper sphere of the other, will each be free to work for his own and for the common good, and that the powers of the individual employee may be developed to the utmost." An implicit symmetry between the public sphere and the workplace was becoming apparent in his thinking. He equated civic virtue with a citizen's involvement in public affairs; industrial virtue consisted of employing one's powers "to the utmost" in the workplace. Neither employers nor employees ought to dominate the relationship; the "sense of unrestricted power is just as demoralizing for the employer as it is for the employee. Neither our intelligence nor our characters can long stand the strain of unrestricted power"; that is, absolute power corrupts in the economic as well as in the political sphere. For that reason, "The employer needs the union 'to stay him from the fall of vanity,'" and union leaders will be "reasonable and conservative" only if they represent strong unions.[8]

Brandeis had begun to speak of "industrial democracy," which he equated with the checks and balances of the political sphere: putting employers and employee unions on an "equal" basis by balancing the financial power of employers with the power of the unions to keep businesses from functioning unless they paid fair wages. He was certain that the leaders of strong unions and the employers dealing with them would act rationally as long as they talked together. Thinking along the same lines, William James was soon to proclaim that the conflict between capital and labor could be solved through mutual understanding. James chided the two sides for being "at cross-purposes all along the line, regarding each other as they might regard a set of dangerously gesticulating automata, or, if they seek to get at the inner motivation, making the most terrible mistakes."[9] The statement contains a quite possibly erroneous assumption of ultimate mutual interest that Brandeis shared. Brandeis's formulation was that "nine-tenths of the serious controversies which arise in life result from misunderstanding, result from one man not knowing the facts which to the other man seem important, or otherwise failing to appreciate his point of view. A properly conducted conference involves a frank disclosure of such facts — patient, careful argument, willingness to listen and to consider."[10] James did not normally enter the world of labor negotiations, but Brandeis did. It is therefore not surprising that Samuel Gompers, leader of the American Federation of Labor, and other leading union organizers as well as many employers lost patience with Brandeis when he in effect told workers who had been shot at by employers' armies and employers whose buildings had been blown up by frustrated workers that they had to "reason together" because their interest in the success of the business was the same.[11]

There was a contradiction in Brandeis's thought of which he was seemingly unaware. He followed Madison in asserting that it was safer to rely upon self-interest than on virtue or altruism and thus argued for unionization rather than for benevolent employers.[12] Pitting one self-interest against another, after all, assumes that the two sets of interests are in opposition to each other. Yet, simultaneously, Brandeis postulated an ultimate congruence of interest between employer and employee, having seen that it was possible to devise solutions that enhanced both the employer's profits and the circumstances under which laborers worked, including their wages; and he assumed this congruence applied to all labor-management situations. The Progressive movement, presupposing a perpetual divergence between the interests of labor and those of management, adopted the idea of balancing them by offsetting the greater power of the employers with governmental intervention and regulation. Brandeis went beyond progressivism to end the duality by merging employer with employee through worker-management, with a slight detour for the purpose of exploring scientific management. But that evolution in his thinking lay in the future.

During the first decade of the twentieth century, Brandeis's mistrust of unbridled power resulted in further postulates that exasperated labor and capital alike. He opposed the closed shop, arguing not only that it was unacceptably coercive but that the presence of nonunion workers would prevent labor from becoming as tyrannical as the employer. He antagonized much of the business community by insisting that businesses had to be small enough so that employers would be in sufficient contact with the workers to remember their humanity and needs. He maintained that labor negotiations had to be conducted by those people who actually owned or managed the business, presumably because they would best understand the relationship of the union's demands to their own self-interest. And rationality necessitated one person or a small group of people being fully familiar with all aspects of the business: a situation attainable only if the business remained small. Another reason for opposing overly large enterprises, including the burgeoning trusts, was that they entailed such massive concentrations of power that countervailing power was impossible, and moral corruption, defined in this context as a lack of care about employees, was the inevitable result.[13]

The negative reaction of many employers and unionists to his ideas was of little interest to Brandeis, who interpreted the hostility as reflecting their regrettable lack of understanding about where their welfare lay. He equated rationality with a common-sense awareness of the solutions that would prove best for all concerned and believed that it eventually would triumph despite the threat presented to it by unlimited power and myopic greed. He saw great possibilities for developing "the powers of the individual employee . . . to the utmost" when rational systems finally came into existence. He urged unions to fight for reasonable hours as well as wages, for as members of a democracy, workers need leisure, "among other reasons, because with us every man is of the ruling class. Our education and condition of life must be such as become a ruler. Our great beneficent experiment in democracy will fail unless the people, our rulers, are developed in character and intelligence." Education requires "freshness of mind . . . and to the preservation of freshness of mind a short work day is for most people essential."[14]

Brandeis's concern for most individuals nonetheless was still paternalistic and his approach to unionization conservative, designed to protect small capitalism. His faith was in union leaders rather than in the rank-and-file worker. He said in 1905 that "democracy is only possible, industrial democracy, among people who think; among people who are above the average intelligence." He mitigated his elitism slightly by insisting on the right of everyone to education and acknowledging that "thinking is not a heaven-born thing. . . . It is a gift men and women make for themselves . . . it is earned by effort. . . . The brain is like the hand. It grows with using." Yet he clearly did not perceive the average worker as being on the same intellectual level as most employers, nor was he ready to give such workers, rather than their presumably wiser leaders, power equal to that of employers. Could one willingly turn power over to the less favored, the less educated, the less intelligent? This question is of course central to democratic political theory, and Brandeis was far from the first or last thinker to wrestle with it.[15]

For the moment, he had no answer. Nor had he come to terms with the contradiction implicit in his belief that the assumption of responsibility by workers would develop their powers of intellect and character and his acknowledgment that "in the unskilled trades and in many so-called skilled trades" within the industrial world, "the limits of development" of responsibility "are soon reached." His unarticulated goal was a method by which the Jeffersonian imperative of economic independence could be achieved in the industrial age. He soon acknowledged that higher wages and an eight-hour workday were insufficient solutions. By 1907 he was telling the Boston Central Labor Union, "Labor unions should strive to make labor share all the earnings of a business except what is required for capital and management." Shareholders should be given a fair return on their investment, but after that and the needs of the business itself had been taken care of, anything remaining belonged to the workers. The former advocate of laissez-faire capitalism had begun to advocate profit sharing. But this approach, however much it might increase worker income, would not result in economic independence. And yet Brandeis could not think of how to go further.[16]

Then came the New York garment workers' strike of 1910, crucial for Brandeis, which he was asked to mediate. Despite the disagreement of mainstream labor with some of his ideas, it considered Brandeis an ally, pointing to his support of unions, decent wages, an eight-hour day, regularity of employment, and pension plans and his opposition to the trusts and to judicial injunctions against strikes. In 1908, in the case of *Muller* v. *Oregon*, he had successfully argued for a state law limiting working hours for women, basing his presentation to the Supreme Court on the special social role of women, and in 1913 he was to win an Oregon court ruling legitimizing a state law setting minimum wages for women.[17]

Brandeis had won the trust of small businessmen by representing many of them and by disdaining the more radical labor positions. He argued, for example, that a single fixed minimum wage for women was uneconomic, believing that "the minimum wage in a department store . . . ought to be higher than the minimum wage in a factory, because the girl in the department store has to dress well all the time and that costs money."[18] He had also demonstrated his integrity to both business and labor. An unidentified typescript in the Felix Frankfurter Papers refers to a statement allegedly made by "Big Bill" Haywood, leader of the Industrial Workers of the World (I.W.W.):

"This fellow Brandeis," he said, "is the most dangerous man in the United States." He was asked to explain. "Brandeis is the kind of man the I.W.W. has got to look out for. Brandeis knows something about capital and labor. He isn't one of these highbrow reformers who is sure to make a fool of himself. That's why I say he is in our way. The workers trust him even when he goes against them. Think of it. He tells them they're wrong here and wrong there, he defends the manufacturers more than half the time, and still they believe him. They even say he was right sometimes when he decided against them. . . . I think they'd follow Brandeis to Kingdom Come because they say nobody can buy him, that he's not in this for himself, and that he's the whitest man who ever mixed up in the class struggle. That's what makes him so damned dangerous. If he were a fool, if he didn't know all about everything, if he were in it for Brandeis, if there were only something the matter with him, he wouldn't be messing things for the I.W.W. wherever he goes.[19]

Haywood was right: Brandeis was not "in it for Brandeis" but was genuinely concerned with the problem of industrial justice — which meant, to him, justice for both employer and employee. And justice was not an abstract conception; it had a human face. Brandeis had many facets: He was a man of the law, a master of facts, a brilliant political tactician, a gifted mediator, a concerned and involved citizen, an educator, a believer in democracy. Above all, however, he was a humanist. He was offended by human suffering and appalled by the waste of human potential.[20] Justice and democracy meant that people would have better lives. His humanism illuminated his approach to the world of employer and employee. He loathed irregularity of employment because it hurt people, and he fought overly long working hours and overly low wages for the same reason. He was closely tied to the world of social reform, as indicated by his relationships with people such as Jane Addams, Florence Kelley, Josephine Goldmark, Meyer Bloomfield, and Henry Moskowitz.[21] At the same time, he viewed each of his business clients as individuals with a need as great as their workers' for economic security and personal fulfillment. His concern for all the people in any given situation, including contentious labor disputes, coupled with his insistent independence, left him free to pursue his own ideas without regard for the self-interested reactions of others. He had a reputation as a fair mediator in labor disputes. In short, both business and labor had reason to trust him. That led to his acceptance as mediator in the New York garment workers' strike by both the International Ladies' Garment Workers Union, which represented approximately 10,000 of the roughly 60,000 workers on strike, and the Cloak, Suit & Skirt Manufacturers' Protective Association, which spoke for 1,500 enterprises, in Brandeis's estimate.[22]

The "protocol" Brandeis worked out for the garment industry contained provisions for maximum hours, minimum wages, holidays, a Joint Board of Sanitary Control to oversee and standardize working conditions, a Board of Grievances and a Board of Arbitration to resolve disputes and avert strikes, and Brandeis's cherished idea, a "preferential" rather than either an "open" or a "closed" shop, giving preference to union workers if equally skilled union and nonunion workers applied for jobs. Brandeis called it "an essay in industrial democracy," but the essay ended in 1916. It failed because it did not bridge the divergent interests of employer and employee at the heart of labor unrest. The experience nonetheless transformed Brandeis's attitude toward the average laborer.[23]

Most of the garment workers were Jewish immigrants from Eastern Europe, as were their employers. Although Brandeis's Jewishness undoubtedly contributed to the willingness of the two sides to have him mediate, both workers and management belonged to a group of Jews totally unknown to him. His family's background lay in the

Austro-Hungarian Empire; his clients and colleagues in Boston were mainly either Jews with origins similar to his or Boston Brahmins or other non-Jews.[24] Suddenly he found himself meeting unskilled laborers who astonished him with their intelligence, rationality, openness to democratic procedures, tolerance for each other's viewpoints, sense of equality, and knowledge. These people were his ideal citizens of a democracy, the workers who could quiet his remaining doubts about the democratic potential of the working class. He was impressed when he heard a disgruntled worker thundering at his employer the words of Isaiah,

> It is you who have devoured the vineyard,
>   the spoil of the poor is in your houses.
> What do you mean by crushing My people,
>   by grinding the face of the poor?
>   says the Lord God of hosts.

Here was no paucity of erudition, no lack of democratic precepts, no inability to grasp economic truths. Brandeis was so enchanted that he spent his evenings relaxing with the negotiating committee and, even though he had supposedly given up alcohol years before as unnecessary, drinking beer with them while he recounted stories of the Pinchot-Ballinger hearings.[25]

Perhaps his mental picture of workers from that time on was of the literate, articulate Jews he found in the garment industry; perhaps his theories of industrial relations were postulated on the assumption that such workers would be the norm; perhaps his intellectual sympathy for the worker was reinforced by the emotional tie that he, who had placed no importance on his Jewishness, was surprised to find himself feeling for these fellow Jews. It was easy for Brandeis to envision them as participants in his ideal industrial democracy, and the theory of labor relations he began to articulate reflected his new attitude.

He had long since dismissed state socialism as an evil to be avoided in political and industrial democracies because of the large bureaucracy and concentration of power he thought it necessarily entailed. In 1913 he wrote to an attorney who thought social reform might stave off socialism, "It seems to me that the prevailing discontent is due perhaps less to dissatisfaction with the material conditions, as to the denial of participation in management, and that the only way to avoid Socialism is to develop cooperation in its broadest sense."[26] "Cooperation," or worker-management, would be adopted by him both as a liberating mechanism and as a way of preventing socialism. Oligopolistic and monopolistic capitalism were equally to be avoided because they were too big to be efficient and because the power implicit in their size permitted them to ignore the best interests of both workers and consumers.

Brandeis gradually had altered his definition of democracy in the economic sphere, changing it from small-scale laissez-faire capitalism to a balancing of power between employer and employees and then adding profit sharing to the formula. Because his interest lay in individual autonomy as well as in justice for employees, however, he had to grapple with the fact that getting more money for their work did not necessarily ensure workers' autonomy in the workplace. Shorter hours and more money would bring them the leisure for involvement in public affairs and self-fulfillment that he considered necessary to a democratic state and to the individuals within it, but such working conditions, although desirable, would not bring democracy to the workplace. In 1911, testifying before a congressional committee chaired by Sen. Moses Clapp, he expressed his approval of profit sharing.[27] In 1912 he wrote a letter to the editor of Human Engineering, saying that there had to be "two lines of development consistent with industrial democracy." One was unionism; the other, cooperation, by which he did not mean "mere profit sharing" but "a share of the responsibilities and management, and a utilization of the latent powers" in the worker.[28] At that point, unable to follow the logic of his own thinking, he backed away from any discussion of "cooperation." The following year, however, he was writing that profit sharing was bound to be a disappointment "unless it [could] be combined with a real labor co-partnership." Industrial democracy would not be achieved unless "we . . . overcome the sense of injustice; and I doubt whether a sharing of profit, without a sharing of responsibilities, — in other words, without real cooperation, — will accomplish what we long for."[29]

Brandeis had begun thinking in ways that would differentiate him from most Progressives. He agreed with them that there was too great a disparity between the incomes of the wealthy, particularly corporation executives, and the wages of the workers. The Progressive goal, and that of the New Deal, was to divide the economic pie into a far greater number of slices even if that meant reducing the size of some of the larger pieces. The emphasis was on raising the workers' standard of living; the assumption was that having done that, maintaining a regulatory system would preclude a return to the earlier level of inequality and exploitation. Brandeis, though agreeing with the absolute necessity to ensure workers an adequate standard of living, was equally concerned about the quality of their lives and their role as citizens of a democratic state. That was his reason for emphasizing sufficient leisure for workers to develop their talents and to engage in the pastimes they considered to be fulfilling while continuing to educate themselves for intelligent participation in the political sphere. He may best have summarized the differences he would have with other Progressives and New Dealers years before he became identified with either movement. "Mr. Gompers quoted some time ago the saying of Heine that 'Bread is Freedom,'" Brandeis stated, referring to labor leader Samuel Gompers. "The ancient Greeks, recognizing that 'Man cannot live by bread alone,' declared that 'Leisure is Freedom.'" He added, again highlighting emphases that would be widely divergent, "The American standard of living demands not only a high minimum wage, but a high minimum of leisure, because we must meet also needs other than material ones."[30]

A number of goals converged in Brandeis's thinking about how to reorganize the workplace: equitable distribution of earnings, the need for a decent income level, provision of leisure time. Two additional factors included the question of fairness, of who should benefit from the toil of the workers, and the issue he referred to as responsibility; a later generation would call it empowerment.

John Locke had insisted that land "belonged" to those people who worked it.[31] Brandeis's ideas about profit sharing suggested that in 1911 and 1912 he felt the fruits of industry "belonged" in part to shareholders and in part to the workers. He obviously continued to ponder the question of responsibility as well as profit, however, and three years later, in January 1915, his testimony before the Senate Commission on Industrial Relations indicated that his ideas were beginning to solidify. He lambasted large corporations as inefficient, unable to deal with their problems intelligently, interfering with the growth of unions, permitting themselves to be dominated by financial interests that had no personal involvement in their work, and relying on wide-scale stockholding that constituted a form of irresponsible absentee ownership. In the course of his testimony, he also sketched his emerging vision of industrial democracy.[32]

One of the commission's concerns was industrial unrest. Brandeis was opposed to solutions that did no more than "improve . . . the physical and material condition of the workingman" because they would also "reduc[e]" the "manhood" of the workers. This was undesirable since a democracy required whole human beings: "Their mental condition is certainly equally important."[33] The paternalism implied in progressivism, which assumed workers' concerns would be satisfied if a governmental elite assured them of a decent wage, might put more food on the workers' tables but would do nothing for their sense of self or for their participation in the democratic process. The goal of the United States' polity, as he saw it, was not merely material improvement per se, but a democracy that would enable its citizens to take control of their material conditions. Here economic and political democracy came together:

> The social justice for which we are striving is an incident of our democracy, not the main end. It is rather the result of democracy — perhaps its finest expression — but it rests upon democracy, which implies the rule by the people. And therefore the end for which we must strive is the attainment of rule by the people, and that involves industrial democracy as well as political democracy.[34]

He had said elsewhere that "we cannot successfully grapple with the problem of democracy if we confine our efforts to political democracy . . . the ideals which we have can be attained, only if side by side with political democracy comes industrial democracy."[35] Industrial democracy meant involvement of workers in the problems of the enterprises that employed them. "The problems of his [the employer's] business, and it is not the employer's business alone, are the problems of all in it," he told the commission. This was more than profit sharing, although Brandeis still favored it:

There must be a division not only of profits, but a division also of responsibilities. The employees must have the opportunity of participating in the decisions as to what shall be their condition and how the business shall be run. They must learn also in sharing that responsibility that they must bear the suffering arising from grave mistakes, just as the employer must. But the right to assist in making the decisions, the right of making their own mistakes, if mistakes there must be, is a privilege which should not be denied to labor. We must insist upon labor sharing the responsibilities for the result of the business.[36]

His remarks reflected an element of confusion. Brandeis spoke about "a division of responsibilities" and workers "participating in the decisions," which he specifically said meant not only wages and hours but "how the business shall be run," and yet he also referred to "the right to *assist*" in the decisionmaking process. It was no wonder that one of the commissioners sought clarification by asking if Brandeis defined industrial democracy as "a condition whereby the worker has a voice in the management of the industry," and Brandeis replied that it did: "not only a voice but a vote; not merely a right to be heard, but a position through which labor may participate in management."[37]

Conceivably, participation could consist of little more than one representative of labor sitting in on management decisions. This was quite valid as an argument against paternalism but far less so as a description of democracy, which presumably implies the right to effective participation by all rather than token representation. At another point, he implied greater employee-participation, describing the protocol in the garment industry as creating a system in which employers and employees "come together to determine the problems of the trade in precisely the same way that members of the legislatures and the judges of the courts come together to decide the matters for the Nation or of the State or of the city." He was asked if he had found that the protocol resulted in "an earnest and sincere effort on both sides to find equity." They had "gotten past the point" of merely seeking equity, he replied. They had reached "a desire to solve industrial problems, and the recognition that the problems of the employer can not be solved by shifting them onto the employee, and that the problems of the employee can not be solved by shifting onto the employers; that some way must be found to arrive at the cause of the difficulty, to remove that cause."[38] The picture he painted had begun to look like a collaborative effort rather than the stereotypical labor-management relationship. The advocate of clashing ideas as necessary to the healthy body politic viewed a peaceful sharing of perceptions as more appropriate to the industrial sector. Truth might be achieved when ideas were tested against each other, but industrial strife was a wasteful indication that business and labor had misunderstood each other.

He added, referring to his belief that if employees understood an employer's problems there would be fewer labor disputes, "Put a competent representative of labor on your board of directors, make him grapple with the problems whether to do or not to do a specific thing, and undertake to balance the advantages and disadvantages presented, and he will get a realizing sense of how difficult it is to operate a business successfully, and what the dangers are of the destruction of the capital in the business."[39] His language was misleading. Although he appeared to be saying that the process would be complete if *a* competent worker representative was put on the board of directors, closer scrutiny suggests that he meant that *any* competent worker put on the board would understand the business' problems; i.e., workers— or at least those whom their colleagues considered sufficiently competent to represent them—could match the employers' understanding of the business.

His language was misleading, however, because his ideas were not yet fully formed, although he was certain of the goal. This became evident as he continued, extolling the unions' success in exercising some control over wages, hours, and conditions and in eliminating child labor from the coal industry. These achievements, Brandeis said, "are all gains for manhood; and we recognize that manhood is what we are striving for in America. We are striving for democracy; we are striving for the development of men. It is absolutely essential in order that men may develop that they be properly fed and properly housed, and that they have proper opportunities of education and recreation. We can not reach our goal without those things. But we may have all those things and have a nation of slaves."[40] By speaking of the inclusion of workers in profit sharing and the participation of some in policy-making, Brandeis was in effect beginning to break down the differentiation between the role and status of employers and that of employees. But if he was to move beyond progressivism, which was in many ways a conservative movement aimed at protecting the world of small business by such measures as trust-busting and reinvigorating small-scale competition, he had to go further in eliminating the differentiation.[41]

Brandeis's thinking had not solidified in part because of the paucity of examples in the United States. Despite his constant and eclectic reading, most — but not all — of his ideas were derived primarily from experience, which was in keeping with his belief that experimentation was the key to progress. One example he did have was the Filene Co-operative Association, whose constitution he had helped write in 1903. The Filene brothers had decided to experiment with greater worker involvement in their Boston department store. The 1903 constitution declared that all Filene employees were automatically members of the association and that the association's goal was "to give its members a voice in their government, to increase their efficiency and add to their social opportunities, to create and sustain a just and equitable relation between employer and employe." The plan contemplated profit sharing, but this aspect was dropped in 1913 in favor of an annual bonus. Another feature that failed was the provision of the 1912 bylaws for the association's acquisition of the Filenes' common stock, amounting to 48 percent of all stock, upon the brothers' retirement. A major reason the provision was dropped in practice was the discouragement of the brothers over the unwillingness of the workers to be actively involved in management. In 1930 a Russell Sage Foundation study concluded that the plan had been unworkable because the idea of worker-management had been instituted from above. It might also have noted that although the employees had the right to decide all aspects of employment, their power did not extend to store policy, merchandising techniques, selection of products to be sold, and so on, and so the plan never called for complete worker-management. While the experiment was still young, however, and again because of his emphasis on experience as a major source of knowledge, Brandeis urged Edward Filene to publicize it, arguing that "the best results of any form of industrial co-operation cannot be attained by working out the problem in a single establishment." This goal would be accomplished only "by having your work and ideas supplemented by the independent work and ideas of others that may be started under different conditions and in different places on the same general lines."[42]

At the time of his testimony before the commission in 1915, Brandeis had just begun to learn about workers' cooperatives, particularly from Beatrice Potter's *Cooperative Movement in Great Britain*. Potter described factories and workshops that had "a brotherhood of workers controlling the organization and retaining the profits of their own labour," mills "owned and governed by the men and women who actually worked" there, and fifty-four manufacturing associations and five agricultural associations in existence when her book was written. She argued that the worker-run enterprises that had failed had done so because of insufficient democracy within the enterprise, lack of support from without, too little understanding of economics and market forces, and the absence of a cooperative union that would not only constitute a network of worker-managed enterprises but would also include consumer cooperatives.[43]

This book occasioned one of the relatively few times that Brandeis's basic ideas were affected by something he read. Potter's impression on him was clear in the interview Brandeis gave to the Sunday *Boston Post* shortly after his appearance before the commission. Perhaps he had been thinking about the inconsistencies in his testimony, for in the interview he described the protocol system as "a large step toward industrial democracy, but of course only a step." And, at last, he spoke of the end of the employer-employee distinction, saying that "in a democratic community we naturally long for that condition where labor will hire capital, instead of capital hiring labor."[44]

One way this could be accomplished, Brandeis told the interviewer, was through "co-operative enterprises, private or public, by which the community undertakes to provide itself with necessaries." He referred at length to England's Co-operative Wholesale Society, the worldwide parts of which included flour mills, England's largest shoe factory, apparel factories, manufacturers of prepared food and household articles, creameries, printing plants, coalfields, a Danish bacon factory, an Australian tallow and oil factory, and a Ceylon tea plantation. The society's annual gross of $150 million made it bigger than most American industries. And it not only sold for low prices but operated democratically. Its leaders were selected not by "England's leading bankers or other notables supposed to possess unusual wisdom, but . . . by all the people interested in the operations of the society, and the number of such persons who have directly or indirectly a voice in the selection of the directors of the English Co-operative Wholesale Society is 2,750,000, for the directors of the wholesale society are elected by vote of the delegates of the 1,899 retail societies, and the delegates of the retail societies are in turn selected by the members of the local societies, that is, by the consumers, on the principle of one man, one vote, regardless of the amount of capital contributed." Each of the thirty-two full-time directors elected in this manner was paid about $1,500 in 1915, making their combined salaries less than that of many individual American executives. And that, commented Brandeis proudly, "shows what industrial democracy can do."[45]

Brandeis went on to read *The Consumer's Cooperative Movement* and *The Decay of Capitalist Civilization* by Potter and her husband Sidney Webb and recommended them and their ideas to his economist daughter Elizabeth and to his protégé Felix Frankfurter.[46] He became an admirer of the consumers' cooperatives not only of England but also of Sweden, Denmark, and Switzerland and an advocate of producers' cooperatives, cooperative banks, and credit unions. Producers' cooperatives would tend to merge into consumers' cooperatives, he thought, and the creation of such institutions would distribute responsibility and thereby serve as a force for democracy and individual development.[47] His interest in Denmark's cooperative factories and consumers' cooperatives led him to encourage his wife and one of her sisters to publish a volume entitled *Democracy in Denmark.*[48]

Brandeis had been pleased to learn that the directors chosen by the Co-operative Wholesale Society frequently were "men who have risen from the ranks." He insisted that "we in America must come to the co-operative idea" in both production and consumption. The profit sharing that Brandeis had been advocating for years, enabling workers to own stock in the companies for which they worked, could now be combined with the society's democratic election procedure to result in worker-management. He also had before him another example of worker-ownership. In 1914 he had become head of the American Zionist movement, and he was delighted to discover the Jewish kibbutzim in Palestine. All kibbutz land, equipment, and possessions were owned jointly; all decisions were made in meetings of kibbutz members; the kibbutz bore responsibility for filling its members' needs.

Obviously, these small agricultural settlements in which the workers lived communally, ate their meals together, put their children to sleep in the children's quarters, and had no need of money could not become direct models for industry in the United States. They did, however, give Brandeis a concrete example of communal, nonbureaucratized, democratic living, in which the distinction between management and labor had disappeared.[49]

Brandeis saw the future economy as based on some kind of worker-management or worker-participation: workers owning a business and voting democratically to elect management. He was not entirely clear about ownership. Whether stock would be held by workers alone, or by both workers and consumers, or even by the public in its collective capacity, as suggested in his reference to public as opposed to private cooperatives (and in keeping with his belief that utilities and land should be owned by the public), was not specified. In this connection it must be noted that his comments about absentee ownership, made before the 1911 Clapp hearings, appear to have reflected his discomfort at the idea of receiving money that had been generated by the toil of others. Both an echo of Puritanism and of Brandeis's growing concern for equality can be heard here. Nonetheless, although he would not own stocks, much of the three-million-dollar fortune he amassed came from his investing the money he earned in corporate bonds. He had written to his brother, early in the century, "I feel very sure that *unser eins* ["people like us"] ought not to buy and sell stocks . . . treat investments as a necessary Evil, indulging in the operation as rarely as possible. . . . And when you buy, buy the thing which you think is safe, and will give you a fair return; but don't try to make your money out of investments."[50] This advice initially may have been a matter of safe investments rather than of virtue. He later said that he invested money in bonds "where it will be so safe that I will not have to take time off thinking about it."[51] His letter to his brother indicates that "unser eins" refers to people who "don't know much about the business" and that he advised, "Don't try to make your money out of investments . . . make it out of your business" because "you understand [your business] as much as anybody."[52] He later fulminated against stock ownership because businesses declared large dividends in order to fool stock buyers "for the power conferred to use other people's money."[53]

Brandeis took an initially puzzling bypath in his enthusiasm for scientific management, which he learned about through a 1903 article by Frederick W. Taylor, the movement's progenitor. Brandeis began to read works by efficiency engineers Henry L. Gantt, Frank B. Gilbreth, and Harrington Emerson. Soon he was corresponding and meeting with them and with executives of businesses that had successfully introduced scientific management into their firms. The oddity, as Richard P. Adelstein has argued, is that scientific management might well be understood as diverging from the individual-centered philosophy Brandeis espoused.[54]

Scientific management, as Brandeis explained it, was based on the assumption that the labor performed in modern businesses could be analyzed and rationalized so as to maximize efficiency. "Efficiency engineers" determined the maximum time needed to perform each step of a business' work process; the business then trained employees so that they could complete their jobs in the time allotted. The results included the ability of a business to plan ahead, as it would know how long specific jobs would take and what the costs would be; reduction of inventory, as it would be able to identify the materials needed on precise dates; the end of irregularity of employment, for the plans would include continual and efficient use of machinery and labor; and greater productivity and reduced costs, which benefited management, labor, and consumers.[55]

Brandeis described scientific management as "a revolution in industry comparable only to that effected in the transition from hand labor to machinery." The system would encompass the labor "of the managers and high-salaried officials" as well as that of the workers: "Increased efficiency must begin with those higher up." It would alter the relationship between employer and employee because an employer, having invested in an employee's training, would have "a special incentive . . . to retain his employee and to conserve his powers."[56]

Brandeis used the examples of the Brighton Mills, which had cut costs dramatically as a result of scientific management and had raised wages by 45 to 75 percent; the Tabor Manufacturing Company, which had reduced prices by 10 to 15 percent while raising wages by 25 to 30 percent; the Link Belt Company, where wages had gone up by 25 to 35 percent; and the Manhattan Press, which handed out bonuses (for work performed faster than the norm) on nonpaydays so as to spread income throughout the week. The workers at the Tabor Manufacturing Company's Philadelphia plant liked the system so much that they refused to join other workers in a general strike.[57]

Organized labor was outraged. When Brandeis told a union group that a "great opportunity is offered us" by scientific management and asked, "Shall we seize it? . . . Will organized labor seize it?" the answer was a resounding no.[58] Unions were certain that greater production per worker would result in a loss of jobs. Of equal importance, however, was labor's view of the automatic "speed-up" inherent in scientific management: The pace set by the fastest workers would become the standard, those who did piecework would find their wages reduced, and slower day laborers would be fired. Brandeis replied that once the amount of time spent on a job was established, it would remain fixed; laborers able to work faster would receive bonuses. The unions were understandably skeptical. Having dealt with hostile employers, they saw no reason to assume that introduction of scientific management or anything else would transform management into bastions of beneficence. Here Brandeis's sense of reasonable people deliberating together to develop a system that would work in the best interests of all was confronted by the unions' more realistic assessment of management's mentality. Brandeis and the unions were speaking different languages. If rationality prevailed, there was every reason to believe that scientific management would indeed better the workers' lot; and Brandeis was a devotee of rationality. The workers, however, had more experience of the workplace. Their reaction was summarized by a union woman who shouted at him, "You can call it scientific management if you want to, but I call it scientific driving."[59]

Upon closer examination Brandeis's adherence to scientific management reflects a lack of realism rather than theoretical inconsistency. He truly believed that scientific management was based on "conserving human effort" and would result in "removing the obstacles which annoy and exhaust the workman. . . . Relieved of every unnecessary effort, of every unnecessary interruption and annoyance, the worker is enabled without greater strain to furnish much more in production. And under the exhilaration of achievement he develops his capacity. . . . He secures the development and rise in self-respect, the satisfaction with his work, which in almost every line of human activity accompany great accomplishment by the individual."[60]

In addition, Brandeis assumed that the profits gained by increased productivity would go in large part to the workers. Scientific management, as he saw it, would improve the lot of the worker. Individual fulfillment was still his goal, however unrealistic this particular method of achieving it may have been. His romance with scientific management constituted one of the few times he ignored the advice he gave to others: "The logic of words should yield to the logic of realities."[61]

When Brandeis was appointed to the Supreme Court in 1916, he gained a national platform for the dissemination of many of his ideas but lost both the time and the forums in which to continue developing his theory of worker-participation. His general method, however, was not to opt for any one possibility until experiments in all had been made and data collected. He believed in evolution, not revolution, and much as he might look forward to the disintegration of the dividing line between labor and management, he would not give up the vocabulary of "labor," "capital," and "management" until experimentation validated his ideas. But he quietly told Felix Frankfurter in the 1920s that the "wage system is doomed" and that consumers ought to go without goods if they could not buy them through cooperatives.[62]

By then he may have seen a source of hope in the experiment undertaken by his friend Norman Hapgood and Hapgood's two brothers in their Indianapolis manufacturing plant. A year after Brandeis joined the Court, Hutchins Hapgood, who bore the major responsibility for the brothers' Columbia Conserve Company, decided to give labor a role in management and found the workers not only enthusiastic but more conservative in their policies than he might have been. When the cost of living rose one year, for example, he asked if they might not like to give themselves a raise. They responded that they still did not know whether the business could afford it; six months later, convinced that it could, they voted themselves the suggested increase. Hutchins, certain that efficiency grew along with the workers' participation in management, started meeting with them to see if the process could not be taken further by selling the business to them outright. A price was set on each share of stock. It was agreed that 7 percent was a fair return for the Hapgoods and that profits beyond that would be used to buy stock for the workers. The system worked; by 1930 a trust established by the workers owned a majority of the stock, dividing the proceeds among them. The initial hostility experienced by the brothers from other business people had faded, and although many were still skeptical, the company's enlarged earnings resulted in Hutchins being asked to give more talks about the experiment than he could manage.[63]

In 1922 Brandeis spoke informally to a group connected with the Department of Research and Education of the Federal Council of Churches in America. The most concise statement of his thinking about worker-participation is in the letter summarizing his remarks that he sent to the meeting's organizer, Robert Bruere. The letter reflects his emphasis on democracy, individual responsibility, human dignity, experimentation, and the collection of facts:

> Do not believe that you can find a universal remedy for evil conditions or immoral practices in effecting a fundamental change in society (as by State Socialism). . . . And do not pin too much faith in legislation. Remedial institutions are apt to fall under the control of the enemy and to become instruments of oppression. . . . Seek for betterment within the broad lines of existing institutions. Do so by attacking evil in situ; and proceed from the individual to the general. Remember that progress is necessarily slow; that remedies are necessarily tentative; that, because of varying conditions, there must be much and constant enquiry into facts . . . and much experimentation; and that always and everywhere the intellectual, moral and spiritual development of those concerned will remain an essential — and the main factor — in real betterment.

Having stated his belief in empiricism as a key element in the search for truth, he went on to discuss the goal:

> The development of the individual is, thus, both a necessary means and the end sought. For our objective is the making of men and women who shall be free — self-respecting members of a democracy — and who shall be worthy of respect.
>
> The great developer is responsibility. Hence, no remedy can be hopeful which does not devolve upon the workers' participation in, responsibility for the conduct of business; and their aim should be the eventual assumption of full responsibility — as in cooperative

enterprises. This participation in and eventual control of industry is likewise an essential of obtaining justice in distributing the fruits of industry.

"Democracy in any sphere is a serious undertaking," Brandeis continued. "It substitutes self-restraint for external restraint. It is more difficult to maintain than to achieve." Democracy is difficult to sustain because it "demands continuous sacrifice by the individual and more exigent obedience to the moral law than any other form of government." Again, the emphasis is on the individual; democracy "is possible only where the process of perfecting the individual is pursued." But individualism went hand in hand with community, for the development of the individual "is attained mainly in the processes of common living."[64] John Dewey commented upon the letter approvingly; he saw its ideal as having to do "with the development, the *making*, of individuals" and agreed that "workers must assume responsibility for the conduct of business if they are to be free to develop."[65]

Although Brandeis supported minimum-wage and maximum-hour laws, he hoped such laws ultimately would be unnecessary, for the employers would be the workers themselves. That was his answer to the question of how Jeffersonianism could be brought into the industrial era, and it was one of the few serious efforts at a response. True liberty necessarily included economic independence, but participation in the twentieth-century American economy meant factory work for great masses of citizens. A formula that would encompass both liberty and the factory therefore had to be found. Brandeis thought he had identified it in the liberty to participate in industrial decision-making.

Seen from the vantage point of the 1990s, it appears that one of the failures of the New Deal was the lack of consideration it gave to the problem of protecting economic liberty and independence as opposed to increasing the economic well-being of workers. Whether even such a charismatic leader as Franklin Roosevelt could have convinced the American public that individual liberty necessitated scaling down the size of businesses and beginning the introduction of worker-management and whether, if he had done so, the political influence of the giant corporations would have prevented Congress from enacting the necessary legislation are yet other unanswerable questions. But no such attempt was made, and the possible solution to the problem of protecting economic liberty and independence in an industrial society received neither full-scale discussion nor meaningful experimentation during the period that may have been the one "window of opportunity" for that attempt in American history.

3

LAW, LAWYER, AND JUDGE
IN A DEMOCRATIC POLITY

Thou hast heard men scorn the city, call her wild
Of counsel, mad; thou hast seen the fire of morn
Flash from her eyes in answer to their scorn!
Come toil on toil, 'tis this that makes her grand.
Peril on peril! and common states that stand
In caution, twilight cities, dimly wise—
Ye know them; for no light is in their eyes!
Go forth, my son, and help.[1]

This verse from Euripides' *Suppliant Women* was sent to Brandeis
by his partner Sam Warren in 1890. Brandeis took its advice so
seriously that within a few years he became known as "the people's
attorney."[2]

It was 1897, and Boston's downtown congestion had become intoler-
able again. It had been bad enough in the early 1890s, when the city
had responded by building its first subway. Now, however, both
population and commerce had grown, and merchants, some of them
Brandeis's clients, were complaining about the difficulty consumers
had getting to their stores.

The Boston Elevated Railway was aware of the problem and eager
to take advantage of it. It secretly obtained a thirty-year franchise
from the state legislature, allowing it to operate on many of the city's
most important thoroughfares for the then exorbitant fare of five cents
a ride. Brandeis reacted to the announcement of the deal with the

49

combination of moral outrage and organizational activity that would typify him and that illuminates his ideal of the "good attorney." He called for public action and was named chairman of the Transportation Committee of the Municipal Transportation League, a group of Boston businessmen opposed to the legislation. Their efforts proved futile. The fight was renewed in 1901, however, when citizens petitioned for an additional line on Washington Street. The Elevated promptly sought the right to build and own the Washington Street line as well as a connecting subway to Cambridge and to lease the already existing subway, which would have given it control over Boston's transportation system.

Brandeis swung into action, opposing the proposal on behalf of the Associated Board of Trade, a group of merchants and manufacturers that included a number of his clients. The fight became complicated, with its first phase lasting until 1902 and later developments continuing until 1911. Brandeis won, getting the legislature to accept the proposal of the Public Franchise League and the Board of Trade for construction of the Washington Street subway by the city, with a lease to the Elevated for no more than twenty-five years and a rental of 4.5 percent of the construction cost.[3]

He represented the Board of Trade pro bono. When Brandeis's friend Edward Filene, speaking for the board, asked for his bill, Brandeis told Filene that "he never made a charge for public service of this kind; that it was his duty as it was mine to help protect the public rights; and when I remonstrated, saying that he and his family were dependent upon his income, he told me that he resolved early in life to give at least one hour a day to public service, and later on he hoped to give fully half his time."[4] At what point "early in life" Brandeis took his resolution is unclear, especially as until that time he had accepted fees for public service but had donated them to charity. In any event, he had now begun to feel that taking no fee might benefit the public but it was unfair to his own law firm, which lost his services and the income it could generate during the hours he spent on public affairs. He also wanted to feel free to use the services of some of the firm's younger attorneys, whom he had encouraged to develop expertise in particular areas of the law. He announced that he would consider himself the firm's client whenever he became involved in public matters and would reimburse the partnership accordingly.

Under this arrangement he paid his firm $25,167.32 for the hours he spent over six years while he was fighting the merger of the New Haven Railroad and the Boston & Maine Railroad.[5] In another instance he both reimbursed the firm for his hours and paid court costs when he represented a consumer group.[6] He had become one of the country's most successful lawyers and was depriving neither himself nor his family by his action, and he frankly delighted in it. "Some men buy diamonds and rare works of art," he told an interviewer; "others delight in automobiles and yachts. My luxury is to invest my surplus effort, beyond that required for the proper support of my family, to the pleasure of taking up a problem and solving, or helping to solve it, for the people without receiving any compensation. Your yachtsman or automobilist would lose most of his enjoyment if he were obliged to do for pay what he is doing for the love of the thing itself. So I should lose much of my satisfaction if I were paid in connection with public services of this kind." His relish of public affairs was perhaps partly responsible for his insistence that all good citizens had to be involved in them.[7]

Brandeis would spend the rest of his pre-Court years combining private practice with representation of the public interest, earning the soubriquet, "the people's attorney."[8] His years as the public's lawyer would affect his view not only of the good attorney but of the role of law in a democratic state and, eventually, of the nature of American jurisprudence.

Brandeis occasionally made attorneys sound embarrassingly like supermen. "The training of the practicing lawyer," he said in 1916, "breeds a certain virile, compelling quality, which tends to make the possessor proof against the influence of either fear or favor," and legal practice "involves a happy combination of the intellectual with the practical life."[9] A few years earlier he had admonished, "What the lawyer needs to redeem himself is not more ability or physical courage but the moral courage in the face of financial loss and personal ill-will [sic] to stand for right and justice,"[10] for to Brandeis, only just laws could be legitimate. In keeping with this description of the lawyer, Brandeis initially took the elitist position that attorneys, along with the rest of the better-educated population, had a particular obligation to make their talents available in the public arena. Later, he recognized that all citizens, including those without professional training, had a role to play in a democratic society, a role that went well beyond the simple act of voting. But whether because lawyers have always had a peculiarly important position in American politics, or because Brandeis as a lawyer continued to believe they had special gifts to bring to the political process, or simply because he knew so many talented and public-spirited attorneys, he continued to emphasize their special contribution.

Horace Kallen has suggested that Brandeis's shock at the divergence of the law from social need in the Homestead steel strike forced him to choose between legalism and morality.[11] Kallen was mistaken: The strike made Brandeis resolve to bridge the gap between the two, of which he had suddenly become aware. One of his contributions to the legal profession was to remind it of its ethical responsibilities at a moment when new situations were tempting it to accept an amoral role.

Brandeis became an attorney during a transitional period in American legal history. As he noted in 1905, many lawyers in the country's early days were also statesmen who could be relied upon for their awareness of the social good. Alexis de Tocqueville had commented in 1835, "If I were asked where I place the American aristocracy, I should reply without hesitation . . . that it occupies the judicial bench and the bar."[12] The lawyers who more or less gave up practice to serve in official public capacities, however, were never the model for the average attorney. Attorneys throughout the mid-nineteenth century had little opportunity to affect many people beyond their own clients because the largely agrarian society, composed primarily of small economic units, gave almost no one large-scale power.

That of course changed with the Civil War, the completion of the transcontinental railroad link, and the burgeoning of industrialization and urbanization. Suddenly there were large corporations, demanding skills and knowledge about the commercial arena that earlier generations of lawyers did not have or need. A schism developed between lawyers working on the local level and those who were employed by the large commercial entities that sprawled across the country. By the end of the nineteenth century and the beginning of federal governmental regulation of business, corporate attorneys had to know not only the intricacies of commercial law but of regulatory law as well. The sheer volume of work that any one corporation could provide for a substantial number of attorneys made it possible for many lawyers to receive their income largely or solely from one source. Instead of representing a variety of clients in situations that frequently were adversarial, many lawyers became advisers to individual corporations or to combinations of similar big businesses. It was not their courtroom skills or their ability to write legal documents for individuals that was important; now the emphasis fell on advising large corporations how legally to do the things that would maximize their profits and keep them out of court.

This development had two consequences. First, the lawyer who wanted to succeed financially had to be more of a specialist than a generalist, confining himself not only to commercial law but to subsets within it. Specializations developed in areas such as trusts, stock issues, and receiverships. Attorneys became economic advisers, aiding businesses in their attempts to peer into the future and predict which courses would prove most financially profitable and least legally contentious.

The second consequence stemmed from the simple fact that maximization of profits and human considerations were not necessarily compatible; indeed, they were frequently diametric opposites. The question of whether the lawyer had a responsibility to the public that preempted or at least had to be balanced against his obligation to his client was implicit in the situation, a question most corporate lawyers preferred to ignore. Even if they had chosen to face it, however, they might have been unable to provide answers, for their immersion in their area of specialization made it extremely difficult for them to see their responsibilities in a larger social and moral scheme.[13]

The model for most young urban lawyers quickly became the corporate lawyer, who could not have been further removed either from de Tocqueville's vision of citizen-lawyers dedicating themselves to the body politic or from the small town practitioner who had grown up with his clients and was an integral part of his society. The new prototype was the corporate attorney whose concern was to help industrial giants make as much money as possible, who neither litigated nor sought a variety of clients and who did not permit ethical considerations to complicate the work at hand. The profitable was transformed into the moral by both bar and bench, with the Supreme Court leading the federal and state judicial systems in handing down a series of decisions extolling the virtues of private property and the obligation of the courts to interpret the Constitution so as to protect it. Property rights became the new official religion; lawyers prided themselves on serving as somewhat tarnished handmaidens to the triumphant deity.[14]

The changed notion of law and of the lawyer's role had a major impact on the American polity. Morton J. Horwitz has described how judges in the period between the ratification of the Constitution and the beginning of the Civil War made a conscious attempt to turn law into an instrument of social policy.[15] As law became more business-oriented, so, logically, did social policy. The Supreme Court, however, consistently denied that it was in the policymaking business, maintaining instead that the new truths it established merely reflected the intentions of the Founding Fathers.[16] Brandeis opened his Boston law office in 1879, when the legal profession and the courts were beginning to experience these changes. During the next two decades, legal discourse was largely transformed into a discussion of mechanisms for protecting property, the courts demonstrated their approval of this goal, the country's most successful lawyers became specialized hired guns for concentrated wealth, and political colloquy was dominated by those individuals who spoke either in legal terms or as social Darwinists on behalf of the intrinsic social utility of large-scale wealth.

Brandeis gradually challenged all the new truths, in part because they embodied a view of the attorney's role that did not comport with his preferred style. In one sense, Brandeis was a lawyer of his times; his emphasis on facts meant that he grasped fully the complicated economics of his era. As Oliver Wendell Holmes was to comment, the successful lawyer was "the man of statistics and the master of economics," and Brandeis qualified as both.[17] A memorandum in his handwriting, written early in his practice and entitled "The Practice of Law," says in part, "Know not only specific cases. But whole subject . . . know thoroughly Each fact. Don't believe client witness— Examine Documents. Reason. . . . Know the whole Subject. Know bookkeeping the universal language of business. . . . Know not only those facts which bear on direct controversy, but know all facts that Surround."[18]

He would not concentrate only on the facts involved in a case, however; his vision of the good lawyer also encompassed an understanding of human nature in general and, in particular, knowledge of the people with whom he was dealing. "Cultivate the society of men — particularly men of affairs," he wrote to William Dunbar, a young lawyer in his firm who was not doing well. "The man who does not know intimately human affairs is apt to make of the law a bed of Procrustes . . . the law bears to [the lawyers'] profession a relation very similar to that which medicine does to that of the physicians. . . . The great physicians are those who in addition to that knowledge of therapeutics which is open to all, know not merely the human body but the human mind and emotions, so as to make themselves the proper diagnoses — to know the truth which their patients fail to disclose and who add to this an influence over the patient which is apt to spring from a real understanding of him." Brandeis advised Dunbar that "the duty of a lawyer today is not that of a solver of legal conundrums: he is indeed a counsellor at law" — precisely the opposite of the kind of lawyer the corporations wanted.[19] Brandeis used "corporation lawyer" as a term of contempt, contrasting it with "the 'people's lawyer'" who stood "ready to protect" the citizenry. He fulminated against attorneys with specialization "not only in the nature and class of questions" with which they dealt "but also specialization in the character of clientage," i.e., corporations. The "growing intensity" of corporation lawyers' work precluded their participation in public affairs and their gaining the benefit of its "broadening of view," and their highly particularized knowledge resulted in "vast areas of ignorance and grave danger of resultant distortion of judgment."[20] Three years later Brandeis acknowledged the need for law firms to become "more and more a business" with each attorney in it "com[ing] to do those things that on the whole he does most effectively."[21] His contempt for lawyers who were *only* specialists did not preclude his wanting the young associates in his firm to master discrete areas of the law. In this letter he emphasized his simultaneous insistence that they be able to function as generalists, able to give intelligent advice to clients and to persuade the clients to take it. He added:

perhaps most important of all is the impressing of clients and satisfying them. Your law may be perfect, your ability to apply it great, and yet you cannot be a successful adviser unless your advice is followed; it will not be followed unless . . . you impress [clients] with your superior knowledge, and that you cannot do unless you know their affairs better than they do because you see them from a fullness of knowledge. The ability to impress them grows with your success in advising others, with the confidence which you yourself feel in your powers. That confidence can never come from books: it is gained by human intercourse.[22]

It should at least be noted, in an analysis of Brandeis's impressive contributions to the definition of the attorney's function, that he did not address the situation in which the client insisted on a course of behavior the lawyer found distasteful. He proclaimed that he would "rather have clients than be somebody's lawyer," and he turned away prospective clients if he thought them wrong and they refused to accept his advice.[23] He did not suggest, however, what resort they would have in an adversarial legal system if all lawyers shared his approach and his beliefs. And he could literally afford to urge upon other lawyers the "moral courage" to "stand for right and justice" even at the cost of "financial loss and personal ill-will," for the combination of his creative brilliance, his outstanding reputation, his ability to work quickly and well, his frugality, and his investment in relatively secure bonds had made him a millionaire by 1907.[24] He took his own advice, however. When some of the Boston Brahmins who had been important to him, realizing that he was serious about attacking their institutions and beliefs, turned their backs, he quietly ignored them and went on doing what he thought was right.[25]

A break with the Brahmins was inevitable once Brandeis became uncomfortable with the emphasis the law placed on the protection of property and the limited role this left for the lawyer, as well as with the assumption that answers to all political-legal problems could be found in the intentions of the Constitution's authors. To him, law made no sense unless it reflected social necessities. As Harold Laski commented to Oliver Wendell Holmes, Brandeis's "method of analysis does magnificently relate law to the life of which it is the expression."[26]

Brandeis wanted to reform the lawyers and the courts not only because they were morally unacceptable but also because their distance from the realities of social need threatened the rule of law. He argued for a radical rethinking in order to conserve a democratic system he believed could work but that he feared was being jeopardized by the law's partiality to the wealthy elite. He noted that in other "periods of rapid transformation, challenge of existing law, instead of being sporadic," had become general. "Such was the case in Athens, twenty-four centuries ago," he reminded the Chicago Bar Association, "when Euripides burst out in flaming words against 'the trammelings of law which are not of the right.'" It had been the case during the German Reformation and after the French Revolution, and it would continue to be the case in the United States until courts stopped relying on "early nineteenth-century scientific half-truths like 'The survival of the fittest,' which, translated into practice, meant 'The devil take the hindmost.'"[27]

Ironically, Brandeis, who scorned social Darwinism, was greatly influenced by Holmes, a social Darwinist. Holmes's seminal *Common Law* broke new ground by declaring, "The life of the law has not been logic; it has been experience." That assertion, according to Holmes, suggested that instead of basing its decisions on what today would be called the "original intent" of the Constitution's writers as reflected in their specific words, the judiciary was obligated to refashioning of legislation according to new perceptions of social needs or the "felt necessities" of the time.[28] Holmes's view fit well with Brandeis's boyhood belief that the law had to be altered because it permitted slavery and that the best people to ensure congruence between law and morality were lawyers like his uncle Dembitz. One of the differences between the jurisprudence of Holmes and Brandeis was the latter's assumption that social necessities included morality. Holmes, the skeptic who numbered survival of the fittest among his few acknowledged beliefs, doubted that morality made any difference. Writing to Frederick Pollock, Holmes declared, "I am so skeptical as to our knowledge about the goodness and badness of laws that I have no practical criterion except what the crowd wants. Personally I bet that the crowd if it knew more wouldn't want what it does—but that is immaterial."[29]

Holmes and Roscoe Pound were the major American exponents of sociological jurisprudence, which is an analysis of the law that describes it not as a collection of legal tenets but as a reflection of social needs in differing historical eras.[30] Their jurisprudence illuminated the approach that Brandeis and others believed was proper to constitutional litigation. The Constitution, as John Marshall had said, was "framed for ages to come, and is designed to approach immortality as nearly as human institutions can approach it."[31] This view implied that the Constitution was expected not only to remain in existence long after the historical facts reflected in it had changed but that it was written with an awareness that the precise meaning of the clauses it included would undergo similar transformations.[32] It was the function of judges to understand society sufficiently to permit the Constitution to be adapted to "felt necessities." If a law was passed because people considered it useful in light of current circumstances, the courts could not strike it down unless it clearly violated a constitutional provision. In Holmes's formulation, the courts had to interpret the Constitution as permitting any law unless "a rational and fair man necessarily would admit that the statute proposed would infringe fundamental principles as they have been understood by the traditions of our people and our law."[33] Holmes recognized that the clauses of the Constitution are relatively vague; the implication was that the courts would have little reason to strike down many laws as being inconsistent with them. Holmes neglected, however, to answer the questions of how "reasonableness" was to be ascertained or of what criteria the judges would employ to differentiate "a rational and fair man" from one less able to reason.

His acceptance of Holmes's analysis did not mean Brandeis saw courts as having little or no function. Holmes may have seen the judges as merely looking at a statute, asking whether it clearly violated the Constitution, and, if it did not, upholding it as valid. This was not quite Brandeis's view.

If the logic of Holmes and Pound is followed, it is not sufficient simply to adopt a stance of judicial restraint, the term used to describe the disposition of judges to minimize their interference with legislative policymaking. Holmes's and Pound's starting point, after all, was the congruence of law and social conditions. The unspoken and therefore unaddressed element of their jurisprudence is the question of what happens when a legislature misperceives social need. Holmes's cynicism about the ability of human beings rather than natural forces to affect their fate illuminated his devotion to judicial restraint. He would no doubt have answered that as long as a law did not conflict with the

Constitution the judicial function was to uphold it; and if it was based on a misperception, the electorate had an obligation to make its dissatisfaction clear to the enacting body.[34] It was a jurisprudence that would later be enunciated, without the element of social Darwinism, by Felix Frankfurter.[35] Again, this view would not have satisfied Brandeis because it denied the logical underpinnings of sociological jurisprudence; unlike Holmes, he did believe in the necessity for the law to be moral, and as a reformer, he had all too close a view of the corrupt legislatures of the late nineteenth and early twentieth centuries.

Brandeis had the additional burden, unshared by Holmes and Pound, of being a practicing attorney attempting to convince the courts of his time that sociological jurisprudence was proper. The approach to judging and particularly to constitutional litigation that was taken by most courts was either historical, based on what judges thought the clauses' writers meant, or mechanistic, relying on what judges believed to be the plain meaning of the words. Brandeis and the attorneys who shared his views had to cope with judges who regarded the Constitution as a static document and who interpreted it as delineating retention of property as the highest good. "Original intent" and mechanical jurisprudence are not approaches sprung full-blown from late twentieth-century jurisprudents;[36] their genesis can be found in the earliest days of constitutional interpretation. More important for Brandeis, they were being enunciated by the judges before whom he had to appear and with whom he would later sit on the Supreme Court. Justice Owen J. Roberts declared, in 1936, that "All the court does" when a statute is challenged as unconstitutional is to "lay the article of the Constitution which is invoked beside the statute which is challenged and to decide whether the latter squares with the former."[37] Brandeis would have denied that such a process was either possible or desirable.

Brandeis the litigator recognized that although the judges did not accept the doctrine of sociological jurisprudence, they might be persuaded to accept its application in specific instances. He had an opportunity to test his theory in 1908.

Oregon had passed a statute limiting women's work in manufacturing and mechanical establishments and laundries to no more than ten hours a day. Kurt Muller's Grand Laundry in Portland was held by the Oregon courts to have broken the law when one woman was required to work more than ten hours. Muller appealed his misdemeanor conviction to the Supreme Court on the grounds that it violated his Fourteenth Amendment right to the "liberty of contract," which the Court proclaimed it had unearthed in the depths of the due process clause.[38] Brandeis's sister-in-law Josephine Goldmark, who worked with the National Consumers' League, and Florence Kelley, the league's secretary general, asked him to defend the statute. The result was the famous "Brandeis brief."[39]

Although he would have preferred workers' hours to be decided jointly by employers and unions, Brandeis considered state regulation of hours legitimate because unions were not yet sufficiently strong to demand such working conditions successfully. He thought it only logical for both men's and women's work hours to be limited. He had good reason to believe, however, that the Court would ignore the argument that overly long hours were bad for all workers. It had recently struck down a New York maximum-hours law with an opinion that made clear its hostility to "interference on the part of the legislatures of the several States with the ordinary trades and occupations of the people," particularly when the "interference" took the form of labor legislation.[40] Brandeis was aware that the Supreme Court and lower courts had said that maximum-hours statutes might be constitutional where the state demonstrated that specific injury to the workers could result from long hours.[41] He decided the best tactic would be to focus on women, emphasizing the particular health problems caused for them and their families by long hours.[42] By far the largest share of the work on the brief was done by Goldmark, who turned up substantial data demonstrating the negative effect of long hours on women. She was also prepared with material showing that long hours were bad for *all* workers and that the sex of the worker was irrelevant. Brandeis deliberately left the second part of the data out of the brief but considered it so important a tool in the fight for maximum-hours laws that he applauded the Russell Sage Foundation's decision to publish it.[43]

The brief resulted from a conscious decision to take a risk and departed from recognized style in devoting only two pages to the traditional legal arguments and citations. Then came fifteen pages of state and foreign laws that limited women's hours, followed by a ninety-five-page section entitled "The World's Experience upon which the Legislation Limiting the Hours of Labor for Women is Based." The numerous subtitles, covering every aspect of the issue from "The Dangers of Long Hours" and "Laundries" to "The Reasonableness of the Ten-Hour Day," introduced copious quotations from reports by American and English commissions, bureaus, committees, and authors. Almost all of the ninety-five pages, in fact, consisted of quotations, designed to demonstrate both the social utility of maximum-hours legislation for women and the general acceptance of the idea.

The gamble paid off; the Court upheld the law.[44] Brandeis had not only won a case, however, nor had he only set a precedent for sustaining other maximum-hour laws for women. He had also persuaded the Court to depart from its usual posture that the Constitution was an unchanging entity, and he had set a precedent for bringing into the courtroom the kind of information that reflected what was really going on in the world outside. The Court could scarcely admit that it had abandoned its static jurisprudence, however briefly, but it praised Brandeis by name in its opinion and took note of "the course of legislation as well as expressions of opinion from other than judicial sources." The Court appended to its opinion a list of the laws he had cited. Justice Brewer, writing for the majority, denied that constitutional questions could be settled "by . . . a consensus of present public opinion" but admitted that "a widespread and long continued belief" about a question of fact "is worthy of consideration" — or, to put it differently, the Court would use sociological jurisprudence if the facts were sufficiently persuasive and if it did not have to acknowledge doing so.[45]

The legal profession and labor experts were electrified. Requests for copies of the brief poured in from lawyers, unions, and universities around the country. Illinois reenacted a women's maximum-hours law that had been struck down by the Court in 1895, and the league asked Brandeis to defend it. Doing so, and winning, he acknowledged the centrality of Goldmark's endeavors to the cases by naming her on the title page of the brief as his assistant, in spite of her lack of a law degree. Brandeis and Goldmark went on to defend similar statutes as well as laws setting minimum wages for women[46] until Brandeis was named to the Court in 1916 and Felix Frankfurter took on the League's cases.[47]

One reason for the success of the Brandeis approach, and for its subsequent emergence as the basis for the dominant jurisprudence and of most modern constitutional litigation, was the brilliance of Brandeis himself. After hearing Brandeis argue one of the league's cases before the Supreme Court, a friend wrote to Felix Frankfurter, "I have just heard Mr. Brandeis make one of the greatest arguments I have ever listened to, and I have heard many great arguments. . . . When Brandeis began to speak, the Court showed all the inertia and elemental hostility which Courts cherish for a new thought, or a new right, or even a new remedy for an old wrong, but he visibly lifted all this burden, and without orationizing or chewing of the rag he reached them all. . . . He not only reached the Court, but he dwarfed the Court."[48] This was typical of Brandeis. An attorney commented about another one of his oral arguments, "It had not gone far before, as usual, Brandeis was in full command by common consent."[49] One of his former law partners considered "the prime source" of Brandeis's power to be his "intense belief in the truth of what he was saying,"[50] and he clearly had the ability to convey that belief to the judges. Brandeis had strengths in addition to his mastery of oral argument. One of his opponents on the Supreme Court, Justice George Sutherland, was to remark ruefully, "My, how I detest that man's ideas. But he is one of the greatest technical lawyers I have ever known."[51] Roscoe Pound added, writing about the *Muller* brief, "The real point here is not so much his advocacy of these statutes as the breadth of perception and the remarkable legal insight which enable him to perceive the proper mode of presenting such a question."[52]

Creation of the Brandeis brief is sufficient evidence of Brandeis's "remarkable legal insight," but he would have disagreed with Pound that the "real point" was "not . . . his advocacy of these statutes." That was at least part of the main point, Brandeis might have said, because he could not draw a line between substance and methodology. Had he not possessed an "intense belief" in the cause he was espousing, he would not have bothered himself with the case.[53] It was, after all, one of the many he took without fee. When Brandeis was on the Supreme Court, Harold Laski described him to Holmes as "a prophet, I suspect, rather than a judge; a grand player for a side in which he believes both disinterestedly and with all his might."[54]

The "side" in which Brandeis believed was the side of socially responsive law. In *Muller*, form followed substance: Brandeis invented the new kind of brief because he wanted to win a particular case. Nonetheless, the particular configuration of the brief reflected Brandeis's larger approach to the law in a democratic political system.

If the premise of democracy is that the people know best what is good for them, then it is logical for that premise to be reflected in the laws that are a major component of public policy. Legislators thus had an obligation to produce laws based on "felt necessities," and judges had a concurrent obligation to interpret laws—including the Constitution—according to the same criterion. The kind of judicial restraint implicit in sociological jurisprudence puts a substantial burden on all judges in its assumption that they will recognize social needs and be prepared to legitimize their expression in statutes. But judges were meant to be removed from the popular will as well as from the popular whim, and this distancing was particularly true of federal judges, appointed by the president and the Senate for life. How were they to assess a statute in the light of "felt necessities?"

Here Brandeis the attorney added a crucial element to Holmes's and Pound's thought, and his answer was plain; it was the attorney's duty to bring courts the facts available to the legislature, which was the social information judges had to have if they were to make the right decision, "right" meaning accepting the statute if it was a rational response to a social problem and not one specifically forbidden by the Constitution. Although Brandeis did not address the problem directly, he presumably would have followed his own logic and said that if the legislature failed to amass factual data before enacting the statute and its lawyers could not themselves demonstrate its social rationality, the law should be struck down. Brandeis's contribution to sociological jurisprudence was to spell out the way it would work in practice by informing lawyers and judges how to ascertain felt necessities. A judge, he asserted, "rarely performs his functions adequately unless the case before him is adequately presented."[55] With one brief, Brandeis heralded a major change in the function of constitutional lawyers in a democratic system. Their job was to explain the policies desired by the sovereign people, bridging the gap between the people and the judges who presided over the people's courtrooms.

The mechanism they would use, so natural to "the man of statistics and the master of economics,"[56] would be facts: facts that would show the judges why it was reasonable for legislatures to respond to social problems with the statutes at issue. Brandeis had told the Massachusetts legislature as early as 1891, "No law can be effective which does not take into consideration the conditions of the community for which it is designed."[57] Laws had to be firmly based in social realities; by extension, laws that ignored social needs were bad. Brandeis assumed that unarguable facts were obtainable and that they were the basis for all intelligent decisions; surely judges should understand that. He was not so naive as to assume they necessarily *would* understand. "A judge is presumed to know the elements of law, but there is no presumption that he knows the facts," he had jotted in one of his notebooks while he was still a law student.[58] He added, in 1911, "In the past the courts have reached their conclusions largely deductively from preconceived notions and precedents. The method I have tried to employ in arguing cases before them has been inductive, reasoning from the facts."[59] The twentieth century was the age of science, and science was dependent upon facts. John Dewey's instrumentalism was an attempt to adapt the techniques of scientific experimentation to social problems.[60] Brandeis's goal was to bring science into the courtroom.

Brandeis's assumption that the ties binding law and morality had to be seamless, his strong desire for legislation protective of labor, and his belief that workers could neither experience the liberty necessary to their own fulfillment nor perform their responsibility to participate in the political process without sufficient leisure came together in the creation and articulation of a jurisprudence that was quintessentially democratic. The courts existed to facilitate the enactment of the popular will. The sole exceptions to this general principle were those troubling occasions when to do so would be to violate both the word and the spirit of the Constitution. Among those occasions might well be the misguided desire of the majority to infringe the civil liberties of others. (The posture he considered appropriate for the courts in such circumstances is discussed in chapter 6.)

After Brandeis joined the Supreme Court in 1916, he acknowledged that his prescription for lawyers was not being followed. Eager though he was to accept the social facts he expected to be given by statistics-conscious attorneys, he encountered what he considered too little factual information in the briefs presented to the Court. His theory of attorney responsibility therefore was broadened to include a theory of judicial responsibility.

Clearly, Brandeis saw law as anything but static. He recognized that major cases brought before the Court reflected not merely differences about legal doctrine but disputes about alternative social policies. Thus, the Court had not only to collect facts but to discipline itself not to substitute its own preferences for that of other equally capable bodies such as legislatures and administrative commissions. The Constitution provided the country with the power to handle all situations but divided that power between the states and the federal government and among branches of the federal government. The Court, he warned, should not elevate "the performance of the constitutional function of judicial review" into "an exercise of the powers of a super-legislature." Nor should it insist on doctrines simply because it had created them. "*Stare decisis* ["reliance upon precedent"] is ordinarily a wise rule of action," he commented, but it "does not command that we err again when we pass upon a different statute."[61] This was particularly true when it came to the corporation and its constitutional "rights." Both corporations and their "rights" were artificial constructs, legitimated by government; both could be undone if government and the people it served found that action proper. Mill had urged, "Let us remember . . . that political institutions . . . are the work of men. . . . Men did not wake on a summer morning and find them sprung up."[62] Mill argued that a legitimate government had to reflect social circumstances;[63] Brandeis's approach implicitly brought Mill's thought into the economic sphere. The "rights of property and the liberty of the individual must be remolded, from time to time, to meet the changing needs of society." Facts were needed so that the Court could know whether its doctrines had become outmoded.[64]

In 1929 the Court heard a case challenging an Oklahoma statute that required new ice companies to obtain a certificate of public convenience and necessity from the state. The law's purpose was to avoid the kind of duplication of plants and delivery service that resulted in higher costs for consumers. Given his emphasis on competition, Brandeis might well have been expected to applaud the Court action striking the law down. But substitution of judicial beliefs for the will of the majority in economic policy ran counter to his thinking about the nature of democracy, and he dissented. He did not consider the briefs before him sufficient to bolster his point that the social problems that prompted the Oklahoma law could lead reasonable people to believe that the statute embodied an appropriate solution. He was certain that the reasonableness of state regulations "can ordinarily be determined only by a consideration of the contemporary conditions, social, industrial and political, of the community to be affected thereby. Resort to such facts is necessary, among other things, in order to appreciate the evils sought to be remedied and the possible effects of the remedy proposed." His clerks therefore found themselves spending as much time in the Library of Congress gathering sociological and economic material as they did in the law library, and that now became the lot of his current clerk.[65]

Brandeis used much of the extralegal material when he wrote fourteen heavily footnoted pages to demonstrate the Oklahoma statute's rationality. He did not agree that it was the right answer. He stated that "whether that view [embodied in the statute] is sound nobody knows," pointing out that among the dangers of the law were the demands it placed on human intelligence and character, and reminded the Court, "Man is weak and his judgment is at best fallible." But that was not his — or the Court's — business. Calling the depression "an emergency more serious than war," he noted, "Economists are searching for the causes of this disorder and are re-examining the basis of our industrial structure." He slipped in a hint about his preferred remedy. "Most of them realize that failure to distribute widely the profits of industry has been a prime cause of our present plight." Many people disagreed, however, and "rightly or wrongly, many persons think that one of the major contributing causes has been unbridled competition." Since they thought so, they had a right to experiment with a limit upon competition.[66]

He was concerned that in stifling such experimentation, the Court was interfering with the search for solutions, and he chided his colleagues, "Some people assert that our present plight is due, in part, to the limitations set by courts upon experimentation in the fields of social and economic science. . . . To stay experimentation in things social and economic is a grave responsibility" that might be "fraught with serious consequences to the nation. . . . This Court has the power to prevent an experiment. . . . But in the exercise of this high power, we must be ever on our guard, lest we erect our prejudices into legal principles." Experimentation was crucial to progress, and the best place for experimentation was the states, which were still the small laboratories suitable to experimentation that Jefferson had envisaged. Experiments could be dangerous, precisely *because* "man is weak and his judgment is at best fallible." But human fallibility was everywhere, even on the Supreme Court, and so the wisest and most democratic approach was to minimize judicial limitations on reasonable experimentation: "If we would guide by the light of reason, we must let our minds be bold."[67]

Brandeis's approval of competition and his support for experimentation by the states came together in his dissent from the Court's overturning of a Florida law that imposed heavier license fees on stores that were part of multicounty chains than on independent shops. The majority of the Court found the law to be an unconstitutional violation of the Fourteenth Amendment's equal protection and due process clauses, holding that the state had no reasonable basis for placing stores into the categories of "independent," "part of an intracounty chain," or "part of an intercounty chain." Brandeis's dissent was a parade of facts designed to demonstrate not only that there was a rational relationship between the problem identified by the state and the statute designed to solve it but that the state was correct in perceiving bigness as antisocial. He traced the history of corporations in the United States and the states' early policy of denying the right to incorporate to businesses, as opposed to religious, educational, and charitable organizations. "It was denied because of fear. Fear of encroachment upon the liberties and opportunities of the individual. Fear of the subjection of labor to capital. Fear of monopoly."[68]

To demonstrate that the fears were legitimate, Brandeis drew on studies such as Adolph A. Berle and Gardiner Means's *The Modern Corporation and Private Property*, Thorstein Veblen's *Absentee Ownership and Business Enterprise*, on works by Stuart Chase, J. A. Hobson, and Arthur Dahlberg, on articles in journals such as *Editorial Research*, *Labor*, *American Economic Review*, *Annals of The American Academy of Political and Social Science*, and *Retail Ledger*, and on numerous congressional hearings, speeches, and government reports. They showed, he argued, that after "the desire for business expansion created an irresistible demand" for corporate charters and the states capitulated, corporations had grown to fearsome size: "Through size, corporations, once merely an efficient tool employed by individuals in the conduct of private business, have . . . brought such concentration of economic power that so-called private corporations are sometimes able to dominate the State . . . the lives of tens or hundreds of thousands of employees and the property of tens or hundreds of thousands of investors are subjected, through the corporate mechanism, to the control of a few men." This power brought about a "negation of industrial democracy" and its replacement with "the rule of a plutocracy." "Such is the Frankenstein monster," Brandeis wrote, "which States have created by their corporation laws."[69]

He continued to marshal facts. Two hundred nonbanking corporations controlled more than one quarter of the country's wealth. Five of the twelve plaintiffs in the case, each with assets of more than $90 million, were among those corporations; their collective assets were $820 million. One of the corporations operated over 15,000 stores; together, they owned 19,718 throughout the country. How, in the light of such facts, could the Court maintain that concentration of wealth was not a problem or that the Florida law was an unreasonable solution to it?[70] Judges had a responsibility to know their facts and to decide accordingly.

Perhaps the best example of Brandeis's use of factual evidence occurred when the Court was asked to determine the constitutionality of a Nebraska consumer-protection law that set weight standards, including maximum-weight limits, for commercially sold loaves of bread. The majority of the Court, much opposed to state regulation of commercial entities, held that the law took bakers' and dealers' property without due process of law. Brandeis disagreed and chastised his brethren for not examining the relevant facts. "Unless we know the facts on which the legislators may have acted," he declared in dissent, "we cannot properly decide whether they were . . . unreasonable, arbitrary or capricious." And to know those facts, the justices had "merely to acquaint ourselves with the art of breadmaking and the usages of the trade; with the devices by which buyers of bread are imposed upon and honest bakers or dealers are subjected by their dishonest fellows to unfair competition; with the problems which have confronted public officials charged with the enforcement of the laws prohibiting short weights, and with their experience in administering those laws."[71] Brandeis fulfilled this "mere" task by presenting the Court with fifteen pages of information about the baking industry, most of it in lengthy and forbidding footnotes.[72]

Brandeis insisted on ferreting out facts to support social experimentation because of his belief that experimentation was one of the keys to human progress. As Frankfurter described his approach, "Problems, for him, are never solved. Civilization is a sequence of new tasks."[73] But his friend and colleague Holmes was more skeptical about the possibility of progress. "Generally speaking, I agree with you in liking to see social experiments tried," he wrote to Brandeis, "but I do so without enthusiasm because I believe it is merely shifting the pressure and that so long as we have free propagation Malthus is right in his general view." He saw democracy as giving the majority the right to have the laws it wanted, but, a true social Darwinist,[74] he did not much care what the experiments were about or what effects they would have. His disdain for the futile efforts of mortals was expressed to Frederick Pollock when he wrote, "Long ago I decided that I was not God. When a state came here and wanted to build a slaughter house, I looked at the Constitution and if I couldn't find anything in there that said a state couldn't build a slaughter house I said to myself, if they want to build a slaughter house, God-dammit, let them build it." He therefore saw no need for an accumulation of factual material. Complaining to Pollock that Brandeis was pushing him to put his interest in philosophy aside temporarily and immerse himself in the facts of his society, Holmes grumbled, "I hate facts. I always say the chief end of man is to form general propositions — adding that no general proposition is worth a damn. . . . I have little doubt that it would be good for my immortal soul to plunge into them [facts] . . . but I shrink from the bore."[75]

Brandeis, far from finding facts boring, thrived on them and believed, given the educability of human beings, that experimentation was a precondition and harbinger of human progress. He was far more pragmatic and optimistic than Holmes about both the possibility of social improvement and the role to be played in it by law, lawyers, judges, and government. David Riesman, who clerked for Brandeis after graduating from Harvard Law School, wrote to his former professor Felix Frankfurter, "Holmes was skeptical of action and thought but seemed to have faith in the inevitable, — Brandeis is skeptical of power and of human abilities but he does not believe that things are inevitable." Holmes, he added, saw "the actions of others" as "merely the inevitable coming to pass," but "Brandeis is not so absolute, — he does not believe that human beings are the prey to unconquerable forces. As you say, he puts his trust in reason."[76] Even more, he put his trust in the democratic process and argued that law had to be a part of it.

His trust in the democratic process led him to treat the Court as an educational institution. It was as much the Court's function to explain its decisions as to make them, to use its opinions so the electorate could understand why the Court's actions were both wise and correct. Progress was possible only if people with ideas made them available to whatever segment of the electorate was willing to listen. Brandeis viewed public officials, including judges, as teachers with the obligation to make their lessons accessible. One of the functions of a justice was to write opinions that would educate the legal profession and other members of the intelligentsia; public education was an important element of judicial civic virtue.

Paul Freund remembered his early clerkship for Brandeis when, after working on one revision after another of Brandeis's opinion for the Court in *National Surety Company* v. *Corielli*, he then heard the justice ask, "Now I think the opinion is persuasive, but what can we do to make it more instructive?" Brandeis told Dean Acheson, when the latter was clerking for him, "The whole purpose, and the only one, is to educate the country." His other clerks recalled similar sentiments; one was astonished at, and presumably educated by, the sixty changes Brandeis made in a draft opinion of ten pages.[77]

Similarly, when the Court erred, it was the duty of a dissenting justice to explain to both the justices and the public where the error lay. He dissented frequently when the Court upheld governmental suppression or punishment of speech and became so disheartened at his colleagues' unwillingness to adopt his position that he told Dean Acheson, "We may be able to fill the people with shame, after the passion cools, by preserving some of it on the record. The only hope is the people; you cannot educate the Court."[78] Although all of Brandeis's opinions laid out his reasoning in detail, his dissents clearly were designed as lessons for the public or at least that part of it that reads Supreme Court opinions. It is therefore in Brandeis's dissents that one finds not only the meticulous workmanship that is a hallmark of his opinions but, in addition, clear statements of political thought.[79]

Brandeis's approach to law reviews also reflected his omnipresent interest in education. His 1917 dissent in *Adams* v. *Tanner* was the first instance of a justice citing law review articles in an opinion.[80] He frequently referred to articles that neither party to a case had mentioned, considering it a part of the responsibility of the justice (or his clerk) to ferret out relevant information.[81] He was particularly wont to turn to law reviews when he was writing an opinion that altered the law significantly. The articles provided factual information and helped bolster Brandeis's arguments. His references to them, a practice gradually adopted by other justices, undoubtedly encouraged more articles to be written in part for judicial perusal. They were of course also read by lawyers and scholars, presumably furthering the debate among them and thereby enhancing the educational process.[82]

His use of law reviews was simply one of the many corollaries of Brandeis's revolutionary thinking about the nature of law and the judicial process. He argued that the good society had to be based on morality and that its laws could be neither moral nor useful unless they reflected changing social circumstances. As a pragmatic matter, if legislators and the judges who assessed the constitutionality of laws distanced themselves from the realities of felt necessities, the rule of law itself would be threatened. He assumed that the Founding Fathers must have shared his views and insisted not only that the Constitution could be used to respond to altered social needs but that it had been designed to do so. Lawyers and judges shared the legislators' responsibility to educate themselves about social facts and to base their arguments and judgments upon them. Democracy required no less. Judges were obligated to hand down socially responsive judgments and then to explain and justify their decisions to the public, educating them in the process.

Frankfurter called Brandeis's sociological jurisprudence "an organic constitutional philosophy, which expresses his response to the deepest issues of society."[83] It reflected a view of law as both growing out of and affecting an endlessly evolving social reality. A jurisprudence that anchors law in the public will while limiting the public's power to abridge individual rights is quintessentially democratic.[84] By translating his perception into lawyers' briefs and judicial opinions, Brandeis helped democratize the judicial process and permanently altered both American jurisprudence and American political thought.

4

THE CURSE OF BIGNESS

If the Lord had intended things to be big, he would have made man bigger—in brains and character.[1]

Neither our intelligence nor our characters can long stand the strain of unrestricted power.[2]

President Franklin Roosevelt was incredulous. The Supreme Court had just struck down the cornerpiece of his New Deal legislation, a statute giving industries the right to adopt federally approved codes regulating wages, hours, conditions of employment, and prices. The National Industrial Recovery Act (NRA), one of Roosevelt's attempts to deal with the depression, he saw as a way to help labor while enabling businesses to charge fair prices. But the Court, including Brandeis, had voted unanimously to overturn it. Referring to Brandeis by the nickname commonly used by many New Dealers, Roosevelt asked, unbelievingly, "What about old Isaiah?"[3]

"Isaiah," for his part, was busy lecturing Thomas Corcoran, a former clerk of Oliver Wendell Holmes and now one of Roosevelt's chief aides. "This is the end of this business of centralization," Brandeis told Corcoran. "I want you to go back and tell the President that we're not going to let this government centralize everything. It's come to an end. As for your young men [from all over the country, many of them recent Harvard Law School graduates recruited for the New Deal by Felix Frankfurter], you call them together and tell them to

72

get out of Washington—tell them to go home, back to the states. That is where they must do their work."[4]

His vote against the NRA made perfect sense to Brandeis. The act neither specified wages, hours, and other standards, nor included guidelines for determining them, leaving the president completely free to decide whether proposed codes were acceptable. Brandeis liked Roosevelt enormously, but no human being should have that kind of concentrated power, nor did the road to democracy lie through creation of a mammoth bureaucracy in Washington. Pulling together bright young people from all over the country and giving them the power to run things might seem to the New Dealers like a good way to revive and rationalize the national economy quickly, but Brandeis disagreed. It was an easy "fix," undertaken without considering the consequences that would follow when power was overcentralized and the states had been deprived of any meaningful ability to experiment.[5] "Human nature, like the inanimate, seeks the path of least resistance," he had said long before. "To think hard and persistently is painful."[6] Now he sent the pained New Dealers back to do some more hard thinking. Creating a big government to regulate big business was not the answer; bigness in any form, however beneficent its purpose, was bad. Brandeis thought the second Roosevelt was making the same mistake his cousin Theodore had, assuming that big business was inevitable and attempting to regulate it instead of cutting it down to size. The conviction that Theodore Roosevelt was wrong had led Brandeis to throw himself into Woodrow Wilson's successful campaign for the presidency. Now he was using his vote on the Court, and Corcoran as his messenger, to warn Franklin Roosevelt against falling into similar error.

One of the themes most important to Brandeis's thought was summed up by the title "The Curse of Bigness," given, with his permission, to an edited collection of his speeches, articles, and judicial opinions.[7] The four other volumes of collected works published during his lifetime under different titles expressed essentially the same views.[8]

Brandeis did not initially tie together bigness, corruption, misuse of power, and monopoly or oligopoly although he eventually would do so. He was exposed to government corruption almost as soon as he became involved in public life. The fights over the Massachusetts liquor laws and the Boston transportation system made him aware that legislators' votes were being bought by public service corporations that guaranteed their minions jobs. It was easy enough to see that the larger the corporation, the greater its ability to use its revenues to enact legislation that ran counter to the public interest.

While he was unearthing and battling public corruption, he was also learning about bigness and concentration of power in the private sphere. He was awakened to the dangers of monopoly by his 1886 fight against Boston's paper monopoly. That particular monopoly was not terribly large, but its nature gave it unrestricted power in its sphere, and neither Boston's Common Council nor the local courts would take action against it.[9] He was speaking out against the concentrated power of trusts at least as early as 1892, when he included criticism of them in his business law lectures at MIT, arguing that price-fixing agreements among companies contain the seeds of monopolistic trusts, in which all the companies are merged into one huge monopoly. He pointed specifically to the Diamond Match Company, the sugar trust, and the Standard Oil trust, lamenting the effect of trusts on consumers.[10]

Recognition of the harm that could be done by those people with governmental power and those in private industry who combined to form trusts was an early element in his thinking; the notion that bigness as such was evil was not. His fight in the first decade of the century against the large life insurance companies that were victimizing workers convinced him that the sheer size of the insurance companies had made them overly powerful. He thought they should be made smaller, but he was not ready to extend the prohibition to all businesses.[11] One of the many lessons he learned in his years-long war with the New Haven Railroad, however, was that size meant unaccountable power. The fight began for him in 1902, while he was battling against the attempts of the Boston and Maine Railroad (B&M) to own trolley as well as railroad lines. Brandeis was startled when the B&M protested that it was only trying to do legally what the New Haven was already doing illegally, for the New Haven had bought up about a third of Massachusetts's trolley mileage through holding companies. When it was discovered that the New Haven was quietly buying enough stock in the B&M to give it control, an investor hired Brandeis to fight the takeover. Brandeis agreed but then decided that the merger was "a matter of public interest in which I am undertaking to influence the opinion of others" and refused to accept any compensation or to act as the attorney for anyone but the public. [12]

His war against the New Haven continued for nine years, during which the railroad aimed some fairly big guns at him. It already had bought votes in the Massachusetts legislature; next it commissioned anti-Brandeis articles and magazines and hired a Harvard Law School professor to deliver "scholarly" lectures on the virtues of the New Haven. Brandeis, convinced that more was at issue than a monopoly, countered by becoming an expert on the financial details of the New Haven and other railroads. He discovered that the New Haven was not an economically viable entity but was being kept alive as a mechanism that could be used for stock watering and high dividends. The consumers were losing; labor, which was not getting a fair wage from the company, was losing; the railroad's passengers were losing; the only people who were winning, and whom he began to see as the villains of the piece, were financiers such as J. P. Morgan, who manipulated the New Haven and other companies for the benefit of their banking houses. This was the "money trust" that Brandeis began to consider a dangerous evil. [13]

Brandeis's education about bigness and corruption continued when he came into conflict with another huge economic entity, the Morgan-Guggenheim syndicate, during the Pinchot-Ballinger affair of 1910–1911. The genesis of the scandal was the syndicate's attempts to gain control of 5,000 acres of government-owned coal and timber land in Alaska, but the congressional hearings that followed also uncovered dishonesty on the part of President William Howard Taft. Brandeis was convinced once again that the trusts and other big monied interests were not only inefficient but, worse, concentrations of power not susceptible to democratic control; they could reach as high as presidents. Thus both political and economic factors led Brandeis to oppose the trusts and to outline the remedial action that would later become central to Woodrow Wilson's New Freedom.

His opposition was due also to his perception of human limitations. "Many men are all wool, but none is more than a yard wide," he liked to say, occasionally adding of man that "nature sets a limit to his possible achievement. As the Germans say: 'Care is taken that the trees do not scrape the skies.'" He concluded that human beings therefore had to "adjust our institutions to the wee size of man." He assumed that if an institution was so big that no one person knew what was going on in it, it was out of control. "No matter how good the organization," he believed, "the capacity of an individual man usually determines the success or failure of a particular enterprise." He approved of delegation of power and a degree of specialization, agreeing that "organization can do much to make concerns more efficient [and] larger units possible. . . . But . . . organization can never supply the combined judgment, initiative, enterprise and authority which must come from the chief executive officer."[14] Organizations, after all, were created and run by human beings. Without individual leadership, no institution would function as intended, nor was there any reason to assume that it was operating well.

Brandeis's definition of "well" for economic institutions was efficiency, which meant operating at the lowest possible cost so as to pay workers an adequate salary and owners a fair profit while making goods and services available to consumers cheaply. Lack of control would result in waste and costliness. For their part, political institutions worked "well" in a democratic state when they were responsive to the will of the people. Again, if no one was in control, the door would be open for the kind of corruption, both financial and moral, that he had seen in the Massachusetts legislature and during the Pinchot-Ballinger affair. The people's will would be negated; democracy would be damaged or even lost.

The more he investigated, the more certain he became that huge corporations and democracy could not coexist because of the corporations' power to corrupt. The belief made him unfashionable with many people, as the current orthodoxy treated these enterprises as almost God-given natural entities. Brandeis rejected the claim that corporations emerged organically from the society and were by definition desirable. Far from being natural, Brandeis replied, the trusts were artificial constructs: the Supreme Court had fostered them by giving them the rights of "persons" under the Fourteenth Amendment; state governments had aided them by permitting them to incorporate; federal laws had contributed to their growth by protecting them with tariffs and by enforcing contracts destructive of competition.[15]

Robert La Follette, the Progressive senator from Wisconsin, was one of Brandeis's allies during the Pinchot-Ballinger hearings. In December 1910 La Follette asked Brandeis to join a still secret group, the

National Progressive Republican League, which was being founded for "the promotion of popular government and progressive legislation." Its Declaration of Principles listed the enemies and the goals that had become Brandeis's:

> Popular government in America has been thwarted, and progressive legislation strangled by the Special Interests. . . . Under existing conditions legislation in the public interest has been baffled and defeated. This is evidenced by the long struggle to secure laws, but partially effective, for the control of railways lines and services, the revision of the tariff in the interest of the producer and consumer, statutes dealing with trusts and combinations, based on sound economic principles . . . a wise, comprehensive and impartial reconstruction of banking and monetary laws, a non-subsidized merchant marine, the conservation of coal, oil, gas, timber, waterpowers and other natural resources belonging to the people, and for the enactment of all legislation solely for the common good.[16]

Brandeis disagreed with other goals, such as popular initiatives, referenda, judicial recall, direct nomination of officials, and direct election of senators and delegates to party conventions, espoused by La Follette Progressives. Still profoundly conservative in his desire to protect small capitalism and in his preference for the existing representative governmental system rather than for direct democracy,[17] he nonetheless put aside his differences to make common cause with the larger Progressive aims he shared and joined the group.

Brandeis's major economic goal had become the elimination of bigness, an achievement he viewed as central to industrial liberty. Unions, however big, would never be able to match the power of great economic combinations supported by the money trust. Even if the trusts failed in their endeavors to keep unions outlawed, their power would be so great that unions would have no chance of negotiating fair treatment for their workers. His opposition to trusts stemmed from a variety of strands in his thinking: his desire to protect small businesses and consumers, his fears for political democracy, the belief first in fair treatment for workers and then democracy in the workplace that lay behind his opposition to the trusts.

He enlarged his argument to encompass the assertion that bigness produced the additional evil of inefficiency. Subsequent events have shown that though he was largely correct, there are sectors of the economy in which bigness can be extremely efficient,[18] and the attack on Brandeis's economics has concentrated on this argument.[19] The critics, however, fail to understand two important points. First, Brandeis was largely right; growth beyond a certain stage in most industries did and does make for economic inefficiency.[20] Second, even in those sectors where bigness may be an economic boon, it is inherently anti-democratic. This point was summed up by Brandeis's friend Norman Hapgood in his foreword to the 1933 edition of *Other People's Money*:

> When, exploring the principles of Justice Brandeis, we say that every business, every institution, has a unit of greatest efficiency, we are not using the word efficiency as if the business existed in a vacuum. We are talking about it . . . as part of a social organism; and it is inefficient, socially considered, if it injures the whole. Even, therefore, if it makes for itself more money than a small unit, it may be a social liability where the smaller business or institution is a social asset. . . . Frequently size gives power . . . that no business ought, for the general welfare to have.[21]

That was the point: the negative effect of size on the "general welfare," including the citizen-laborer, the small competitor, and the consumer. In the early 1900s, however, his theory of worker-participation not having solidified, Brandeis concentrated on the argument against trusts of which he was certain, the decline of efficiency in overly large corporations and their inability to produce affordable products.

A few months after Brandeis joined La Follette's Progressives, the Supreme Court held that only those trusts engaged in "unreasonable" restraints of trade could be considered in violation of the Sherman Antitrust Act. Although the Court found the restraint of trade by the plaintiff, Standard Oil Company, sufficiently unreasonable for it to be liable under the act, Progressive members of Congress, who had thought the act made all combinations in restraint of trade illegal, recognized that the definition of "unreasonable" now lay completely in the hands of whoever happened to be sitting on the Supreme Court when the government decided to prosecute a particular company or trust. Aided by La Follette and a number of other Progressives, Brandeis began to draft legislation to restore the Sherman Act's intent according to their understanding. Simultaneously, Sen. Moses Clapp, chairman of the Senate Committee on Interstate Commerce, wrote to Brandeis, urging him to suggest amendments to the Sherman Act before weaker measures could be introduced and passed. Upon receiving Brandeis's reply about the bill he was already working on with La Follette, Clapp arranged an investigation into trusts and the federal policy toward them, largely so that Brandeis would have a public forum for his ideas.[22]

When the Clapp Committee hearings opened, however, Brandeis was preceded by George W. Perkins, a partner in J. P. Morgan and Company and the representative of the Morgan interests and Big Steel. His presentation was a useful summary of precisely the widely held beliefs about trusts and efficiency that Brandeis challenged. Perkins argued that trusts were good, that they had grown because they were efficient, that it was inevitable for the most efficient businesses to drive out competitors and seek to gain control over their share of the market, that the efficiencies made possible by trusts would provide improved products at lower costs, and that since trusts were both good and inevitable the government should attempt to regulate rather than to destroy them.[23]

Brandeis's rebuttal took three days. He maintained flatly that "there are no natural monopolies in the industrial world." Artificial manipulation of credit rather than efficiency or fair competition had created trusts. The laws of the United States had been skewed to nurture them; the law should now be used to undo what it had helped create. The law had permitted seemingly unconnected businesses to agree among themselves on high prices; law could now forbid price fixing. Brandeis denied that trusts resulted in lower prices. Such prices existed only temporarily; once competitors had been driven out, prices rose.[24]

Brandeis insisted that trusts were not efficient and that many had failed. He named them: the Newspaper Trust, the Writing Paper Trust, the Upper Leather Trust, the Sole Leather Trust, the Wool Trust, the Paper Bag Trust, the International Mercantile Marine Trust, the Cordage Trust, the Mucilage Trust, and the Flour Trust. Trusts that were still in existence remained so only because they had acquired virtual monopolies over their market areas and were able to raise prices high enough to cover their costs. Efficiency in the absence of factual information was impossible, Brandeis argued, and the huge size of trusts prevented their nominal leaders from knowing enough about the business to exercise informed judgment. Then Brandeis turned to the human component. Human limitations made trusts inefficient: "Nature sets a limit to their [human beings'] possible accomplishment. . . . Whatever the business or organization there is a point where it would become too large for efficient and economic management. . . . Organization can do much to make larger units possible and profitable. But the efficiency even of organization has its bounds; and organization can never supply the combined judgement, initiative, enterprise, and authority which must come from the chief executive officers." Brandeis was not arguing for horse-and-buggy-sized businesses but for businesses large enough to be efficient and small enough to remain susceptible to human control. One could not design a formula for the optimal size of all businesses any more than one could say trusts were good; the desired size of each business would have to be ascertained through trial and error.[25]

Brandeis placed much of the blame for existing trusts on the money trust; the trusts' ability to manipulate capital to put competitors out of business enabled them to thrive. Deprived of the help of the money trust they would collapse, for in fact they lost money. In a litany whose echoes are uncannily familiar in the 1990s, Brandeis pointed to the many failures of the American way of business. He cited the Department of Agriculture's findings about the poor quality of fence wire made for farms, the declining percentage of the market held by the supposedly efficient steel trust, and the turning of foreign purchasers to non-American sources of steel. Ten years after the steel trust completed its takeover of the steel industry by absorbing the Carnegie Company, the United States had fallen five years behind Germany in iron and steel metallurgy, creation of updated machinery, and methods of production. The number of deaths and injuries due to derailments of trains had led to an investigation by the Interstate Commerce Commission, which found that derailments due to broken rails had increased dramatically to 2,059 and had resulted in the death or injury of 106 people during the decade since the steel trust had taken over. Similarly, when confronted with a more efficient system of shoe manufacturing, the shoe machinery trust bought out the system and killed it. The lesson, to Brandeis, was obvious. Trusts were incapable of operating properly because they were too big, and they became lazy. They discouraged invention, or the process a later generation would call research and development; they made little attempt to reduce costs because as monopolistic industries they knew their profits to be secure. The result was neither efficiency nor rapid progress but poor consumer products, and the United States economy was losing ground to other producers that operated more efficiently.[26]

Although asserting that the giantism that destroyed competition necessarily would result in inefficiency, Brandeis did not argue that competition inevitably would be efficient. On the contrary, it would involve waste: "What human activity does not?" But to Brandeis, who believed himself to be echoing the Founding Fathers, efficiency was a means, not a goal, and on this point his critics ignore a vital part of his thinking. Competition brought compensatory benefits: "The margin between that which men naturally do and which they can do is so great that a system which urges men on to action, enterprise, and initiative is preferable in spite of the wastes that necessarily attend that process." If efficiency was lost in pursuit of a higher goal, the loss was worth absorbing. The writers of the Constitution thought that the inefficiencies of a democratic republic were more than compensated for by other advantages. Implicit in Brandeis's advocacy of free speech was acceptance of inefficiency because it is inefficient, in the search for the best policies, to have the same idea expressed repeatedly by the same or even by different people. The educated choices that would result from exposure to all ideas, however, could only be attained at the cost of preventing the government from interfering with speech, however repetitive. Brandeis brought that calculation into the economic field by asserting that the inefficiencies attendant upon competition would be more than offset by the incentives and progress fostered by competition.[27]

Brandeis rejected the claim that a higher level of general economic well-being and affordable consumer goods would be attained, albeit at the price of temporary dislocation of workers, as the economy moved from a small to a larger scale. He would have denied that a choice had to be made between economic efficiency and a system detrimental to human beings. But if he had to choose, his choice would have been easy; his major indictment against the trusts was that they hurt human beings.

Brandeis reminded the Clapp Committee about James and Joseph McNamara. In 1910 they had dynamited the *Los Angeles Times* building, killing twenty-one workers, because of the antiunion stance of the *Times'* publisher. Brandeis told the committee that as long as men like the McNamaras believed that their only recourse was to dynamite, there would be violence instead of industrial liberty:

> You cannot have true American citizenship, you cannot preserve political liberty, you cannot secure American standards of living unless some degree of industrial liberty accompanies it. And the United States Steel Corporation and these other trusts have stabbed industrial liberty in the back. . . . This social unrest is what is really the matter with business. Well-founded unrest; reasoned unrest; but the manifestations of which are often unintelligent and sometimes criminal. . . . Until we had these great trusts, or the great corporations which preceded them, workers could secure justice through unions.[28]

Bigness destroyed liberty, and so Brandeis condemned it. He frequently spoke about consumer costs, and he cared about owners of small businesses driven out by large corporations, but his primary concern was for the workers. First industrialization and then the giant trusts made possible by it had amassed so much economic power that most Americans would spend their lives working for faceless employers in huge enterprises to which they felt no personal connection beyond that symbolized and encompassed by their weekly pay check. Brandeis was angered not only because workers were being exploited, having no leisure with which to fulfill and educate themselves, but also because they were being turned into automatons unable to learn about and participate in the political process, with the result that the country was becoming far less democratic.

Brandeis's concern for democracy led him to conclude that government had to involve itself to rectify the wrongs being committed in the industrial sector. By 1912 he was convinced that the trusts had become so politically potent that even if workers had sufficient leisure to involve themselves in the political process, the trusts would prevent the votes of workers and other citizens from really counting. He was anxious to help elect a president who shared his views. In June 1912 the

Democratic party adopted William Jennings Bryan's resolution denouncing "the privilege-hunting and favor-seeking class." It then nominated Woodrow Wilson for president, and Wilson endorsed the program aimed at the financiers Brandeis had been fighting for years. Brandeis promptly issued a statement calling Wilson's nomination "among the most encouraging events in American History."[29] Within weeks, the two men met for lunch and a three-hour discussion, and Brandeis began fashioning the program that became known as Wilson's "New Freedom."[30]

Wilson declared after the meeting that their joint goal was not regulation of the trusts but destruction of them through regulation of competition. The basis for Wilson's proposals was laid down in a lengthy summary Brandeis sent him of the problems with the existing Sherman Act and the virtues of the La Follette-Brandeis proposed amendments. Wilson's biographer Arthur Link credits Brandeis's memorandum with being the source of "all of [the] ideas that [Wilson] expressed during the presidential campaign."[31]

The difference between Theodore Roosevelt's platform and the Brandeis-Wilson approach went beyond the former's assumption that trusts could be controlled. Brandeis, with his experience of illegal ties between governments and corporations, did not believe that trusts were manageable by government. Even if they were, however, the entity regulating them would itself have to be so large that the problems of bigness would be repeated. The regulators would grow to be as big as the businesses; bureaucracies would develop; it would be impossible for anyone to be in charge. Again, Brandeis returned to human limitations. The citizen had to be as wary of the evil of bigness in government as in business. With their complex combination of creativity and limited intellect, human beings could create institutions that were too big to monitor for efficiency and effectiveness, too big to assess for value or liability to society, too big to control, too big to care about the policies necessary to protect individual liberties. Such were the trusts; such, without care, could be the federal government.

In spite of Brandeis's experience with state legislatures, he preferred that power be lodged with them rather than with the federal government. Again, the problem was bigness and centralization of power. It was not merely that corruption followed bigness all too easily; it was also important to remember that experimentation was crucial if progress was to be made. Here Brandeis followed Jefferson in extolling the wisdom of the system that enabled a relatively small entity, a state, to begin an experiment that, if promising, could be picked up and perfected by other states. If the experiment failed, its limitation to one state meant that relatively little had been lost. Ideas were exciting but they were not to be put into effect before they had been adequately tried. Brandeis was so insistent on thorough experimentation that even though he had invented savings-bank life insurance and worked hard to establish it in Massachusetts, he warned twenty years after its inception that it had not been sufficiently tested to be introduced in other states.[32]

By the time Brandeis met Wilson, then, his ideas about human limitations, his fear of bigness in both government and business, his detestation of the trusts, his faith in democracy, and his assumption that the government had to undo the privileged position it had given the trusts and regulate competition, coupled with an understanding of the economics of the trusts, had come together in proposed policies that would destroy the trusts while keeping the federal government down to a manageable size.

For his part, Wilson sounded much like Roosevelt until he met Brandeis. He worried about the control over economic life that the trusts might give to a few people, but he considered trusts inevitable and could find no solution to the problem of concentrated economic power. In 1905 the aristocratic Calvinist had stated, "We can't abolish the trusts. We must moralize them," but he had little in the way of concrete ideas about how to do so. In 1912 he was still talking about nothing more than lowering the tariff and applying the criminal provisions of the Sherman Act.[33] His understanding of the relationship between political and economic forces in the state went little beyond his certainty that socialism and government ownership of the means of production were wrong. Norman Thomas, a former student of Wilson's at Princeton, reported about him that "if he had ever heard Harrington's dictum that the distribution of power follows the distribution of property, he never discussed it with his students in the classroom."[34]

Earlier in his scholarly career, Wilson had described Congress as the dominant if unorganized and inefficient branch of the national government.[35] By 1908, however, he had moved so far as to see the Senate as the bastion of economic interests and the president as the desired "political leader of the nation." He had also realized that many state legislatures were corrupt but nonetheless advocated reforming them rather than transferring their powers to the national government.[36] He thus shared Brandeis's emphasis on federalism and was ready to be tutored by him about modern American economics.

The two major actions Brandeis urged upon Wilson were stronger antitrust laws and the kind of currency reform that would negate the use and abuse by the money trust of "other people's money," and Wilson stressed these themes in his campaign speeches. After Wilson won the election, Brandeis continued his tutoring as a key unofficial adviser on economic matters. In June 1913 Brandeis was summoned to the White House to help Wilson choose between two competing proposals for a Federal Reserve Board. Brandeis dismissed the plan for a privately controlled and decentralized reserve system supervised by a Federal Reserve Board that would be elected by bankers. He threw the weight of his approval behind the second proposal, which sought to establish a reserve system that would issue notes, to be considered government obligations, and that would be supervised by a board appointed by the government.[37] He told Wilson that "the power to issue currency should be vested exclusively in Government officials," with the bankers limited to a strictly advisory role. He added that businesses other than the money trust would applaud such a move because they would know that "whatever money is available, will be available for business generally, and not be subject to the control of a favored few." Wilson was convinced and asked Brandeis to put his arguments in writing. The resultant bill was passed by Congress and signed by Wilson on December 23, 1913.[38]

Brandeis then began to push Wilson on general antitrust legislation. He advocated establishment of an Interstate Trade Commission with the power to investigate agreements in restraint of trade, use of information to aid the Justice Department in litigation against the trusts, and action to secure compliance with the law at the request of injured parties. He also called for creation of "industrial experiment stations and other bureaus for research and for the dissemination of education in industry." These were necessary if smaller businesses were to have the kind of access to research currently available only to large corporations with their own research laboratories. In addition, he advocated repeal of the law prohibiting price fixing of trademarked merchandise by its producer or distributor. He differentiated price maintenance by a producer, who had a stake in the quality and reputation of his product, from price cutting and price fixing. Price maintenance would promote competition, he believed, but price cutting was "the most potent weapon of monopoly — a means of killing the small rival to which the great trusts have resorted most frequently," and price fixing was used by monopolies to force consumers to pay high prices. Presumably, he distinguished legitimate independent producers from trusts by the over-40 percent of the market criterion that he had suggested to La Follette when they were devising antitrust proposals.[39]

Then Brandeis turned to a particular bête noire: interlocking directorates. He was convinced that no one could serve two masters, as was required by these directorates, because people could not act in one capacity without considering an action's effects on their other interests and because to sit on numerous boards of directors strained the resources and abilities of any one individual beyond human limitations. An executive of one company sitting on the board of directors of others could not possibly possess enough facts to make intelligent decisions about all of them. Brandeis sent Secretary of the Interior Franklin K. Lane an example of the dishonesty inherent in interlocking directorates:

J.P. Morgan (or a partner), a director of the New York, New Haven, & Hartford Railroad, causes that company to sell to J.P. Morgan & Co. an issue of bonds. J.P. Morgan & Co. borrow the money with which to pay for the bonds from the Guaranty Trust Company, of which Mr. Morgan (or a partner) is a director. J.P. Morgan & Co. sell the bonds to the Penn Mutual Life Insurance Company, of which Mr. Morgan (or a partner) is a director. The New Haven spends the proceeds of the bonds in purchasing steel rails from the United States Steel Corporation, of which Mr. Morgan (or a partner) is a director. The United States Steel Corporation spends the proceeds of the rails in purchasing electrical supplies from the General Electric Company, of which Mr. Morgan (or a partner) is a director. The General Electric sells supplies to the Western Union Telegraph Company; and in both Mr. Morgan (or a partner) is a director. The Telegraph

Company has an exclusive wire contract with the Reading. . . .
The Reading buys its passenger cars from the Pullman Company. . . . The Pullman Company buys . . . locomotives from
the Baldwin Locomotive Company. . . . The Reading, the General Electric, the Steel Corporation and the New Haven [also]
buy locomotives from the Baldwin. . . . The Steel Corporation,
the Telephone Company, the New Haven, the Reading, the
Pullman and the Baldwin Companies, like the Western Union,
buy electrical supplies from the General Electric. The Baldwin,
the Pullman, the Reading, the Telephone, the Telegraph and the
General Electric companies, like the New Haven, buy steel products from the Steel Corporation. Each and every one of the companies last named markets its securities through J.P. Morgan &
Co.; each deposits its funds with J.P. Morgan & Co., and with
these funds of each, the firm enters upon further operations.[40]

Wilson read Brandeis's articles on the money trust and then
delivered a special message to Congress on January 20, 1914. The
president proposed creating a Federal Trade Commission (FTC), giving the Interstate Commerce Commission the power to regulate railroad financing, outlawing interlocking directorates and price cutting
that would destroy competition, and strengthening the penalties for
violation of the Sherman Act. Brandeis wrote triumphantly to his
brother that Wilson's message "has paved the way for about all I have
asked & some of the provisions specifically are what I got into his
mind at my first interview."[41] Brandeis then helped persuade Wilson
that the FTC should be a regulatory rather than a purely investigatory
body. This ran counter to Brandeis's usual disapproval of extensive
governmental regulatory involvement. He was nonetheless convinced
that no law could cover all possible violations of antitrust policy, and
an agency with the power to expand upon basic legislative policy should
be created. Brandeis's congressional testimony and lobbying aided
passage of the Clayton Antitrust Act, the Covington Bill (FTC) and
the Rayburn Bill (Interstate Commerce Commission), although the
Clayton Antitrust Act was somewhat watered down. Wilson then had
to choose commissioners for the FTC. At that point Brandeis and
Wilson began to part company. Wilson decided, largely on the basis
of other political considerations, not to name activist Progressives to

the FTC. Consequently, the commission functioned so much less effectively than Brandeis had hoped that he held Wilson responsible for ruining it.[42]

Brandeis's fear of bigness accompanied him when he joined the Supreme Court in 1916. He saw the Court's economic role as reinforcing governmental efforts to return American businesses to the size they would have been without the artificially created giant corporations. The Court had the responsibilities not to interfere with state and federal experiments in limiting bigness, such as antitrust laws; to encourage the growth of nongovernmental forces, such as unions, that would aid in curbing the power of bigness; and to help those governmental policies, like antimonopoly statutes, that fostered economic competition. Only a year after taking his seat on the Court, he dissented from its grant of a decree that in effect permitted a coal company to prevent its employees from joining a union. Brandeis argued, as he would continue to do in subsequent cases, that the Court was wrong to favor business over labor and that the company's policy was as unacceptably coercive as the Court had found the closed shop to be.[43]

His ideas about the evils of bigness and the need for the Court to permit state experiments that attempted to deal with it ensured his being regularly in dissent when the Court decided cases involving regulatory legislation. In 1928, for example, the Court overturned a Pennsylvania statute that taxed corporations more heavily than individually owned businesses and partnerships. Brandeis dissented, writing angrily that "there are still intelligent, informed, just-minded, and civilized persons who believe that the rapidly growing aggregation of capital through corporations constitutes an insidious menace to the liberty of the citizen; that it tends to increase the subjection of labor to capital; that, because of the guidance and control necessarily exercised by great corporations upon those engaged in business, individual liberty is being impaired and creative power will be lessened; . . . that the evils incident to the accelerating absorption of business by corporations outweigh the benefits thereby secured; and that the process of absorption should be retarded."[44]

In case after case he emphasized the virtues of federalism and decentralized power and argued for the right of the states to experiment.[45] The limits federalism imposed on the central government applied to the

Supreme Court as well as to the other branches. For almost one hundred years, the Court's holding that federal courts could ignore state common law had been the law of the land.[46] This led businesses seeking to evade local law to obtain charters in more than one state and then claim under the "diversity of citizenship" doctrine that cases involving them could be heard only by federal courts. Brandeis, along with Holmes, had long protested the power given to federal courts by this decision, and he was pleased to write for the Court in 1938, overturning the doctrine.[47] Brandeis told his current law clerk that he regarded his opinion in *Erie*, stopping federal courts from making their own law, as his "last major contribution to the law" and a triumph for state power.[48] He advocated judicial restraint because the Court, as all other bodies in a democratic society, had an obligation to be moderate in its use of power[49] and, perhaps, because he himself approved of many of the experiments that the state and federal governments undertook.

It has been suggested that Brandeis exercised restraint for the latter reason alone[50] and that he might well have approved a more active judicial role if, for example, states experimented with limitations on labor union activity or encouragement of industrial bigness. It is true that this was not a situation he often faced, but he did show in the Oklahoma ice case that he was quite capable of putting his personal beliefs aside in the name of experimentation and judicial restraint.[51] What he would have done had he lived in another era is not germane because his entire political thought, including his jurisprudence, grew out of his experiences at a particular historical moment. The development of American sociological jurisprudence during the last decades of the nineteenth century and the first ones of the twentieth was not accidental.

In one sense, sociological jurisprudence was part of a larger political and intellectual reaction against some of the consequences of the alteration of the American economy from a system based on farming and small-scale business to one in which great industrialized corporations and trusts played a major role. The concentration of power that resulted from the change was one of the engines that fueled the Progressive movement. Lawyers such as Brandeis were particularly concerned about the propensity of courts to endorse that concentration and to hand down decisions supportive of big business while they denied legitimacy to state experiments designed to minimize the negative human consequences of industrialization. Brandeis could counsel judicial restraint because it implied judicial endorsement of experiments he thought were important. Yet the soundness of sociological jurisprudence, and the corollary doctrine of judicial restraint, has been demonstrated by its continued use in later historical eras when the questions faced by the Court have been quite different from those of 1916–1939. Brandeis's insistent belief in democracy, in the ability of the people to find truths, and in the necessity of experimentation as part of that process suggest that, had he been confronted with experiments he disliked, he would quietly have deplored them but would have considered them constitutionally permissible as long as they did not violate the basic principles of dispersion of power and protection of civil liberties.

Brandeis joined Holmes's dissent in *Hammer* v. *Dagenhart*, in which the Court struck down the federal law prohibiting shipment in interstate commerce of articles produced by child labor. Presumably use of federal power was permissible here because it was clear that the states were unable or unwilling to deal with a practice that, as Holmes pointed out, was widely acknowledged to be shocking, and the statute neither concentrated power nor abridged civil liberties.[52] Brandeis viewed emergency as another appropriate occasion for the exercise of federal power and for experimentation. Thus he frequently dissented from the Court's overturning of President Franklin Roosevelt's New Deal legislation.[53]

Brandeis had a major opportunity to influence public policy during Roosevelt's presidency. By the time FDR was elected in 1932 the country was in the midst of the depression, and emergency measures clearly were needed. Brandeis met with Roosevelt on November 23, 1932, at the president-elect's request and urged him to finance public-works programs by taxing large estates. There were relatively few meetings of the two thereafter;[54] Brandeis, after all, was a Supreme Court justice, and should not be seen as politicking.[55] But he received regular visits from a host of New Deal officials and advisers — high-ranking officials including Secretary of Labor Frances Perkins, Secretary of the Interior Harold Ickes, National Recovery Administration heads Gen. Hugh Johnson and Donald Richberg, Tennessee Valley Authority director David Lilienthal; lesser officials such as Thomas Corcoran, Benjamin Cohen, and James Landis; brain trusters Felix

Frankfurter, Samuel Rosenman, Raymond Moley, and Huston Thompson. Through them and the numerous members of Congress who also sought his conversation and advice, he had a major effect on such New Deal legislation as the 1933 Public Securities Act, the 1934 Securities Exchange Act, the 1935 Holding Company Act, and the 1935 Social Security Act.[56]

Brandeis also made two private explicit statements of his preferred program.[57] The first was outlined in part on December 8, 1933, to his clerk Harry Shulman. Again, the themes centered on actions the federal government could take while still avoiding a dangerous centralization of power, on the necessity to keep experimentation alive, and on the vital importance of continuous employment. Brandeis told Shulman, as he had Roosevelt, that the government ought to rely heavily on the federal taxing power to minimize concentration of power. Taxation, he believed, should be used to keep the banks from doing more than one kind of banking: "This would avoid all the evil of great concentration of financial power in the hands of bankers." The bankers had to be the first object of governmental action, he thought, because at the moment the government was in the bankers' hands. The government could get money elsewhere: through postal-system savings accounts, checking accounts, commercial accounts, and the issuance of securities. Once freed from the control of the money trust, the government ought to impose excise taxes of other kinds upon overly large corporations. Brandeis retained his belief that the federal government usually should not regulate corporations because this would concentrate too much power in federal hands,[58] but he advocated using the powers of the central government to keep the corporations small enough to be regulated by the states. In addition, Brandeis suggested using federal taxes to curb the size of inheritances.[59]

Harold Laski had written to Oliver Wendell Holmes in 1922 that Brandeis "is really a Jeffersonian Democrat, trying to use the power of the State to enforce an environment in which competition may be really free and equal. This," commented Laski, "I take to be an impossible task," and he labeled Brandeis "a romantic anachronism."[60] Shulman echoed Laski and others by asking Brandeis if reducing the size of corporations would be "attempting to do the impossible, to turn the clock back." "Why shouldn't we turn the clock back?" Brandeis immediately demanded. "We just turned the clock back on a 'noble experiment' [Prohibition], which was unanimously adopted in the country and was being tried for some time." And then he added, in effect defining the difference between the thinker and the pragmatist, "To have that objection raised only confuses the proponent and directs his mind away from the real issue. First, we must determine what is desirable to do and then we can find ways and means to do it."[61]

They turned to the enormous unemployment caused by the depression. Brandeis envisioned action by both the states and the federal government. The states should be encouraged to adopt the Wisconsin unemployment plan, drawn up in large part by Brandeis's daughter Elizabeth and her husband Paul Raushenbush. Technically, the plan was voluntary for employers; however, nonparticipating employers were taxed.[62] Elsewhere, Brandeis advocated a massive program of public works, including a program similar to the Tennessee Valley Authority. He was certain such a program could get two million people to work within two months. He also urged credit for small businesses, help for small farmers and sharecroppers, and, returning to ideas he had been advocating since early in the century, elimination of holding companies and interlocking directorates.[63]

His New Deal prescriptions demonstrated that Brandeis could differentiate between his constant fear of bigness and the kind of emergency situations that might require emergency measures. But the perils of bigness were not to be ignored, even during emergencies; thus the federal taxing power could be used to limit the size of corporations, but the powers of the states rather than the federal commerce power should be used to regulate them. Emergencies were not to be the excuse for a massive concentration of power in the federal government—a situation that in fact did happen, with Brandeis's warnings being brushed aside.

The second Brandeis document suggesting postdepression policy, a letter to his daughter Elizabeth, also reflected his continuing fear of bigness. The states were to play a major part in ending the depression and were to continue as important elements in the American governmental system. As he emphasized in his letter, "Curb of bigness is indispensable to true Democracy & Liberty. It is the very foundation also of wisdom in things human. . . . 'Nothing too much.'" Unless this was remembered, he warned, "we may get amelioration, but not a working 'New Deal.' And we are apt to get Fascist manifestations.

Remember, the inevitable ineffectiveness of regulation, i.e. the limits of its efficiency in regulation." After all, he added, "If the Lord had intended things to be big, he would have made man bigger — in brains and character." The letter continued:

My idea has been that the Depression can be overcome only by extensive public works.

(a) that no public works should be undertaken save those that would be effective in making the America of the future what it should be,

(b) that we should avail [ourselves] of the present emergency to get those public works which Americans would lack the insight & persistence to get for themselves in ordinary times.

These public works are, for every state,

(1) afforestation

(2) running water control

(3) adult education

(4) appropriate provisions for dealing with defectives and delinquents.

It is absurd to permit either floods or droughts, or waste of waters. We should so control all running waters, by reservoirs, etc., so

(a) as to prevent floods & soil erosion

(b) to make it possible to irrigate practically all land

(c) to utilize the water for power & inland navigation

(d) & for recreation.[64]

Most of Brandeis's major ideas are reflected here. People were major "natural resources," and to give them the knowledge and living conditions necessary for informed participation in the democratic process, slum clearance, and adult education were added to land use and natural resources as targets for short-term federal programs. The federal government could use its money to stabilize the economy during the existing emergency, but the income derived from federal taxation had to be shared with the states instead of remaining in Washington to build up the national government's power. Public-works programs were of major importance because governments were the only bodies with sufficient money and motivation to fund the workers necessary to these "unprofitable" but socially desirable projects. Initially, public-works programs would be sponsored both federally and by the states; presumably, after the emergency had been ended, the states could take over almost all such programs, not forgetting to use natural resources for the recreation needed by well-rounded citizens.

Perhaps one reason the economists and other policymakers around Roosevelt could not understand Brandeis's ideas and thought he was merely advocating a return to nineteenth-century laissez-faire economic theory was that instead of offering a panacea he couched his thinking in terms of experiments and multistage developments. The New Dealers, to the contrary, correctly saw their mandate as finding fast solutions to the economic and political emergency of the depression. Their attitude was exemplified by the rapidity with which bills were proposed by the White House during Roosevelt's first "Hundred Days," and it was encouraged by the popular approval and congressional action generated by the legislation.

Brandeis recognized that fast action was necessary, but he remained aware of the possibly undesirable indirect effects of governmental measures. The celerity of the governmental response should not be permitted to conceal tendencies toward long-lasting concentration of power. He also declined to mistake quick fixes, however essential they might be at the moment, for permanent solutions.[65] He had been willing to defend Oregon's maximum-hours law for women in *Muller* v. *Oregon* only because the legislation was on the state rather than the federal level. As he had done in warning other states not to adopt the Massachusetts savings-bank life insurance system until it had been used long enough for its strengths and weaknesses to be demonstrated, so he supported experimentation by the states in regulating labor but opposed a federal statute mandating minimum wages for women as premature and possibly unconstitutional.[66] At the time of *Muller*, he was still dubious about governmental regulation of men's working hours or wages, contending that such matters were best handled through labor-management negotiations, at least until investigatory commissions established a need and an appropriate procedure, e.g., an approach similar to the Oregon statute tying the minimum wage for women to the actual cost of living.[67] Although he advocated an eventual move to worker-participation and consumer cooperatives, he knew there had to be not only many experiments with such systems but education of the public about their desirability. He therefore gradually came to endorse state — again, not federal — establishment of minimum wages and maximum hours, but only as a temporary measure, with the thought that government-mandated standards eventually would become unnecessary when the workers had enough time to teach themselves how to run corporations.[68]

Although he supported use of governmental power during the New Deal period, he would not countenance what he saw as unbridled power. He made this clear with his votes in *Panama Refining Co.* v. *Ryan*, *Schechter* v. *United States*, and *Louisville* v. *Radford*.[69] He was particularly concerned about the growing tendency to address problems by delegating power to the executive branch, even when it was run by Roosevelt. He commented to Frankfurter, when Congress was out of session, "There is some comfort in the thought that each day brings Congress' convening nearer. It was a terrible thing to vest absolute power in one man, and adjourn for so long a period." He added a week later, writing about Roosevelt policies he disliked, "They were the inescapable penalties paid for conferring absolute power."[70] Some years earlier, he had written an impassioned dissent in *Myers* v. *United States*, when the Court permitted a president unilaterally to fire a civil servant even though a statute required Senate advice and consent before such a removal. The Court argued efficiency; Brandeis countered with democracy and a statement that echoed Madison's belief in balancing power with other power: "The doctrine of the separation of powers was adopted by the Convention of 1787 not to promote efficiency but to preclude the exercise of arbitrary power. The purpose was not to avoid friction, but, by means of the inevitable friction incident to the distribution of the governmental powers among three departments, to save the people from autocracy."[71]

Brandeis opposed early New Deal attempts to limit production and to raise prices. If the government removed laws making unions illegal so that workers could negotiate sufficient wages for themselves, and if prices were lowered and jobs and goods were made available in part through public works, consumption would equal production. Concomitantly, of course, the end of the artificial maintenance of trusts by repealing laws supportive of them would encourage the redevelopment of smaller corporations that would set reasonable prices on the products they chose to stand behind. He was also willing, for the

moment, to permit states to operate transportation and banking
systems, to tax estates and profits in order to prevent the overac-
cumulation of wealth and power, to extend credit to small business
and farms, to accumulate and disseminate information about industries
and agriculture, and to limit the activities of bankers and stockbrokers
so that the money trust could not be resurrected. These moves would
help correct past mistakes while avoiding the trap of creating a huge
government. Brandeis saw a vital role for government while industrial
democracy was being fashioned. It was not, however, as centralized,
as extensive, or designed to be as permanent as that envisaged by
the framers of the New Deal.

There was nonetheless a major role for the central government to
play. Speaking to two journalists in 1935, he argued for the imposi-
tion by the federal government of heavy taxes on out-of-state corporations, on directors who did business with their own corporations,
on intraorganizational transactions within a holding company, and
on public utility holding companies. The object of all the taxes was
to end the practices and institutions taxed. Thus the federal taxing
power could be used to eliminate wrongs.[72] As Chief Justice John
Marshall had counseled much earlier in the country's history, "The
power to tax is the power to destroy."[73] Brandeis was urging that it
be used as such. As he told Alfred Lief, "By taxation bigness can be
destroyed. The power is there: what we create we can destroy."[74] Some
of the New Dealers were listening or at least thinking along similar
lines, as was demonstrated by the Brandeisian use of the taxing power
in the Walsh-Healy Public Contracts Act, the Public Utility Holding
Act, the 1936 Revenue Act, the Guffey Coal Act, and the post-1935
versions of the Agricultural Adjustment Act, the NRA codes, and the
Farm-Foreclosure Moratorium Act. And Brandeis also envisioned a
long-term federal governmental role in transportation, utilities, and
land development. But the basic economic function of the central
government was negative: It had an obligation to keep citizens free
from tyranny that might otherwise be imposed by some of their fellow
human beings, and the best way to accomplish this was to keep businesses from becoming too big.

One of the differences between Brandeis and the ultimately triumphant New Dealers such as Adolph Berle, Jr., Rexford Tugwell,

Raymond Moley, and Donald Richberg was this group's unarticulated assumption that government was best served by a monopoly over policymaking by a group of bright, dedicated men with expertise in economics and politics—in short, the New Dealers. The idea that democracy implied constant citizen-involvement was not one of their central political principles. They viewed Washington as the home of the enlightened and the state capitals as benighted outposts. Brandeis, who knew better than most of them how corrupt and uninterested in modernization state legislatures could be, nonetheless recognized that the kind of citizen-participation he considered crucial in a democracy was unlikely if the seat of most major decisionmaking was Washington. He concentrated on state models such as Massachusetts' savings bank life insurance system and the more recent socioeconomic reforms such as unemployment insurance that his daughter Elizabeth and others were creating in Wisconsin. He was reminiscent of Jefferson in emphasizing the need for dynamic governmental entities that were geographically accessible to a concerned citizenry. It was precisely because he knew that many state legislatures and bureaucracies were corrupt that he mistrusted their federal counterparts, with the far greater resources they were amassing through federal taxes on individuals and corporations.

The New Dealers could not comprehend Brandeis's insistence on federalism, which they viewed as a regrettable vestige of historical necessity. They made no effort at mass mobilization. Instead, the electorate was asked to vote for New Dealers, wait for them to solve the country's problems, and try to avoid fear in the interim. The big government created by and in Washington not only signaled a decades-long negation of meaningful federalism, but it also implied the end of a practice Brandeis considered vital: experimentation by the states. He regretted the lure of Washington for the young politically involved elite. He startled the young New Dealers who came to him expecting praise for their accomplishments in the nation's capital by admonishing them to return to the "provinces" from which they had gratefully escaped. "But Mr. Justice—Fargo, North Dakota!" one young man exclaimed in horror. To the protest of another that "I have no hinterland. I'm from New York City," Brandeis replied implacably, "That is your misfortune." Even his law clerks were advised to take their talents, much admired by him, back to the states from which they came.[75]

Brandeis's thought, as Paul Freund later commented, was all of a piece; or, to use Frankfurter's metaphor, "To quote from Mr. Justice Brandeis' opinions is not to pick plums from a pudding but to pull threads from a pattern." His theory of democracy, centered on the individual, encompassed both a recognition of the kinds of innovative governmental action required by the industrial age and an awareness of the limitations that had to be placed on business and on government if the individual was to be emphasized, the economy was to work well, and efficiency and freedom were to be kept in a proper balance. The New Dealers preferred to work piecemeal. C. Herman Pritchett has noted that the chief failure of the New Deal was the lack of "any consistent social and economic philosophy to give meaning and purpose to its various action programs." James MacGregor Burns has depicted Roosevelt as a man who "hated abstractions." Arthur Schlesinger has described how the president "wriggled away" when confronted with the differences between the Brandeis and the Berle camps and defined the New Deal as the "satisfactory compromise" between Theodore Roosevelt's New Nationalism and Woodrow Wilson's New Freedom. Brandeis knew that such a compromise was impossible, and in effect that is what he told the president, through his votes on the Supreme Court.[76]

Brandeis was fortunate in being able to take the economic policies he fashioned first to a presidential candidate, then, in a sense, to the White House; and, finally, to the Supreme Court. He was less so in getting either the White House, the Court, or the public to understand and support his ideas, particularly about the perils of bigness and the need for industrial democracy. Americans have remained insistently social Darwinists in their thinking, accepting giant economic combinations and their mistakes as an inevitable part of the nature of things. An Edsel or a thalidomide is seen as an aberration rather than as a symptom. The increasingly rare person who "makes it" after developing an ingenious invention in his garage and marketing it to millions is regarded as a hero worthy of the Horatio Alger myth he helps to perpetuate. The centralization of governmental power is perceived as a hallmark of civilization as long as it buries its scandals and makes no dramatic forays into the taxpayer's pocket. Brandeis loathed tycoons, he deplored public apathy, he condemned invasions of privacy, he feared big government, and he seems not to have thought much of television.[77] What he did care about, passionately, was the individual, and thus he was unceasing in his efforts to educate both the governors and the governed about the curse of bigness.

5

ZIONISM AND THE IDEAL STATE

Let us insist that the struggle for liberty shall not cease until equality of opportunity is accorded to nationalities as to individuals.[1]

Brandeis's one trip to Palestine, in 1919, lasted only sixteen days, but it was a triumphal tour. Brandeis had become the leader in the United States of the Zionist movement — the drive for a Jewish homeland in Palestine — and the Palestinian Jews outdid each other in their eagerness to applaud him. There was a whirlwind of activity as he visited all the Jewish cities and twenty-three of the forty-three Jewish settlements, being greeted at every stop as a hero. He was met by singing children and an honor guard at the settlement of Motza. There were singing children again at Rishon LeZion. Other children, many in Boy Scout and Girl Scout uniforms, along with adults dressed in their holiday best lined the roads as he arrived in flag-bedecked Tel Aviv. He was welcomed to Lod by doctors from Hadassah and by forty members of the Jewish Brigade. From the Lemel School in Jerusalem he received a silver-cased parchment extolling his virtues. The settlement of Zichron Yaacov built a special gate in his honor. He was as enthusiastic about what he saw as his hosts were about him. "It is a wonderful country, a wonderful city," he wrote to his wife from Jerusalem, and from Haifa he declared to English Zionist leader Chaim Weizmann, "Palestine has won our hearts. . . . It is no wonder that the Jews love her so."[2]

100

Brandeis, a thoroughly assimilated Jew who had never considered Jewishness as a key element of his identity, had become the acknowledged leader of American Zionists and the hope of the Jewish immigrants to Palestine. His transformation resulted at least as much from the opportunity to apply his political thought as from his ethnic emotionalism.

He displayed little interest in Jewish causes until summer 1910 when he mediated the New York garment strike and discovered the Eastern European Jewish workers who were the backbone of the American Zionist movement. His enthusiasm for their potential as citizens of his ideal democratic state began to grow. Everything about them, including the Zionism that was new to him, piqued his curiosity, and when a reporter for *American Hebrew* asked his opinion of Zionism, Brandeis replied, "I have a great deal of sympathy for the movement." He spent most of the interview, however, emphasizing that in the United States, "there is no place for . . . hyphenated Americans" and that "the opportunities for members of my people are greater here than in any other country."[3] His close friend Elizabeth Glendower Evans was certain that the strike was a "profound emotional experience that gave birth to his realization of himself as a Jew," and Benjamin V. Cohen attributed Brandeis's newly emerged Jewish consciousness to his experience with the Jewish workers. Labor leader Henry Moskowitz said that Brandeis's meetings with the workers "became almost a mystic experience for him." Brandeis acknowledged that the strike showed him "the true democracy of my people, their idealistic inclinations and their love of liberty and freedom."[4]

Shortly after the strike ended, Brandeis met Jacob de Haas, former secretary to Theodor Herzl, the father of modern Zionism. De Haas was the editor and publisher of a Jewish newspaper and interviewed Brandeis about savings-bank life insurance. At the conclusion of the interview de Haas asked if Brandeis was related to Lewis Dembitz, whom he described as a "noble Jew." Brandeis listened enthralled as on that day and at other meetings over the next months de Haas explained Dembitz's Zionism and the Zionist cause. Herzl had founded the formal Zionist movement in the 1890s, and Dembitz had joined it only after Brandeis left Louisville, so Brandeis had not known about his uncle's involvement. He later said that he was "eternally grateful" to de Haas for "unfold[ing] the Zionist cause" to him.[5]

The talks with de Haas, coupled with his experience of the garment strike, led Brandeis to enlist in the Federation of American Zionists in 1912, becoming a member of its Associate Executive Committee. He also joined the Zionist Association of Greater Boston, the Menorah Society, and the advisory board of the Hebrew Sheltering and Immigrant Aid Society. None of this activity was seen as important by the Zionist community, which was not particularly excited when his membership was announced at the Zionist convention of 1912, because he had not yet become an activist and was not known as being interested in Jewish causes. In spring 1913, however, he presided when the well-known Polish Zionist Nahum Sokolow spoke for two hours to an audience in Boston and gave Sokolow a letter of introduction to Secretary of State William Jennings Bryan. He began lecturing to Jewish and Zionist groups and was elected a delegate to the Zionist Congress meeting in Vienna in 1913. Although unable to attend it, he sent the Congress a message firmly advocating Jewish immigration to Palestine.[6]

During this period Brandeis was busy advising President Woodrow Wilson and actually gave little time to Zionism. In summer 1914, however, disheartened by Wilson's loss of interest in antitrust and other Progressive measures, Brandeis went on his annual vacation. It was typical for him to immerse himself in books and articles about each new enthusiasm, and he decided to spend much of the month reading intensively in Zionism and Jewish affairs. World War I broke out that summer. On August 30, Brandeis went to an emergency conference of American Zionists concerned about the wartime plight of European Jews and was asked to become chairman of the Provisional Executive Committee for General Zionist Affairs that the conference had created. It was assumed he would be a figurehead, interesting his wealthy friends in the cause while an administrative committee did the real work. But much to the surprise of everyone, he threw himself into the endeavor with total commitment and quickly became the acknowledged leader of American Zionism.[7]

Zionism proved to be a key part of Brandeis's life and one of his major activities for years.[8] His view of Zionism is crucial to an understanding of his political thought, and I argue here that Brandeis envisioned the Jewish Palestinian settlements as a potential re-creation of Periclean Athens and that Alfred Zimmern's *Greek Commonwealth* was central to his thinking.[9]

Three factors appear to have been primary in Brandeis's involvement in Zionism. One was his reaction to the Eastern European garment workers, the first working-class Jews he had met. He found them "possessed of those very qualities which we of the twentieth century seek to develop in our struggle for justice and democracy—a deep moral feeling which makes them capable of noble acts; a deep sense of the brotherhood of man; and a high intelligence, the fruit of three thousand years of civilization."[10] The second factor was the knowledge, gained from de Haas, that his adored Uncle Dembitz had considered Zionism a worthy cause. The third was his developing economic and political ideology, based on Jeffersonian and Progressive principles but going further to worker-participation. Zimmern's *Greek Commonwealth*, expressing political ideas much like Brandeis's and calling attention to notable similarities between Palestine and Greece, played a major role in Brandeis's Zionism by enabling him to pull together his growing interest in the movement and his view of the ideal state. For both Brandeis and Zimmern, the ideal had existed in Periclean Athens.

Brandeis thought of that period as the high point of democratic civilization. The great tribute he paid his Uncle Dembitz was to say that "he reminded one of the Athenians." He used a sentence from Pericles' "Funeral Oration" in *Whitney* v. *California*, his impassioned defense of his ideal democracy; in fact, as Pnina Lahav has demonstrated, much of the structure and message of Pericles' Oration is reflected in *Whitney*. He turned regularly to ancient Athens for wisdom. A journalist who followed Brandeis around for two days in 1916 reported wryly, "Euripides, I now judge, after having interviewed Brandeis on many subjects, said the last word on most of them."[11] The poem that Brandeis liked best and quoted most often because it expressed his view of citizenship and public service came from Euripides' *Suppliant Women*. Brandeis looked toward Periclean Athens to discover how the model citizen would function in the model political society.

Periclean Athens is the subject of *The Greek Commonwealth*, and Brandeis read it during winter of 1913–1914, just months before he startled the Zionist movement by expressing his interest in active participation. He later wrote to Zimmern that the book had been his only recreation while he was investigating the New Haven Railroad that winter and that it gave him more pleasure than almost anything he had read in recent years other than Gilbert Murray's translation of the *Bacchae*. Brandeis added that Horace Kallen had informed him of Zimmern's interest in Zionism and that they shared a friend in Norman Hapgood.[12]

Brandeis apparently learned of Zimmern through the latter's role as a translator of Guglielmo Ferrero's *The Greatness and Decline of Rome*. After reading *The Greek Commonwealth*, he used his photographic memory to quote Zimmern's words and urged the book upon all the people important to him.[13] He tacitly acknowledged Zimmern's centrality in his formulation of Zionism and the ideal state by arranging for Zimmern to be one of his only companions when he went to Palestine in 1919, even though the two men had not yet met when the trip was organized. Brandeis, the leader of American Zionism, was viewed by European Zionists as the potential head of the World Zionist Organization; he was known throughout American political and legal circles and was a member of the Supreme Court. It seems fair to assume that many people would have liked to accompany him on his trip, but he chose only de Haas and Zimmern.[14]

His choice of Zimmern was made despite the fact that Zimmern was interested in Zionism but was not a Zionist. The Oxford classicist occasionally advised London-based Chaim Weizmann, but his major goal was World Federalism.[15] In the meantime, however, he saw no contradiction in aiding the effort for a Jewish homeland because Jews had enriched the common culture and were an important element in it.

Zimmern's pan-nationalism was more accepting of cultural differences than was the pan-Americanism Brandeis favored until he became a Zionist. Brandeis had condemned ethnic separatism, telling the New York Century Club on the occasion of the 250th anniversary of the first Jewish settlement in the United States, "There is room here for men of any race, or any creed, of any condition in life, but not for Protestant-Americans, or Catholic-Americans, or Jewish-Americans, nor for German-Americans, Irish-Americans, or Russian-Americans." This attitude was not surprising from the son of a successful and assimilated immigrant family, and it also was in keeping with Brandeis's belief in universal truths and values that superseded nationalisms: human dignity, the personal and social benefits of fulfilling human potential, the need of a democratic electorate for a shared ethos.

Hyphenated Americans were not for Brandeis. Nor were they for most successful German-Americans like Jacob Schiff, Felix Warburg, Louis Marshall, *New York Times* publisher Adolph Ochs, Henry Morgenthau, or Brandeis's brother-in-law Felix Adler, the head of the Ethical Culture Society and teacher of ethics and morals at Columbia University who had performed the Brandeis's wedding ceremony.[16]

Brandeis's vision of a Jewish state seems to have been based in good part on the Jeffersonianism that runs throughout his thought, but *The Greek Commonwealth* helped alter his attitude toward hyphenated Americans and enabled him to connect his political beliefs and his dreams for the ideal society with the possibilities presented by Palestine. Zimmern's book paralleled Brandeis's thinking about the United States and brought it together with his love of Greece. Palestine as Brandeis envisioned it would become the new Periclean Athens, resembling Athens as Zimmern described it.

Zimmern waxed lyrical when he described Periclean Athens: "For a whole wonderful half-century . . . Politics and Morality, the deepest and strongest forces of national and of individual life, had moved forward hand in hand towards a common ideal, the perfect citizen in the perfect state."[17] He went on to examine the reasons the Athenians were able to scale such lofty heights; each factor paralleled one of Brandeis's basic beliefs.

The Greeks "grew up unable to conceive of any . . . state of government" other than local independence, Zimmern wrote; Brandeis championed decentralization and federalism. Zimmern argued, "The record of civilized States seems to show that no sub-division of the community . . . is sufficiently well informed or wise or tolerant or unselfish to be entrusted for long, without control or responsibility, with the powers and temptations of government"; Brandeis feared political centralization because fallible human beings inevitably would falter and be corrupted by an excess of power and responsibility. Zimmern noted, "Public business is much the same as private; and men are not able to transact business in hordes. Large companies are much the same as small, only more uncomfortable." Brandeis had called big government and big business equally inefficient. Zimmern declared that "it is only in a state where men are jealous for the maintenance of justice that the freedom of the individual can permanently be secured," that "it was Pericles' boast that his fellow-citizens found time to do justice both to public and private responsibilities, that they were at once (what is nowadays considered impossible) the most active political workers and the most many-sided individuals of their time," and that "democracy is meaningless unless it involves the serious and steady co-operation of large numbers of citizens in the actual work of government." This could have been Brandeis speaking about the concern for justice and public affairs that had to exist for the protection of democracy or about the worker-citizens to whom he wanted to give the leisure time necessary for participation in public affairs.[18] Zimmern spoke in Brandeisian terms about the need for industrial reform, castigating the "modern industrial system" as typified by "'soulless organization'" and the decline of the worker's liberty. He also wrote of the corruption of conspicuous consumption and of the necessity to concentrate instead on individuals' minds and physical abilities.[19]

Zimmern made the connection between Periclean Athens and Palestine by describing the latter as possessing all the physical elements found in the Athenian state. Both were in the Mediterranean area; both relied "on the unsettled weather of winter and the big rainfalls in the autumn and spring, the 'former' and 'latter' rains of the Bible"; Greece's "threefold division" into distinct geographic areas was "as true of Palestine as of Greece." Zimmern traced one cause of the decline of Pericles' Athens to the plague that killed a quarter of the citizens. Brandeis, whose family had kept a bowl of quinine tablets on a table in Louisville, would make one of his first priorities in Palestine the eradication of malaria, declaring that a workable civilization could not be developed where malaria thrived.[20] Again and again, Zimmern compared Palestine with Greece, quoting Greek poets alongside Hebrew prophets and maintaining, "It is true to assert of all these regions that, even if they have not preserved their independence or attained to popular government, they yet provide conditions which will prove helpful at any time to their successful exercise."[21]

The new Athens Brandeis envisioned would have the benefit of lessons he had learned in the United States. He was never more Jeffersonian than in his approach to Palestine, which he described in terms, although not specifically the same, that the American Founding Fathers might well have used in speaking of the colonies. There was arable land; there were determined pioneers; there was the newness of a society that might escape class divisions; there was a chance to make democracy work, far from the corrupting forces of existing regimes. His speeches demonstrate that in many ways the Jewish community in Palestine had become, for him, the fourteenth colony or, perhaps, the colonies as they should have been. He extolled the "Jewish Pilgrim Fathers," "the pioneers in Palestine," and called Palestine "a miniature California" and Zionism "the Pilgrim inspiration and impulse over again."[22] He reminded audiences that democracy prevailed during "the early days of the colonies and states of New England" because "the Puritans were trained in implicit obedience to stern duty by constant study of the Prophets."[23] Applauding the equal value given to civic duty, education, and democracy by the early New Englanders and the Jewish settlers in Palestine, he admonished Zionist audiences, "The Pilgrims had faith, we should have it."[24] He repeated the analogy, declaring, "The twentieth century ideals of America have been the ideals of the Jew for more than twenty centuries. We have inherited these ideals of democracy and of social justice."[25]

One might raise the question of exactly how much Brandeis understood about Athens and the New England colonies or whether his romanticized conception of each existed in spite of his extensive reading. There were slaves in Athens and in the colonies; indeed, the Athenian economy was based upon slavery. The two societies treated women as inferior.[26] Although few if any classicists of Brandeis's era discussed slavery and chauvinism in Greece and there was still a paucity of feminist writing about early American history, the man who had grown up hating slavery and who was a champion of women's suffrage might have been expected to perceive for himself the inequities that underlay the two societies. But his usually fierce intelligence seems to have faltered here. Perhaps he assumed that the virtues of Athens and Plymouth Rock could be replicated without their vices.

In any event, Brandeis had moved from distaste for "hyphenated Americans" to advocacy of what he called "inclusive brotherhood" and his colleague Horace Kallen referred to as "cultural pluralism." He had in fact come to view anti-Semitism as reflecting a failure of liberalism that did not protect groups as well as individuals.[27] Had he been on the Supreme Court in the second half of the twentieth century rather than the first, whether this view might have led him to approve the extension of constitutional rights to include groups as well as individuals is a matter for speculation. There is some evidence, however, in Kallen's assertion that Brandeis "turned to Zionism out of an interest partially philanthropic and humane" but remained a Zionist "because he came to apply the conceptions of the Declaration of Independence, which were among the postulates of his faith, to all sorts of human associations and groups of individuals, as well as to individuals."[28]

The program that Brandeis fashioned for Jewish Palestine also grew out of his Americanism. During the Pinchot-Ballinger hearings, for example, Brandeis not only uncovered government giveaways of natural resources in Alaska but realized that the larger problem was ownership and conservation of land and other natural resources. As usual, he created his own solutions. He spoke of the need to keep land, mineral deposits, and development of transportation and utilities in Alaska's relatively untouched terrain away from the "capitalists" who were certain to use land and mines for speculation and who had exploited New England by turning its transportation systems and utilities into monopolies. "We must devise some system," Brandeis wrote to his ally Sen. Robert La Follette, "by which those who are willing to go to Alaska, with a view to working there and developing its resources, shall have not only the assurance of fair treatment, but the opportunity of operating without undue oppression through monopolistically inclined competitors."[29]

There is again an echo of Locke and the idea that the land should belong to the person willing to work it, but that was not a realistic option given the relative monopoly of investment resources by the capitalists. Brandeis's answer was government ownership of land, with only a small return required from those individuals who used it, and a government-owned but privately operated transportation system. The government might own at least one mine, to compare with those that were private, running it as an experimental station.[30]

Once the government had established a system for protecting the interests of the community from the ever-present threat of big money, it was the people who should rule the territory that had not yet become a state. Brandeis asked La Follette:

My dear Bob: How would this do for the Progressive slogan:
"Alaska; the Land of Opportunity.
Develop it by the People, for the people.
Do not let it be exploited by the Capitalists, for the Capitalists."[31]

What mattered was democratic decisionmaking, which would ensure that the profits went to those people who had earned them through their labor. There was to be small-scale communal responsibility, with decisions about land use to be made communally. This pattern was precisely the approach that Brandeis tried to accomplish in Palestine.

The outline of his goal appeared in the Pittsburgh Program he drew up for the June 1918 Zionist convention held in that city.

First: We declare for political and civil equality irrespective of race, sex, or faith of all the inhabitants of the land.

Second: To insure in the Jewish National Home in Palestine equality of opportunity we favor a policy which, with due regard to existing rights, shall tend to establish the ownership and control by the whole people of the land, of all natural resources and of all public utilities.

Third: All the land, owned or controlled by the whole people, should be leased on such conditions as will insure the fullest opportunity for development and continuity of possession.

Fourth: The co-operative principle should be applied so far as feasible in the organization of all agricultural, industrial, commercial, and financial undertakings.

Fifth: The system of free public instruction which is to be established should embrace all grades and departments of education.

Sixth: Hebrew, the national language of the Jewish people, shall be the medium of public instruction.[32]

The platform may be the closest thing to a short summary of Brandeis's political thought that exists. It begins with a notable assertion of human equality. Political and civil equality apply to all people: not just men, not just Jews. Brandeis's realization that there were Palestinian Arabs already living on much of the land was reflected in both the first and second paragraphs, the second including "due regard to existing rights" of land ownership. Presumably he hoped enough contiguous land could be obtained "by the whole people," meaning the Jewish community, but the reference to "due regard to existing rights" made it clear that Palestinian Arab landowners were not necessarily expected to give up their holdings.

The bulk of the land was to be owned "by the whole [Jewish] people," not by private companies, and the same was true for all natural resources and public utilities. The community's governing entity was not to work the land or develop the resources or run the utilities, however; these were to be leased, with the requirement for lessees being their willingness to develop resources as fully as possible.

The principle of communality went further. Institutions—agricultural, industrial, commercial, and financial—were to be run along cooperative lines, which meant communal decisionmaking, as it already existed in the two major types of Palestinian Jewish agrarian communities. The first, the kibbutz, held land entirely in common, and decisions as to what crops would be planted, which jobs would be done by whom, what percentage of any profit would be put back into the land and infrastructure and what would be used for less pressing necessities were made by the entire community in general assemblies. The second, the moshav, held the land communally but sold shares and individual plots to families who would live on the land and either work both on their plots and on communal land or farm their plots alone while returning a percentage of their crop to the community. The moshav's members decided jointly about membership in the community, use of communal profits, and so forth. In Brandeis's day, the kibbutzim and moshavim existed only as agricultural endeavors. He nonetheless anticipated the existence of industrial, commercial, and financial institutions, some of which were already present in early form (e.g., small-scale banks, usually linked to a political party, that helped finance the settlements),[33] and he was thinking ahead about worker-participation in them.

Brandeis expressed his belief that a democratic system could not survive without educated citizens; hence the inclusion of "free public instruction." And it was to be in Hebrew, as the revival of Hebrew as a living language and as one that would be common to Jewish immigrants from various countries was a major goal of the Zionists. But Brandeis did not comment upon, and possibly did not consider, the effect of this measure upon Arab citizens.

The "whole people" who, according to the Pittsburgh Program, would own and control land, natural resources, and utilities clearly were the Jewish people. Although the platform also stated that there would be "political and civil equality irrespective of race, sex, or faith of all the inhabitants of the land,"[34] there is no indication of the place the Palestinian Arab population would occupy under a social contract that rested upon the specified pattern of land ownership and education.

Brandeis, along with many Palestinian Zionists and almost all American Zionists, apparently knew little about the number and situation of Palestinian Arabs. He seems to have been as unaware as the other Zionists around him of the extent to which the Palestinian Arabs' land was being acquired through questionable dealings, particularly after the Balfour Declaration in 1917; of the suffering being caused Palestinian Arabs by the development of the Jewish entity; or of the existence of a well-developed Palestinian Arab economy, dependent in part on the land that was being turned into Jewish settlements.[35] He clearly accepted the general Zionist assumption, self-serving as it may have proved to be, that Jewish economic efforts were benefiting the Arabs and that Palestinian Arab anger was generated by absentee Arab landowners opposed to the improvements in the lives of the fellahin.[36] As a Zionist, his major concern was the creation of a Jewish homeland in Palestine. Unlike some other Zionists, however, he was equally certain that a Zionist entity ought to recognize the rights of all inhabitants. He thought Arabs and Jews could live together, that Arabs should be permitted to buy stock in Jewish enterprises and to join Jewish labor unions.[37] Shortly before he died he donated money for playgrounds in Palestine to be used by Jewish, Moslem, and Christian children.[38]

Brandeis could assert that Jews might want and need a Palestinian homeland, rather than simply helping to build democracies wherever they found themselves, because he gradually realized that much of the world would not permit their participation. He had not experienced anti-Semitism himself and had not been particularly concerned about it.[39] He discovered it, however, in talking to the New York garment workers, and he was shocked at the depth of European anti-Semitism during World War I. "You cannot possibly conceive of the horrible sufferings of the Jews in Poland & adjacent countries," he wrote to his brother in 1914. "These changes of control from German to Russian & Polish anti-semites are bringing miseries as great as Jews ever suffered in all their exiles. . . . The Jews are having a bad time."[40] He knew anti-Semitism existed in the United States, and at least one of his colleagues has suggested that Brandeis helped create the American Jewish Congress in part to help combat anti-Semitism.[41] He did not think, however, that the level of American anti-Semitism would or should lead many American Jews to move to Palestine; given the American democratic and legal system, he saw no reason for them to leave. Zionism meant an increase in freedom, specifically, the freedom of Jews to live "either in the land of their fathers" or, as a majority Jewish collectivity, under self-rule in Palestine.[42] He considered the United States to be as good a place as Palestine for Jews to live. This belief was one of the elements of his thought that led to his eventual dispute with European Zionists, who thought all Jews should move to Palestine, and to the schism it caused in the world Zionist movement.[43]

Brandeis also recognized a historical "longing for Palestine" among many Jews, "a manifestation in the struggle for existence by an ancient people";[44] this yearning, combined with the Jews' long history in Palestine and with anti-Semitism, was sufficient reason for the establishment of a Jewish homeland there rather than elsewhere. He argued that a group of people sharing a combination of elements such as "'race, language, religion, common habitat, common conditions, mode of life and manners, [and] political association'" have not only a right but an obligation to assert their nationality and that "the . . . internationalism" that "seeks the obliteration of nationalities or peoples" is "misnamed."[45]

Legitimation of the longing for self-determination was a precondition of world peace. "Deeply imbedded in every nation and people is the desire for full development," Brandeis told the Economic Club of Boston in 1915, equating "full development" with nationhood. The predemocratic idea that strong individuals had a right to exercise arbitrary power had been found wanting, he said, and it was time to recognize that the assumption of strong nations "that they possess the divine right to subject other peoples to their sway" was equally outmoded. That assumption resulted in wars and ran counter to the twentieth-century concept of liberty, which was based on the recognition of individuality. The national movements of the nineteenth century had demonstrated that "whole peoples have individuality no less marked than that of the single person." Adherence to the ideal of liberty required that national individuality be recognized and that "equal opportunity for all people as for all individuals" be understood as "the essential of international as well as of national justice upon which a peace which is to be permanent must rest." History demonstrated that people who mistakenly considered their community to be superior frequently turned to violence, attempting to dominate others in the name of civilization and progress; people whose inherent right to nationhood was disregarded were equally likely to fight for self-determination. Global peace depended upon acceptance of the equality of peoples. The Jews sought in Palestine a collective right similar to that of the Greeks, the Rumanians, the Italians.[46]

Brandeis's reasons for the creation of a specifically Jewish entity in Palestine thus encompassed more than anti-Semitism. He insisted that the Zionist goal be seen in light of the national movements that had been a major feature of nineteenth-century Western civilization. His emphasis on the individual *as a member of society* included the belief that maximum individual development could occur only within the community. A community, however, implied group membership, which was one of the bases for Brandeis's support for self-determination. "This right of development on the part of the group is essential to the full enjoyment of rights by the individual," he said in 1915, because "the individual is dependent for his development (and his happiness) in large part upon the development of the group of which he forms a part. We can scarcely conceive of an individual German or Frenchman living and developing without some relation to the contemporary German or French life and culture."[47]

The logic of Brandeis's argument is that self-determination is both a collective and an individual right. Nationalism, properly understood, means "that each race or people, like each individual, has a right and duty to develop, and that only through such differentiated development will high civilization be attained."[48] It was nationalism that "created gallant Belgium . . . freed Greece . . . gave us united Italy."[49] Each individual who shares in a particular nationalism has a presumed right to live in a nation dominated by that nationality.

Beneficial though nationalism might be, however, it is not identical to nationhood; there is a "difference between a nation and a nationality."

Likeness between members is the essence of nationality; but the members of a nation may be very different. A nation may be composed of many nationalities, as some of the most successful nations are. An instance of this is the British nation . . . the French in Canada . . . the Swiss nation . . . the Belgian nation . . . the American nation. The unity of a nationality is a fact of nature; the unification into a nation is largely the work of man. The false doctrine that nation and nationality must be made co-extensive is the cause of some of our greatest tragedies.[50]

Brandeis made it clear that he was arguing for "recognition of the equal rights of each nationality" in every nation;[51] for tolerance, not for separatism or for subordination of any nationality. Nations, like individuals, legitimately can exercise rights only "in such manner and to such extent as the exercise of the right in each is consistent with the exercise of a like right by every other."[52]

Because nationalities had not only a "right" but a "duty" to maintain a homeland, Jews who felt they could best realize themselves in a Jewish homeland should have the opportunity to move to one. The human rights of self-determination and freedom of movement, not formally recognized in theory by many nations until after Brandeis's death and still recognized only in theory by some, were contained in his thought. Because he was speaking in the context of Zionism, Brandeis emphasized that the Jews, like the Greeks, had made major contributions to civilization, among them establishment of at least parts of three great religions, "reverence for law, and the highest conceptions of morality."[53] But again, there was no implication of superiority or inequality, only "that the struggle for liberty shall not cease until equality of opportunity is accorded to nationalities as to individuals."[54] When he was asked what he thought of the concept of the "Chosen People," Brandeis replied, "It would seem to me that even the strictest adherents of the Jewish faith ought to inquire whether their belief respecting the election of Israel is not perhaps based on a misinterpretation of revelation . . . let us teach all peoples that they are all chosen, and that each has a mission for all."[55]

The themes of Brandeis's Zionism echoed the themes of his Americanism and his view of Periclean Athens: the just society, the democratic society, the moral society, equality before the law, participation in public life, regularity of employment, a reasonable income and working hours, opportunity for self-realization, access to education, proper medical care. For him, Zionism was an extension of Americanism. Like all human beings, Palestinian Jews were "capable of noble acts," and, living in the organizational embodiment of "the brotherhood of man," they would create a democratic civilization.[56] Brandeis gradually had become convinced "that Jews were by reason of their traditions and their character peculiarly fitted for the attainment of American ideals," that the culmination of Jewish and American ideals would be found in Jewish Palestine, and that "to be good Americans, we must be better Jews, and to be better Jews, we must become Zionists."[57]

The Jewish Palestinian community would become the ideal state that he hoped would exist, in larger and somewhat different form, in the United States. He recognized that the latter would take longer to achieve if it could be attained at all, in part because a recalcitrant system dependent on bigness and relative inequality was already established, in part because of the size and heterogeneity of the United States and its population, in part because it was urbanized and industrialized rather than agrarian. For the moment, therefore, he would see what he could do about creating the "good society" in Palestine.

6

CIVIL AND ECONOMIC LIBERTIES

In frank expression of conflicting opinions lies the greatest promise
of wisdom in governmental action; and in suppression lies ordinarily the greatest peril.[1]

One of Brandeis's major contributions to law and to political theory
lay in the realm of civil liberties. He viewed free speech and privacy
as necessary to individual development and to the creation of the
educated citizens crucial to the democratic state. Speech, privacy,
education, and democracy were elements of the ideal political system.
Therefore, democracy had to be defined as majority rule with full
protection for the rights of individuals. Equally, sociological jurisprudence, which in other spheres mandated judicial deference to the
will of the majority, required that the judiciary play a central role
in preventing democratically elected officials from interfering with individual rights. If law was to reflect felt necessities and new policies
were to be enacted in response to social developments, free and open
discussion of problems and possible solutions by an educated electorate was vital.

Brandeis's goal was a harmony of individual and community. He
frequently spoke of the citizen's right to speech as if the right flowed
from the need of the community for an informed electorate rather
than from any individual need, a view that has misled some scholars.[2]
The right to speak and hear could not be defended "as a merely individual right," he said.[3] It was, in fact, more a "duty" for the citizen

116

than it was a right, "for its exercise is more important to the Nation than it is to himself."[4] But he was far from a communitarian, because his overarching goal was fulfillment of the individual. Ideas were necessary to individual as well as to social development. People had to be able to explore all available ideas if they were to learn, stretch their intellectual horizons, and fulfill their individual capabilities. The individual's world had to be organized into a community because it was only within that setting that individual fulfillment could be attained. This obligated the individual to participate actively in the democratic state so that it would not lose the democratic nature that made it responsive to individual needs. But means and ends are not identical, however compatible they may be. The free individual was the goal; society, the means by which individual freedom was to be achieved. Society was the framework; the individual, the subject. Ideally, society would be constituted of free individuals living in a community of self-governing equals. Brandeis spoke of the right of speech as belonging to the individual, adding that "exercise of this right by the citizen is ordinarily *also* his duty." The individual was primary.

It is sometimes assumed, because Brandeis and Oliver Wendell Holmes were friends who frequently voted alike in Court cases, that they shared an approach to free speech. The assumption is mistaken. Holmes believed that people's opinions should be tested in the "marketplace of ideas," and he enjoyed watching competing ideologies rising or falling in popularity as the public will decreed. In spite of his delight in reading philosophy and playing with ideas, Holmes's social Darwinism prevented him from considering that the specific ideas the majority adopted would make any difference; the "fittest" human beings would survive and shape society in their image. Thus Holmes was able, while serving on the Massachusetts Supreme Judicial Court and during his early years on the Supreme Court, to sustain governmental interferences with free speech.[5]

This view was anathema to Brandeis. To him, ideas made a great difference. Without the free exchange of ideas, experimentation could not take place, solutions could not evolve, and institutions could not adapt themselves to changing social needs. Only through the airing of divergent ideas could the people know which ones to choose, and only then could they give their government the benefit of their advice.

Choice was difficult. "Differences of opinion are inevitable among thoughtful men," Brandeis reflected, "if the question under consideration is one worthy of discussion." The expression of various opinions about controversial subjects was to be encouraged, not prevented: "Differences in opinions are not only natural but desirable where the question is difficult; for only through such differences do we secure the light and fuller understanding which are necessary to a wise decision." "Good" speech, not government repression, was the antidote for "bad" speech, and so certain was he that the people would be able to distinguish between them that he advocated the setting aside of areas "in every park" for speech making.[6]

Brandeis did not fear dissent; he welcomed it. Absence of dissent in a democratic society is artificial, he thought, and "may be due to indifference"; only a thorough thrashing out of differences could lead to communal unity. "Like the course of the heavenly bodies," he said in *Gilbert* v. *Minnesota*, "harmony in national life is a resultant of the struggle between contending forces. In frank expression of conflicting opinions lies the greatest promise of wisdom in governmental action; and in suppression lies ordinarily the greatest peril."[7] Like Holmes, Brandeis put his faith in the marketplace of ideas; unlike Holmes, he believed that the choices made in it mattered and ultimately would be the correct ones. Robert Cover has noted that Brandeis doubted that government could function wisely, much less democratically, in the absence of input from citizens.[8] As David Riesman said, although Brandeis was "skeptical of power and of human abilities," he also had "an extraordinary faith in the possibilities of human development."[9] Perhaps the difference lay in the backgrounds of the two men, with Holmes's experiences largely confined to the world of the Boston Brahmins except for the traumatic service in the Civil War that helped turn him into a social Darwinist.[10] Brandeis, on the other hand, had worked with laborers whose education had been minimal but whose ideas seemed far more rational to him than did those of many Brahmins. His skepticism was reserved for the "experts" — precisely those people Holmes might have seen as the "fittest" — and for the concentration of power that was based on the assumption that any group of human beings knew what was best for all.

The differences in their approach to ideas and the value of free speech were reflected in their interpretation of the First Amendment's enjoinder, "Congress shall make no law . . . abridging the freedom of speech, or of the press." In 1917 Congress passed an Espionage Act that made it illegal, in part, "when the United States is at war . . . willfully [to] cause or attempt to cause insubordination, disloyalty, mutiny, or refusal of duty, in the military or naval forces of the United States, or . . . willfully [to] obstruct the recruiting or enlistment service of the United States." Two Philadelphia Socialists who had participated in the writing and distribution of an antidraft pamphlet were convicted for violation of the act. When they appealed to the Supreme Court, Holmes, writing for the Court, upheld the conviction and in the course of doing so enunciated the famous "clear and present danger" doctrine.[11]

The question Holmes addressed was whether the limitation on abridgment of speech was meant to be an absolute. He decided it was not. "We venture to believe," he would write in an opinion handed down later that year, "that neither Hamilton nor Madison, nor any other competent person then or later, ever supposed that to make criminal the counselling of a murder within the jurisdiction of Congress would be an unconstitutional interference with free speech."[12] This meant that speech could become an act beyond the protection of the First Amendment. The example he used in *Schenck* was that of "a man . . . falsely shouting fire in a theatre and causing a panic." He offered no criterion for delineating between speech and speech-become-action, observing only that "the character of every act depends upon the circumstances in which it is done." If the speech was made during war, the test was different than it would be during peacetime: "When a nation is at war many things that might be said in time of peace are such a hindrance to its effort that their utterance will not be endured so long as men fight and that no Court could regard them as protected by any constitutional right." If, in the circumstances of war, "the words used . . . are of such a nature as to create a clear and present danger that they will bring about the substantive evils that Congress has a right to prevent," then Congress has the power to punish their use.[13]

"Clear and present danger" was not defined. It is difficult to see how the actions of the little group, which apparently mailed out a few of its leaflets and put the rest on a table in its headquarters for the benefit of anyone who wandered in, constituted a "clear and present danger" of anything more than the most minimal obstruction of recruitment or service in the armed forces. Holmes's belief that the Constitution gave no special protection to speech was spelled out in a letter he sent to Judge Learned Hand in 1918. "Free speech," wrote Holmes, "stands no differently than freedom from vaccination"; that is, given adequate justification, either could be abridged by the state.[14]

Prof. Gerald Gunther has argued convincingly that the correspondence with Learned Hand, of which the preceding quotation is only a small part, altered Holmes's attitude toward the First Amendment. Gunther finds the first indication of this change in the opinion Holmes wrote for himself and Brandeis in *Abrams* v. *United States*, handed down in 1919.[15] Dissenting from the Court's decision upholding the conviction of pamphleteers under the 1918 Sedition Act, Holmes asserted that the Constitution protects free trade in ideas.[16]

Brandeis, who silently went along with Holmes's opinion in *Schenck*, also rethought it later on and regretted having voted to uphold the conviction. He told Frankfurter that "I have never been quite happy about my concurrence. . . . I had not then thought the issues of freedom of speech out — I thought at the subject, not through it." He did more thinking through of the subject of speech during wartime, which resulted in three dissenting opinions during the following year.[17]

The first contained what can only be read as a deliberate misconstruction of the clear and present danger doctrine. *Schaefer* v. *United States* was an appeal by five men convicted under the Espionage Act for printing misleading articles about the war in two German-language newspapers. The government alleged that the articles, contemptuous of the American war effort and suggesting that the war was the doing of the president, violated the act by obstructing recruitment into the armed forces of the United States as well as "willfully mak[ing] or convey[ing] false reports or false statements with intent . . . to promote the success of its enemies." Brandeis, reprinting the articles in their entirety, found it impossible to believe that a jury "acting in calmness" could find that they created a clear and present danger of obstruction or of aiding the enemy. So far he had only applied Holmes's new doctrine; but then he went further, declaring, "The constitutional right of free speech has been declared to be the same in peace and in war." This statement was manifestly a deliberate misreading of *Schenck*, which quite specifically stated that wartime created a different set of "circumstances," justifying the suppression of speech that would be allowed in peacetime. Brandeis, however, warned that it was precisely in time of war that "an intolerant majority" was most likely to be "swayed by passion or by fear," implying that freedom of speech was at least as necessary then as in peacetime.[18]

Brandeis reiterated his dissenting position in *Pierce* v. *United States*. The case involved another Espionage Act conviction, this one for the distribution of Socialist leaflets that had allegedly interfered with the operation of the war effort and had caused insubordination. Brandeis found it difficult to see how insubordination had been caused, as the leaflets had been distributed only to civilians, or how the statements describing the "hopelessness of protest" against the "irresistible power of the military arm of the Government" and counseling acquiescence in its will could have interfered with the war effort. Again, he argued, the test of a grave, imminent, clear and present danger had not been met; moreover, he asserted the need for free speech whether in peace or in war:

> The fundamental right of free men to strive for better conditions through new legislation and new institutions will not be preserved, if efforts to secure it by argument to fellow citizens may be construed as criminal incitement to disobey the existing law.[19]

It was "not until I came to write the Pierce and Schaefer cases," Brandeis told Frankfurter, that he understood the issues of freedom of speech. He mentioned Herbert Hoover's belief that "criticism should end at water's shore. . . . I felt just opposite — wrote those long dissents in Schaefer and Pierce cases to put on permanent record what we were not allowed to say." Rather than putting on record what one was *not* allowed to say, however, the dissents addressed themselves to what one *should have been* permitted to say, and that seemed to be virtually anything that would be permitted in peacetime, when Brandeis could see no reason for limitations on criticism of foreign or any other governmental policies. As he did in *Schenck*, Brandeis had quietly concurred in Holmes's 1919 opinion for the Court upholding the Espionage Act conviction of labor leader Eugene Victor Debs for speaking in such a manner as to prevent recruiting. Now he considered that case also to have been wrongly decided and thought that it should have been "placed . . . on the war power — instead of taking Holmes' line about 'clear and present danger.' Put it frankly on war power . . . and then the scope of espionage legislation would be confined to war." Or, stated differently, the "clear and present danger" doctrine allowed too great a limitation on the right of the citizenry to free speech.[20]

Holmes concurred in the dissents in *Schaefer* and *Pierce*. He disagreed, however, with Brandeis's dissent in the third 1920 speech case.[21] A Minnesota law prohibited any interference with the military enlistment effort. An official of the Nonpartisan League had been convicted under it for telling a public meeting that the average person had nothing to say about whether the United States should have become involved in World War I or whether a draft should have been imposed. Holmes quietly concurred with Justice McKenna's opinion for the Court upholding the conviction. Brandeis's dissent asserted that the Minnesota act violated Congress' exclusive control over the war power and that it was "an act to prevent teaching that the abolition of war is possible." The act in effect outlawed the teaching of pacifism. In doing so, it violated the right of privacy as well as that of speech because it made it a crime "to teach in any place a single person that a citizen should not aid in carrying on a war. . . . Thus the statute invades the privacy and freedom of the home. Father and mother may not follow the promptings of religious belief" by teaching their children that their religion condemned participation in any war.[22]

After the Court issued its decision in *Gilbert* v. *Minnesota*, Holmes wrote to Frederick Pollock, "Brandeis . . . dissented in a state case on free speech in which he had one ground worthy of serious consideration and others that I thought all wrong — while I heartily disagreed with the reasoning of the majority. So I, with some doubts, concurred in the result of the decision." Chief Justice Edward Douglass White had written a separate dissent making the point about the war power having been exercised by Congress by its passage of the Espionage Act. Had that been the "one ground worthy of serious consideration," Holmes could have joined White's dissent. His failure to do so presumably indicates that his agreement with Brandeis came on another point, probably the corollary one that Brandeis made about what he, and to a lesser extent Holmes, considered the Court's misguided use of the due process clause to strike down state economic legislation.[23]

Brandeis's own belief in judicial restraint should have prevented him from getting into a discussion of the due process clause. As he agreed with White that the Espionage Act had already filled the field, leaving no room for state action, he should not have ignored the Court's rule of avoiding constitutional issues and deciding on lesser grounds wherever possible. But he was too angry for rules, lashing out against the Court's relying on the due process clause to negate state laws prohibiting employers from "discriminat[ing] against a workman because he is a member of a trade union" or preventing a businessman from conducting a private employment agency but declining to see that the same logic should apply in the Gilbert case to protect "liberty to teach, either in the privacy of the home or publicly, the doctrine of pacifism." "I cannot believe," Brandeis chastised the Court, "that the liberty guaranteed by the Fourteenth Amendment includes only liberty to acquire and to enjoy property."[24] Brandeis was as infuriated by the Court's limitations on state experiments in the economic sphere as he was by its interference with what he viewed as protected speech. As Walton Hamilton noted, this attitude was the result of the different values he placed on speech and on property rights. "The right to a free and full expression of personal opinion," wrote Hamilton in interpreting Brandeis, "has such value that only a positive case will justify its abridgement; the right of free contract is a business usage which has its important but limited function."[25]

If he could have, Brandeis would have wiped out the Fourteenth Amendment's due process clause entirely, in exasperation over its use by the Court to negate the people's will, especially regarding labor legislation. That became clear in a conversation he had with Felix Frankfurter after the Court handed down its decision in another case in which Brandeis and Holmes were on opposite sides.

In 1923 the Court overturned the conviction of a Nebraska schoolteacher who had violated a state law, passed during the war, that made it a crime to teach German in the public schools. Brandeis did not write in this case but concurred in Justice McReynolds's opinion for the Court. Holmes, however, dissented, saying that this "experiment," ostensibly designed to make English the "common tongue" of all residents, was not unreasonable and therefore was within the state's powers.[26] Brandeis commented to Frankfurter that the right to an education was so fundamental that any impairment of it had to be judged by the clear and present danger test, thereby indicating that he put education on the same high plane as speech. In the course of what Frankfurter described as "long talk on topic of due process as to freedom of speech and foreign language cases," Brandeis expressed his view of the due process clause:

1) d.p. [due process] should be restricted to procedural regularity or

2) in favor of repeal but

3) while it is, must be applied to substantive laws and so as to things that are fundamental.

Right to Speech

Right to Education

Right to choice of profession

Right to locomotion[27]

In other words, if use of the due process clause could not be confined to purely procedural matters (the process by which a law was passed or enforced rather than its substance), it should be eliminated. Failing that, Brandeis would insist that speech be given at least equal weight with property and that the due process clause be used to strike down state limitations on speech.

It is quite possible that however great his belief in the importance of speech, the idea of using the Fourteenth Amendment to protect it from state abridgment would not have occurred to Brandeis had he not been so angry at what he saw as the Court's misuse of the due process clause. It is not an idea of which Holmes appears to have approved, for Frankfurter's notes of the conversation with Brandeis continue, "Holmes says doesn't want to extend XIV"; i.e., Holmes would not have used due process as a basis for striking down state action limiting civil liberties.[28] The *Gilbert* dissent nonetheless laid the foundation for a major alteration of American law and for a reassessment of political values. Five years later, while upholding the conviction of a radical who had published a pamphlet favoring general strikes that was read as violating New York's prohibition on advocating forceful overthrow of the government, the Court declared,

For the present purposes we may and do assume that freedom of speech and of the press—which are protected by the First Amendment from abridgement by Congress—are among the fundamental personal rights and "liberties" protected by the due process clause of the Fourteenth Amendment from impairment by the states.[29]

This was the first time the Court held one of the liberties of the Bill of Rights to be "incorporated" into the due process clause of the Fourteenth Amendment. This case and subsequent ones incorporating liberties protected by the Bill of Rights into the due process clause are responsible for the assumption, now part of American polity, that the Bill of Rights is a barrier to state as well as to federal violation of individual liberties.[30] The Court, adopting Brandeis's earlier reasoning in *Gilbert*, thereby altered theory, practice, and popular perception. Brandeis and Holmes dissented from the Court's upholding of Gitlow's conviction, although they of course both agreed with the newly announced principle that the states as well as the federal government were limited in their power to abridge speech.[31] It was Brandeis's dissent in *Gilbert*, however, that had made yet another major contribution to American jurisprudence and political thought.

In *Schaefer*, Brandeis had altered the clear and present danger doctrine to mean the same thing during war and peace. He attempted to change it further in his concurrence in *Whitney* v. *California*,[32] which is both a major contribution to free speech jurisprudence and a guide to many of his basic ideas about the state.

Anita Whitney was a fifty-two-year-old social worker and clubwoman, daughter of a California state senator and niece of Supreme Court Justice Stephen Field[33]—scarcely the kind of person likely to be considered a threat to the security of the state. Nonetheless, in 1920 she was convicted by California of organizing, assisting in organizing, and being a member of the Communist Labor party, which advocated the use of unlawful force. The statute under which she was tried was one of many passed by states in an attempt to minimize the power of Socialist or Communist parties. In this instance, Whitney was convicted primarily because of her presence at a party convention. During it, she had advocated a purely nonviolent role for the party. The convention adopted a more violence-oriented platform, however, and she was charged and found guilty despite having expressed her continuing disagreement with the platform.

Her appeal reached the Supreme Court in 1927.[34] Justice Sanford, writing the decision of the Court upholding the conviction, asserted that the kind of "united and joint action" implicit in the existence of the party was much more dangerous than individual speech and could legitimately be punished for the "danger to the public peace and security" it presented to the state.[35] Brandeis believed that the statute was an unconstitutional limitation on speech that presented no clear and present danger to the state. Whitney's lawyers had not made that argument, however,[36] and because the Court followed a rule precluding it from deciding cases on grounds not raised by the parties' own attorneys, Brandeis did not dissent but wrote a separate opinion concurring with the Court's decision upholding her conviction.[37] The "concurrence" might well have been a dissent, however, as it not only showed that Whitney did not belong behind bars[38] but also demolished the line of reasoning followed by the Court so completely that California's governor cited it in pardoning her.[39] Some of the paragraphs are lengthy but must be read as a piece if they are to be understood.

Those who won our independence believed that the final end of the State was to make men free to develop their faculties; and that in its government the deliberative forces should prevail over the arbitrary. They valued liberty both as an end and as a means. They believed liberty to be the secret of happiness and courage to be the secret of liberty. They believed that freedom to think as you will and to speak as you think are means indispensable to the discovery and spread of political truth; that without free speech and assembly discussion would be futile; that with them, discussion affords ordinary adequate protection against the dissemination of noxious doctrine; that the greatest menace to freedom is an inert people; that public discussion is a political duty; and that this should be a fundamental principle of the American government. They recognized the risks to which all human institutions are subject. But they knew that order cannot be secured merely through fear of punishment for its infraction; that it is hazardous to discourage thought, hope and imagination; that fear breeds repression; that repression breeds hate; that hate menaces stable government; that the path of safety lies in the opportunity to discuss freely supposed grievances and proposed remedies; and that the fitting remedy for evil counsels is good ones. Believing in the power of reason as applied through public discussion, they eschewed silence coerced by law — the arguments of force in its worst form. Recognizing the occasional tyrannies of governing majorities, they amended the Constitution so that free speech and assembly should be guaranteed.[40]

There are at least seven ideas implicit in Brandeis's concurrence. First, human beings are simultaneously "good" in their ability to act intelligently and "bad" in their susceptibility to the pitfalls of power and illogical thinking. Second, government is properly created by human beings to achieve goals unattainable without a state, among them the liberty necessary to develop individual talents. Third, and following logically from the second idea, government must be democratic, i.e., responsive to the expressed will of the people. The fourth idea, again following logically from earlier premises, is that government must not act arbitrarily or in an illegitimately repressive manner, and mechanisms must be incorporated into its structure to prevent such behavior because it constitutes a threat to liberty. Fifth, the state inevitably is an imperfect instrument, not only because arbitrary forces will challenge deliberative forces and because institutions are run by fallible human beings but because it is in the nature of humanity to generate and heed "evil counsels," at least temporarily. No government is to be trusted, no matter who its administrators are, and every democratic government must be subjected to constant examination by the people. For that reason, one of the functions of government is maintenance of the free flow of ideas. Sixth, "examination by the people" includes exchange of ideas about current and possible governmental policies and actions. Citizens have an obligation to participate in the discussion, which is possible only if they also have free speech. As Charles Miller has written, Brandeis thought that "civic virtue for the individual and political value for the society consisted in the exercise of freedom. Participation in the formation of public policy through freedom of expression was the high duty as well as the sacred right of citizens in a democracy."[41] Seventh, government stability is desirable because instability may be harmful to liberty, but stability is of lesser value than the liberty for whose sake it is sought. Prof. Vincent Blasi argues persuasively that another and key element of the concurrence is the belief that democracy can work only if it retains the ideal of civic courage.[42]

There are overtones here of Madison and his recognition that if human beings were angels, government would not be necessary. Brandeis was explicating and acknowledging his agreement with the ideas he rightly believed to be those of at least many of the Founding Fathers. But Brandeis was a creature of the second half of the nineteenth century and the first decades of the twentieth, and his thought would be of little use if it simply echoed that of American thinkers two hundred years earlier. Brandeis insisted that the state ought not merely to be negative, that it could be the agent of liberty as well as its enemy, and the question was how to enhance the first possibility without encouraging the second. By the time he began to address the problem, the American national state had become far more active than it had been during the government's Founding period. The thoughtful citizen had now to be concerned with how to keep the government within acceptable boundaries and, in addition, with ways to employ as much governmental power as was necessary to foster individual liberty. A balance had to be struck between two social imperatives: one, a government strong enough to protect citizens from overzealous majorities and the institutional embodiments of economic greed; the other, the kind of protection needed by citizens from that very government. Expanding upon the section already quoted, Brandeis argued that "fear of serious injury" was insufficient justification for punishing speech and suggested a different standard:

> Fear of serious injury cannot alone justify suppression of free speech and assembly. Men feared witches and burnt women. It is the function of speech to free men from the bondage of irrational fears. To justify suppression of free speech there must be reasonable ground to fear that serious evil will result if free speech is practiced. There must be reasonable ground to believe that the danger apprehended is imminent. There must be reasonable ground to believe that the evil to be prevented is a serious one. Every denunciation of existing law tends in some measure to

increase the probability that there will be a violation of it. Condonation of a breach enhances the probability. Expressions of approval add to the probability. Propagation of the criminal state of mind by teaching syndicalism increases it. Advocacy of lawbreaking heightens it still further. But even advocacy of violation, however reprehensible morally, is not a justification for denying free speech where the advocacy falls short of incitement and there is nothing to indicate that the advocacy would be immediately acted on. The wide difference between advocacy and incitement, between preparation and attempt, between assembling and conspiracy, must be borne in mind. In order to support a finding of clear and present danger it must be shown either that immediate serious violence was to be expected or was advocated, or that the past conduct furnished reason to believe that such advocacy was then contemplated.[43]

There are a number of important ideas in this paragraph. First, speech cannot be suppressed unless it is "reasonable" to believe that "serious" and "imminent" evil is about to occur. If this implies that all reasonable people must agree that specific speech will cause serious and imminent evil, an agreement that a governmental limitation on speech was "reasonable" would be extremely hard to reach. It is not enough for the danger to be "clear"; it must be "serious." Similarly, it has to be more than "present"; it has to be "imminent." Elaborating on the meaning of "imminent" and once again citing the beliefs of the Founding Fathers, Brandeis continued,

Those who won our independence by revolution were not cowards. They did not fear political change. They did not exalt order at the cost of liberty. To courageous, self-reliant men, with confidence in the power of free and fearless reasoning applied through the processes of popular government, no danger flowing from speech can be deemed clear and present, unless the incidence of the evil apprehended is so imminent that it may befall before there is opportunity for full discussion. If there be time to expose through discussion the falsehood and fallacies, to avert the evil by the processes of education, the remedy to be applied is more speech, not enforced silence.[44]

The two excerpts indicate that Brandeis was not naive about the power of ideas. On the contrary, he counted on good ideas being adopted, for it was the only way progress would be made toward the achievement of democracy. He well understood they could be dangerous to existing laws and institutions; that, he might have said, was part of their function. Political change, however, was not to be feared; liberty was more important than protection of the existing order. Speech therefore could not be abridged or punished as long as there was time for other voices to respond. It could not legitimately be stopped, he went on, if the only danger was "some violence or . . . destruction of property"—an admonition that perhaps should have been better remembered during the sit-ins of the 1960s and the student protests of the 1970s and that might well be kept in mind today when dealing with racist or sexist speech. The sole triggering element that would permit suppression of speech was "the probability of serious injury to the State," and that could occur, as Brandeis had said in *Gilbert*, only if there was an "emergency [that] does not permit reliance upon the slower conquest of error by truth." Speech that resulted in violence or destruction of property might be punished but it could not be suppressed. People could be silenced only if there was imminent "probability of serious injury to the State" because "among free men, the deterrents ordinarily to be applied to prevent crime are education and punishment for violations of the law, not abridgement of the rights of free speech and assembly." Brandeis trusted that truth ordinarily would conquer error; otherwise, democracy made no sense. Perhaps more important, he believed that the difficult job of engaging in debate and refuting error, unlike the comparatively easy method of suppressing it, would contribute to building democratic habits and character. The answer to bad speech was good speech, and lots of it.[45]

The importance of this idea is not in the niceties of legal doctrine, particularly as the phrase "clear and present danger" has been notable primarily for the paradox of having been incorporated into the American political vocabulary at the same time that it has been virtually ignored as the real basis for judicial decisionmaking.[46] The Brandeis-Holmes debate over clear and present danger, conducted in the opinions written by the two men, is significant for the information it provides about a major element of Brandeis's political thought. Much of his concurrence originally was written for a dissent in *Ruthenberg* v. *Michigan*, an appeal not by a seemingly harmless person like Anita Whitney but by a top Communist party leader who believed in illegal action in the name of the cause. Brandeis indicated his awareness that the party was a conspiracy aimed at the training of cadres for infiltration of the government. That did not matter; there was no evidence that Ruthenberg's actions caused immediate danger, and there was time to rebut his beliefs through discussion. The case was mooted when Ruthenberg died before the Court could hand down its decision.[47]

Brandeis probably was as fervent a democrat as has ever sat upon the Supreme Court, if democracy is defined as a willingness to rely upon the wisdom of the electorate while at the same time recognizing that the electorate will not always be correct. Because the majority may be wrong Brandeis insisted on the individual's right to free speech even in defiance of the majority will. One is again reminded of Winston Churchill's comment that democracy is the worst form of government ever invented, except for all the others. Holmes might have responded that the form of government does not much matter as the human future inevitably will be determined by the forces of Darwinian struggle. Brandeis probably would have chided Churchill for belittling democracy. As Alvin Johnson said, Brandeis was an "implacable democrat." Donald Richberg went further, writing that to Brandeis, "democracy is not a political program. It is a religion."[48]

One of the tenets of the religion was the centrality of education. Consciously or not, Brandeis followed both Jefferson and John Dewey in seeing a vital connection between democracy and education.[49] Like Jefferson, Brandeis emphasized free speech and press because he believed both in democracy and in the possibility of creating the knowledgeable electorate crucial to it. It is not surprising, therefore, that he elevated the "Right to Education" to the same high plane upon which he placed the "Right to Speech."

Democracy, speech, and education went hand in hand. One scholar has suggested that Brandeis's insistence on small-scale businesses would have resulted in fewer consumer goods and that Americans, in buying the products of business, have in effect answered him by demonstrating their preference for the fruits of bigness over the economic liberty that inevitably would have been accompanied by economic rigors.[50] Brandeis would have replied that the solution in both cases was more education. "Education is necessary to save democracy from economic wrongs," he had told the Civic Federation of New England in 1906. "The citizen should be able to comprehend among other things the many great and difficult problems of industry, commerce and finance, which with us necessarily become political questions. He must learn about men as well as things." Only in this way could the society be "saved from the pitfalls of financial schemers on the one hand or of ambitious demagogues on the other." Education was unlikely to result in immediate improvement, he wrote two decades later, because "democratic methods are necessarily slow" and the instrument of democracy was "man with his weaknesses and defects." But democracy and education were inextricably linked because the first could not succeed without the second.[51]

Brandeis joined or helped to found numerous organizations while he was "the people's attorney" — the Public Franchise League, the Election Laws League, the Good Government Association and its Aldermanic Association, the Industrial League, the Advisory Committee of the National Municipal League's Municipal Taxation Committee, the Civic Federation of New England, the National Committee of Economic Clubs, the People's Lobby, the Municipal Transportation League, the Savings Bank Insurance League. They revolved around public problems of concern to him, and he used them as educational mechanisms. When he was fighting the proposed Boston subway monopoly, for example, he wrote to Edward Filene, then head of the Public Franchise League's Publicity Bureau, "Have editorials and similar notices in various papers, particularly the Springfield Republican, the Worcester Spy, and the Pittsfield papers. . . . Have the labor organizations repeat their protest. . . . Have personal letters written to members from the Metropolitan District, particularly from Boston, by their constituents. . . . We rely upon you for hard work."[52] He sent similar letters to supporters all over the state.[53] Such action was typical of his battles on behalf of the public, as was his role as an educator. During the fight for savings-bank life insurance in Massachusetts he wrote to his brother about speaking before the Central Labor Union, the Unitarian Club, the Amalgamated Sheet Metal Workers, the Industrial League, and a Unitarian church. A few weeks later he reported that he had spoken at two meetings the night before and had six more lectures coming up.[54]

One of his key allies in educating the public was the press. After Norman Hapgood, editor of *Collier's Magazine*, wrote favorably about one of Brandeis's insurance speeches, Brandeis began to send Hapgood letters and copies of articles. Eventually he suggested, "In considering the best method of undertaking to secure to our working people life insurance under proper conditions, it seemed to me that you might deem it wise to have Collier's lead in the movement."[55] *Collier's* hired Brandeis as counsel in the Pinchot-Ballinger affair, during which Brandeis made extensive use of other representatives of the press. Each evening, he would invite the newspapers' Washington correspondents up to his hotel room, explaining which parts of the day's proceedings he considered it important for them to report. They responded with articles that both enhanced Brandeis's national reputation and "educated" their readers, leading Brandeis to call the members of the press "our real Chorus."[56] When the Senate committee rejected his arguments, Brandeis calmly sent hundreds of copies of his brief to newspapers and magazines with letters urging that they make use of them.[57] He turned *Collier's*, *Harper's Weekly*, and *La Follette's Weekly* into regular outlets for his views on a wide variety of subjects.[58] In addition to giving numerous campaign speeches during Woodrow Wilson's 1912 campaign, Brandeis wrote articles, letters to the editor, and even unsigned editorials for *Collier's*.[59] He could no longer give lectures or write articles once he joined the Supreme Court, so he had others do so for him, bombarding Felix Frankfurter in particular with suggested topics for editorials and articles in weekly magazines and law reviews.[60]

Both his belief in the press as a force for education and his certainty that wrong ideas would not triumph became apparent when he intervened during the 1931 oral argument in *Near v. Minnesota*. The *Saturday Press*, published by Jay Near, had been enjoined from publication under a Minnesota statute aimed against periodicals that were "malicious, scandalous and defamatory." Minnesota acted after the newspaper accused public officials by name of being participants in a gambling ring. The publication was also noted for its virulent anti-Semitism, and many Court watchers expected Brandeis, by then known not only as the Court's first Jewish member but as the leader of American Zionism as well, to take the side of the state. But Brandeis interrupted Minnesota's deputy attorney general's presentation to the

Court. It was common knowledge, Brandeis declared, that "just such criminal combinations" involving public officials did exist, "to the shame of some of our cities." Brandeis could not tell whether this was true in Minnesota, but he did know that Near and his partner had exposed what they believed to be such a combination. "Now, is that not a privileged communication, if there ever was one?" he asked. "How else can a community secure protection from that sort of thing, if people are not allowed to engage in free discussion in such matters? . . . You are dealing here not with a sort of scandal too often appearing in the press, and which ought not to appear to the interest of any one, but with a matter of prime interest to every American citizen."[61]

The attorney general responded that citizens ought to be concerned if the allegations were correct, but that in this instance they had been defamatory. "Of course there was defamation," Brandeis replied. "You cannot disclose evil without naming the doers of evil. It is difficult to see how one can have a free press and the protection it affords in the democratic community without the privilege this act seeks to limit. As for such defamatory matter being issued regularly or customarily, how can such a campaign be conducted except by persistence and continued iteration?" Brandeis, the veteran of battles with a corrupt Massachusetts legislature, praised the publishers for their "campaign to rid the city of certain evils." "So they say," the lawyer commented. "Yes, of course," Brandeis agreed, "so they say. They went forward with a definite program and certainly they acted with great courage. They invited suit for criminal libel if what they said was not true. Now, if that campaign was not privileged, if that is not one of the things for which the press chiefly exists, then for what does it exist?"[62]

Brandeis did not write an opinion in *Near*, simply adding his name to Chief Justice Charles Evans Hughes's opinion for the Court, which struck down the statute. His comment during oral argument, however, indicates either that he believed all speech had to be allowed but that some speech could be punished or that in *Near* he merely appeared to accept the idea of libel laws for the sake of argument. A later Court's decision in *Times* v. *Sullivan*, establishing the doctrine that the standard of proof in a successful libel action was higher for public officials than for private individuals and contemplating only civil libel as a remedy,[63] might well be read as a logical extension of Brandeis's approach to speech. It is possible that his thinking would have developed in this direction; admittedly, however, that is speculative.

Perhaps his apparent acceptance of libel laws, which strikes a somewhat dissonant note for someone as convinced as he that the people ultimately would be able to differentiate truth from falsehood, stemmed from his attitude toward privacy. Brandeis and his partner Samuel Warren had written the 1890 article that Harvard Law School's dean Roscoe Pound later credited with "nothing less than add[ing] a chapter to our law," that chapter being the one about privacy.[64]

The Brandeis-Warren article on "The Right to Privacy" was written in outrage at the lurid newspaper coverage given to Samuel Warren's personal life. It combined the issue of privacy with a conception of the law as a changing entity, arguing that new inventions with the potential for violations of privacy had to be brought under law: "Instantaneous photographs and newspaper enterprise have invaded the sacred precincts of private and domestic life; and numerous mechanical devices threaten to make good the prediction that 'what is whispered in the closet shall be proclaimed from the house-tops.'" The article became "perhaps the most influential law journal piece ever published." It made Judge Thomas M. Cooley's phrase "the right to be let alone" part of American political discourse.[65]

In 1890 "the right to be let alone" could be seen as a right that people might want to assert against the press. By 1928 government had grown bigger, and still newer inventions enabled it to be at least as great a threat to privacy as the press. The reactions of Holmes and Brandeis to the threat again reflected the differences between the two, illuminating the latter's thinking.

The public stage for their disagreement was set when the Court heard the case of *Casey* v. *United States*, in which a Seattle attorney was convicted of violating the federal Harrison Antinarcotic Act. The warden of a county jail suspected Attorney Casey of supplying his clients with drugs. The warden took his suspicions to federal narcotics agents, who induced two prisoners to offer Casey money for morphine and arranged to record their conversations, in which a deal was struck. A relative of the prisoners testified that she then picked up the drugs from Casey's office.[66]

Holmes wrote for the Court, sustaining the conviction, there being no question that Casey had violated the act. Brandeis, however, dissented on the grounds that the government had instigated the crime and that, absent government action, there would have been no evidence for the government to record. It was one thing for the government to "set decoys to entrap criminals," Brandeis argued, but here "the act for which the Government seeks to punish the defendant is the fruit of their criminal conspiracy to induce its commission. . . . [The Government] may not provoke or create a crime and then punish the criminal, its creature." Casey had not pleaded entrapment, although his lawyer did raise the question of the wiretap's constitutionality. It might have seemed logical for Brandeis, who, in *Whitney*, had meticulously followed the Court's rule that issues not raised by the parties would not be decisive, to concur here. But he dissented, he explained, "not because some right of Casey's has been denied, but in order to protect the Government. To protect it from illegal conduct of its officers. To protect the purity of its courts." Presumably the difference between *Casey* and *Whitney* was that the California legislature that had passed the act under which Whitney was convicted could be assumed to have acted in good faith, however mistaken its understanding of what the Constitution allowed, but that the officers in *Casey* had not. There was no evidence that the officers knew themselves to be acting illegally and so the distinction appears somewhat artificial. Be that as it may, Brandeis found it sufficient to enable him to dissent in *Casey*.[67]

The Court immediately went on to consider the case of *Olmstead* v. *United States*. The government suspected that a group of men were violating the National Prohibition Act. For almost five months, it tapped their home and office telephones, making 775 pages of notes. Here, the men did raise a constitutional issue at trial, asserting that wiretapped evidence violated the search and seizure clause of the Fourth Amendment. They were nonetheless convicted.

Chief Justice William Howard Taft wrote for the Court, sustaining the conviction. The question that had been discussed in the justices' conference was whether the Volstead Act was constitutional, and they could find no reason to believe it was not. Taft and the four justices who agreed with him considered the Fourth Amendment argument specious. There had been no physical trespass, nothing had been physically seized, and no one had forced the men to talk over the telephone.[68]

Brandeis found both the acts of the government and the decision of the Court incredible in their bland ignoring of privacy. He thought wiretapping far too intrusive: "Whenever a telephone line is tapped, the privacy of the persons at both ends of the line is invaded, and all conversations between them upon any subject, and although proper, confidential, and privileged, may be overheard. Moreover, the tapping of one man's telephone line involves the tapping of the telephone of every other person whom he may call, or who may call him. . . . Can it be," he demanded, "that the Constitution affords no protection against such invasions of individual security?" He recalled the concern of the Constitution's writers about writs of assistance and general warrants. By comparison with wiretapping, such devices were "but puny instruments of tyranny and oppression." Brandeis noted that James Otis had objected to such writs and warrants because "they put 'the liberty of every man in the hands of every officer,'" and Lord Camden had called "a far slighter intrusion [than wiretapping] 'subversive of all the comforts of society.'"[69]

Worse still, greater invasions were undoubtedly on the way. "Discovery and invention have made it possible for the Government, by means far more effective than stretching upon the rack, to obtain disclosure in court of what is whispered in the closet," he warned. "The progress of science in furnishing the Government with means of espionage is not likely to stop with wire tapping. Ways may some day be developed by which the Government, without removing papers from secret drawers, can reproduce them in court, and by which it will be enabled to expose to a jury the most intimate occurrences of the home." Brandeis saw television as such a potential "means of espionage." One of his working folders for *Olmstead* contains a 1928 clipping reporting on the development of that new medium, and an early draft of his opinion included the sentence, "By means of television, radium and photography, there may some day be developed ways by which the Government could, without removing paper from secret drawers, reproduce them in court and lay before the jury the most intimate occurrences of the home."[70]

He considered it irrelevant that the writers of the Fourth Amendment had not specifically mentioned wiretapping. Of course there was no such thing when they wrote, but if a proper approach was taken to constitutional interpretation, it was clear that the spirit rather than the specifics of the Fourth Amendment banned wiretapping. Chief Justice John Marshall had admonished, "We must never forget that it is a Constitution we are expounding," meaning that the country's basic law, designed to last for many years, necessarily was contemplated as sufficiently flexible to encompass new circumstances. Marshall used the phrase in explaining why the powers granted to the federal government by the Constitution had to be understood in the light of altered conditions; Brandeis used it to argue that this idea applied equally to clauses containing limitations on governmental power.[71] "Rights of . . . the liberty of the individual must be remolded from time to time," he wrote in another opinion, "to meet the changing needs of society."[72]

Most important to Brandeis in the *Olmstead* case was the spirit of the Fourth Amendment, which was intended to ensure privacy: "The makers of our Constitution undertook . . . to protect Americans in their beliefs, their thoughts, their emotions, and their sensations. They conferred, as against the Government, the right to be let alone — the most comprehensive of rights and the right most valued by civilized men." Here Brandeis demonstrated the connection he made between speech and privacy, for the protection that was given to "beliefs, thoughts, emotions, and sensations" extended to the expression of them. Both the thoughts and their utterance were necessary not only to the free flow of ideas but also to the growth of the individual, which could not occur if government had a right to invade privacy.[73] The "right to be let alone" had to be given the greatest protection: "To protect that right, every unjustifiable intrusion by the Government upon the privacy of the individual, whatever the means employed, must be deemed a violation of the Fourth Amendment." The argument that government had violated the right in the name of the greater good included in law enforcement was relevant but for a reason quite different from that accepted by the majority of the Court: "Experience should teach us to be most on our guard to protect liberty when the Government's purposes are beneficent. . . . The greatest dangers to liberty lurk in insidious encroachment by men of zeal, well-meaning but without understanding."[74]

The lack of "understanding" was such that government officials not only failed to recognize how wrong their violations of the right to privacy were but, even worse, they also did not see that their own actions encouraged the very disdain for law they intended to punish. Government had to recognize that it inevitably played an educational role, particularly about respect for law. Objecting some years earlier when papers stolen from a defendant and given by the thief to the government were admitted in evidence, Brandeis had written, "At the foundation of our civil liberty lies the principle which denies to government officials an exceptional position before the law and which subjects them to the same rules of conduct that are commands to the citizen. And in the development of our liberty insistence upon procedural regularity has been a large factor. Respect for law will not be advanced by resort, in its enforcement, to means which shock the common man's sense of decency and fair play."[75] Now, in *Olmstead*, he added, "Our Government is the potent, the omnipresent teacher. For good or for ill, it teaches the whole people by its example. Crime is contagious. If the Government becomes a lawbreaker, it breeds contempt for law: it invites every man to become a law unto himself; it invites anarchy." Use of illegal means to attain desired ends was not only immoral but counterproductive: "To declare that in the administration of the criminal law the end justifies the means — to declare that the Government may commit crimes in order to secure the conviction of a private criminal — would bring terrible retribution. Against that pernicious doctrine this Court should resolutely set its face."[76]

Brandeis was distressed once again at the Court's inconsistent use of the Fourteenth Amendment. His brethren were quick to employ it to strike down governmental interference with what they viewed as the right to control property, but they were much more lenient about violations of civil liberties: "I suppose," he lamented to Frankfurter, "some review of the wire tapping decision will discern that in favor of property the Constitution is liberally construed — in favor of liberty, strictly." He was equally concerned at the executive branch's improper behavior. Discussing the case with a niece, he commented, "Lying and sneaking are always bad, no matter what the ends," and "I don't care about punishing crime, but I am implacable in maintaining standards."[77]

It was in the name of "maintaining standards" — standards that the government transmitted to the people through its own acts — that Brandeis condemned government "espionage." He knew that most people would fail to see that the "greatest dangers to liberty lurk in insidious encroachment" by well-meaning zealots. He also understood that, under circumstances such as war, Americans would applaud such acts. Two years earlier he had written to Frankfurter,

> Wouldn't it be possible to interest . . . [Harvard Law School teachers and students to write articles for the Law Review] bearing on the redress for the invasion of civil and political rights through arbitrary, etc. government action, by means of civil suits? I think the failure to attempt such redress as against government officials for the multitude of invasions during the war and postwar period is also as disgraceful as the illegal acts of the government and the pusillanimous action of our people in enacting the statutes which the states and the nation put on the books. Americans should be reminded of the duty to litigate. . . . There are times of ease & prosperity when the pressing danger is somnolence rather than litigiousness. . . . I have grave doubt whether we shall ever be able to effect more than superficial betterment unless we succeed in infusing a sense (A) of the dignity of the law among a free, self-governing people and (B) of the solemnity of the function of administering justice. Among the essentials is that the government must, in its methods, & means, & instruments, be ever the gentleman.

His judgment about government espionage was, "It is un-American. It is nasty. It is nauseating."[78]

Though Brandeis's condemnation of government espionage perhaps unfortunately has not become part of mainstream American political thought, the right to privacy that he asserted in his 1890 article and in his *Olmstead* dissent is now integral to it. It illuminates the case law upholding the constitutional right to privacy[79] and is the basis for provisions in a number of state constitutions.[80] It seems appropriate that his conceptions of speech and privacy have endured, because rights were of key importance to him. During the Pinchot-Ballinger hearings, when he learned that President Taft was part of a cover-up, Brandeis wrote what for him apparently were words of ultimate contempt: "[Taft] is simply impervious to a conception of the people's rights."[81]

The "people's rights" were of key importance to Brandeis, and two points remain to be made about his enunciation of them. The first involves an apparent lapse; the second, an indication of how far in advance of his time his thinking may have been.

Brandeis's great value to American political thought and jurisprudence lay in his creative questioning and analysis of phenomena that were treated as givens by most of his contemporaries. It is therefore somewhat surprising that he took such little note of the extent to which the American political system had been created for the benefit of white men. The Constitution specifically legitimized slavery and, by leaving suffrage criteria to the states, disenfranchised women. The inability of the United States to end slavery without enduring the trauma of the fiercely contested Civil War, the socially condoned brutalization of southern blacks from the post-Reconstruction period through the civil rights movement of the 1960s, and the continuing pervasiveness of racism throughout the United States raise the question of whether the exclusionary nature of the political system was structural or capable of being altered through extension of the franchise. A similar question can be raised about women, particularly in view of the governmental and social resistance first to what ultimately became the Nineteenth Amendment. The fact that the Fourteenth and Fifteenth Amendments made so little difference to the real condition of the former slaves might well have led Brandeis to ask whether the women's suffrage he came to espouse would be sufficient to produce true gender equality.[82] That may be condemning Brandeis for not being even further ahead of his time as most suffragettes assumed with him that the right to vote would go far toward altering the condition of women. The same, however, cannot be said of black Americans.

The southern states had made clear their intention of keeping black Americans in a condition that lacked only the formal name of slavery. In this context, it is puzzling that Brandeis offered no indication of how the excesses and failures of federalism might be confronted. Justice John Marshall Harlan, a fellow Kentuckian, had attacked segregation and argued that it violated the Fourteenth Amendment.[83] Brandeis's dislike of racism was clear. He subscribed not only to the beliefs of "my uncle the abolitionist"[84] but to the ideal of racial equality, as reflected in his admonition, "Let us teach all peoples that they are all chosen, and that each has a mission for all."[85] He suggested action to eliminate racial discrimination and to enhance racial equality to Felix Frankfurter and to the president of Howard University.[86] He did not address either the unlikelihood of piecemeal reform making any major change in the status of nonwhites or the human inequality and suffering that therefore would continue.

Like most politically active white citizens of his day, Brandeis probably knew relatively little about the lives of most black Americans, southern or otherwise. Although his world was largely white after he moved from Kentucky to Boston, he undoubtedly learned something about the situation of black Americans from friends, like Frankfurter and Stephen Wise, who were active in the National Association for the Advancement of Colored People. He was not one of the small number of white Americans involved in the struggle for racial equality; he had more than enough causes to champion. Neither, however, did his belief in federalism normally affect his willingness to strike down state statutes when he considered them violative of rights, and yet his record on racial equality is mixed. Relatively few race cases went to the Court during the years that Brandeis was on it. When they did, he voted with the majority. That meant, in his early years on the Court, going along with decisions that usually but not always struck down discriminatory state or federal statutes and actions[87] as well as joining one that reaffirmed the separate but equal doctrine in transportation and another that upheld a state's insistence that a Chinese student go to a black rather than a white school.[88] It is possible that Brandeis truly believed, along with the rest of the Court during the years he sat on it, that the equal protection clause did not prohibit state segregation. Given his advocacy of judicial restraint and the way formal and informal segregation permeated the United States, it is equally possible that he believed the judiciary was not the proper institution to solve the problem.[89] During his later years, as the Court moved against segregation in primary elections and, gradually, in educational institutions, so did Brandeis.[90] In this, he was very much a man of his historical moment.

Whatever the explanation for Brandeis's seeming failure to appreciate the nature and extent of American racism, a number of his pre-Court speeches indicate that he cherished not only the traditional "political" rights but some of those today subsumed under the heading "economic rights." That is not a phrase Brandeis used, but the evidence that he was thinking in such terms lies in his own words. He spoke frequently of meeting people's economic needs, both because doing so was right and because it was necessary if people were to be able to participate fully in government. An examination of the way his language might be read to indicate that he had begun to think not only of economic needs but of constitutionally protected economic rights follows.

Early in his career, Brandeis had been appalled to discover the plight of Boston's paupers, which had led to his involvement in an 1894 crusade to improve the city's treatment of them. The waste of potential shocked him most. "These people are not machines," he declared; "these are human beings . . . [with] emotions, feelings, and interests. . . . They should have entertainments, they may be literary, they may be musical." He took what was, for 1894 and the heyday of social Darwinism, the rather startling position that their poverty was not of their making but that they were victims of a system that did not provide them with work; that without work and the necessities including leisure they could buy with it, they could not function fully as human beings; and that because society had created the problem, society had a moral responsibility to solve it.[91]

It was one thing to say that a particular approach ought to be policy; another that the Constitution mandated it. Brandeis began moving in that direction at least as early as 1914, when he was quoted by *The Independent* as elaborating upon constitutional protection of what might today be called the quality of life:

The "right to life" guaranteed by our Constitution is now being interpreted according to demands of social justice and of democracy as the right to live, and not merely to exist. In order to live men must have the opportunity of developing their faculties; and they must live under conditions in which their faculties may develop naturally and healthily.

In the first place, there must be abolition of child labor, shorter hours of labor, and regular days of rest. . . . In the second place, the earnings of men and women must be greater, so that they may live under conditions conducive to health and to mental and moral development.[92]

Brandeis went on to suggest that the constitutionally guaranteed "right to life" required a *government* — most likely, given his philosophy, state rather than federal — to be responsive to "demands for shorter working time, for higher earnings and for better conditions." He noted that "men and women must have leisure, which the Athenians called 'freedom' or liberty." Thus he brought together his own strong view of individual autonomy, his admiration of Athenian democracy, and what he suggested was a constitutional mandate. In using the word "liberty" in a passage about the Constitution, he obviously was referring to the Fifth and Fourteenth Amendments' due-process-clause guarantees of liberty. Far from claiming "original intent," he emphasized that the "right to life" was *now being interpreted* in a way that comported with social justice and democracy, suggesting that social justice and democracy were now seen as impossible without the right of citizens to "live under conditions in which their faculties may develop naturally and healthily."[93]

Here, in effect, Brandeis seems to have brought together traditional civil liberties and the beginnings of what today are called economic rights. The goal was "mental and moral development," both necessary in a democratic polity. These qualities could not be developed in the absence of health and leisure, which in turn could not be assured unless workers were required to put in no more than reasonable workdays. A logical extension of this train of thought is that if the Constitution guarantees Brandeis's version of the "right to life," which is both the right "to exist" and much more, those people unable for whatever reason — youth, age, disability, absence of work opportunities — to earn the necessities of life for themselves must be provided with them by the society. And since the whole purpose of the Constitution is to establish a governmental system that will enable the furtherance of social goals, it is presumptively the governmental system that has the obligation to provide for those people who cannot do so themselves.[94]

Brandeis made the same assertion a few months later when he delivered the annual July 4 oration at Boston's Faneuil Hall on "True Americanism."[95] Part of his speech concerned "the American standard of living." Asking rhetorically, "What does this standard imply?" he answered, "the exercise of those rights which our Constitution guarantees, the right to life, liberty and the pursuit of happiness."[96] In fact, he used the formulation found in the Declaration of Independence rather than the "life, liberty and property" of the Constitution's Fifth and Fourteenth Amendments, and it is scarcely believable that he did so by accident. "Life, in this connection," he went on, "means living, not existing; liberty, freedom in things industrial as well as political; happiness includes, among other things, that satisfaction which can come only through the full development and utilization of one's faculties." He spoke of adequate wages and of hours that would not endanger health; but, he continued, "The essentials of American citizenship are not satisfied by supplying merely the material needs or even the wants of the worker."[97]

Note should be taken here of the logic of Brandeis's argument. He began with the premise that the Constitution embodied the right to life, which implied at least a minimal level of freedom from material want, the level no doubt fluctuating with the historical moment and society's perception of felt necessities. As the Constitution was the work of the citizens who created and ratified it and was designed to permit them to continue exercising the rights and responsibilities of citizenship, they must necessarily have included in the "right to life" those aspects crucial to their participation as citizens. The Bill of Rights prohibits the government from interfering with a person's "life" without due process of law. This could have meant no more than that government had the negative obligation not to create the circumstances that would negate the quality of any citizen's life. But he had said, in discussing the Boston paupers, that the entity responsible for depriving someone of a "good" life had an obligation to rectify the wrong. He also argued that the establishment of a democratic government implied the citizen's right and obligation to participate in it and that the government created by the Constitution bore some of the burden for making this possible; e.g., the creation of schools.

Brandeis described the quality of life as a constitutionally guaranteed right. He did not argue that the government was obliged by the Fifth and Fourteenth Amendments not to obstruct a citizen's access to the "right to life" but that the government guaranteed it. He applauded Franklin Roosevelt's program of public works and suggested projects in the states for purposes such as afforestation, flood control, and irrigation. He was strongly in favor of the government-owned Tennessee Valley Authority, an entity that clearly was designed to outlast the emergency conditions of the depression.[98] He did not speak of the government as an employer of last resort in times of normalcy, for he assumed private industry (eventually, of course, worker-owned) would suffice. But he had no objection to substantial numbers of state employees, he approved of the Civilian Conservation Corps that put young unemployed men to work on environmental projects and of the "Wagner-Perkins Federal Employment projects" (the Public Works Administration),[99] and it seems fair to assume he would have condoned government training programs and jobs at other times of large-scale unemployment.

Brandeis saw government in a democratic state as playing a far more positive role than did the Founders such as Madison and Jefferson whom he admired, and in part he was drawing the latter's thought out to some of its logical conclusions. This led him to the subject of education. Foremost among the "essentials of American citizenship," Brandeis declared, was the right to an education, "broad and continuous," and the child had to be "given education adequate both in quantity and in character to fit him for life's work." He was speaking of the schoolroom but of much more as well: "This essential of citizenship is not met by an education which ends at the age of fourteen, or even at eighteen or twenty-two. Education must continue throughout life."[100] Some years before, he had praised the Massachusetts law that made education compulsory through age fourteen, adding that "the intellectual development of citizens may not be allowed to end at fourteen. With most people whose minds have really developed, the age of fourteen is rather the beginning than the end of the educational period."[101]

He did not mean that government had to provide adult education, which could occur "in classes or from the public platform, or . . . through discussion in the lodges and the trade unions, or . . . from the reading of papers, periodicals and books,"[102] although there were situations in which specific forms of adult education could be undertaken by the government. In a speech to the Chamber of Commerce, Brandeis mentioned the federal and state "agricultural experiment stations" that provided information to farmers, and he spoke of the government's "duty to give to the farmer the opportunity of education."[103] Whatever the source of the education, there was one quality without which it could not take place, and that was "freshness of mind," for which "a short workday is as essential as adequate food and proper conditions of working and of living." "Leisure," he stated flatly, "is an essential of successful democracy." There was a clear implication of governmental responsibility for the existence of leisure, which in turn depended upon a "curb . . . upon capitalistic combination." If citizens were to use education as a tool for democracy, they had to have "industrial liberty," and they had to have "some degree of financial independence."[104] Not all of these essentials were the duty of the government: Brandeis spoke of the obligations of unions to fight for working conditions that would result in provision of necessities, including leisure; and in listing the various routes along which education could be pursued he was clearly calling upon private organizations to participate in the educational process.

Judging from his fear of concentrated power, it seems fair to hypothesize that Brandeis would have preferred small private entities to ensure the minimum conditions he viewed as necessary if citizens were to be "free." If, as he came to recognize in the case of minimum-wage and maximum-hours laws, social forces were insufficient to secure them, then the duty devolved on the state governments. The burden should not be that of the federal government because placing it there would only encourage a big bureaucracy. But one way or another, the conditions had to be provided: "The standard worthy to be called American implies some system of social insurance."[105] The standard also demanded medical care. Brandeis declared that the child had to be "not only well fed but well born" and provided with "conditions wholesome morally as well as physically."[106]

This view was in keeping with the "two pillars" that Brandeis saw as differentiating democracy from aristocracy. One was "the principle that all men are equally entitled to life, liberty and the pursuit of happiness; and the other, the conviction that such equal opportunity will most advance civilization." In rejecting aristocracy, he declared, the eighteenth and nineteenth centuries had established "the equal right of every person to development."[107] The implication is that citizens are not merely to be free from government interference; they can demand those things necessary to their development.

This, then, was Brandeis's understanding of one requirement of American constitutionalism. Like his theory of worker-participation, its details were neither fully expressed nor worked out. This was only to be expected, given his belief in experimentation and experience as a guide for social and political action. As a sociological jurisprudent he would scarcely have argued that the Founding Fathers, or the writers of state constitutions, were thinking in terms of a minimum wage; that was irrelevant. They had established a flexible system into which each historical era was expected to read its perception of at least those minimal conditions necessary to enable citizens to pursue life, liberty, and happiness. The leisure to become sufficiently informed to participate in the democratic process was not a newly discovered concept; Brandeis traced it as far back as the Athenians, where he also found the need for citizens to be educated for democracy. The simple recognition that overworked or underfed children or those where not "well born" (that is, medically cared for) could not learn and that overworked or underfed adults could not fulfill their democratic responsibilities meant to him that the government had an obligation to organize society in such a way that basic needs would be met.[108]

This is not to say that the government itself had to meet those needs, but neither could it allow creation and continuation of organizations and entities that would interfere with the fulfillment of basic needs. The Progressive might say that this meant regulating the trusts; Brandeis told Frankfurter that it meant providing an educational system,[109] and he said repeatedly in his letters and at government hearings that it also meant worker-participation.[110] Yet until worker-participation had been experimented with and become the dominant form of economic organization in the country, until the basic socioeconomic underpinnings of the country had altered to the point where workers could protect themselves without intervention of government, the federal judiciary was required to permit states to adopt minimum-wage and maximum-hour laws. Similarly, whatever the mechanism adopted for their protection, citizens had a *constitutional* right to basic necessities.

Brandeis's thought was couched in terms of "industrial liberty" and the political "rights" of citizens. It is precisely his emphasis on the key right of participation in the political process and all the phenomena necessary to it, including adequate education, proper medical care, and the leisure to engage intelligently in the process, that leads logically to governmental protection of economic rights. It seems reasonable, for example, to imagine the advocate of unemployment compensation laws supporting a similar system to provide health care. It is true that his economic theories were not spelled out in great detail. Combined with his thoroughly articulated concept of democracy, however, they provide the beginnings of a theory of economic rights in a democratic society and an intriguing starting place for those individuals concerned with current issues in American political thought and policy.

CONCLUSION:
THE INDIVIDUAL AND
THE DEMOCRATIC STATE

I believe that the possibilities of human advancement are unlimited.

Must we not fight, all of us, even for the peace that we most crave?[1]

American constitutionalism is based on the ideas of individual sovereignty and the social contract, with the latter an agreement among individuals to establish and respect the authority of a government they create for specific and limited purposes. Social-contract theorists postulate the existence of free people who choose to subject themselves to governmental authority because of the benefits that accrue, particularly in the areas of personal and collective physical safety and in the security of property.[2]

Under this theory, the terms of the contract are precise. Government legitimately can exercise only those powers specifically given to it by the people, who retain the right to alter or to revoke the terms of the agreement if and when they choose.[3] The government is the handiwork of the sovereign people and therefore does not share the people's right to unilateral alteration of the contract. This means, for example, that the federal government in the United States cannot abridge freedom of speech or religion (the First Amendment) or exercise powers in areas such as health or education unmentioned in the Constitution.

To present those examples is to demonstrate the disparity between the theory as it existed when the United States was founded and

150

American history and praxis. Societies transform themselves constantly, even if the speed at which they do so varies according to the historical moment. That characteristic was not of great importance to early social-contract theorists, who envisioned the government as so insignificant to the daily lives of the people that there would be no reason for it to respond to most social change. On those relatively rare occasions when social phenomena demanded alteration of the contract, the people were free to modify it. American history, however, has not worked quite that way.

The Bill of Rights, for example, was adopted at the behest of those individuals who were afraid that in its absence the federal government might consider itself entitled to interfere with the liberties of the people.[4] By keeping the federal government from abridging individual liberties, it in effect gave a monopoly over such interference to the states, unless the citizens of each of those states enacted constitutional restrictions on their governments. The First Amendment has not been changed, the social contract has not been altered, and yet the federal government has indeed curbed the liberty of the people to say those things it believes constitute a "clear and present danger" or to practice their religion in ways the government finds unacceptable.[5] Similarly, the federal government plays a major role in health and education policies, subsidizing students, programs, books, hospitals, and providing medical insurance, and the reelection by the people of the legislators and presidents who have enacted the relevant statutes indicates the electorate's approval of the federal programs.

Constitutional scholars agree that the reinterpretation of the constitutional mandate has been made possible largely by judicial review and the willingness of judges, particularly those sitting on the Supreme Court, to read the Constitution in light of "felt necessities." The purpose of the sociological jurisprudence espoused by Brandeis was to solve the problem of how to maintain a social contract with minimal formal alteration and still be responsive to major social changes. Other aspects of Brandeis's thought indicate that implicit in his sociological jurisprudence was the view that the government had in fact violated the social contract by throwing the weight of its power on the side of capital and against labor and that it was now appropriate for the government to take remedial action so that the basic terms of the contract could be restored.

The social contract was perceived by many people as minimalist at the time of the Constitution's ratification. In Jefferson's thinking, that government was best that did least and left the governing of the people to the people themselves. Certainly the government furthest away from the people geographically, i.e., the federal government, was to exercise a minimum of power, because the fact of distance alone made it least responsive to the wishes of the people.[6] When Hobbes typified life before the fashioning of a social contract as "poor, nasty, brutish and short,"[7] he implied that the government had an obligation to keep people from harming each other, not that it had an affirmative duty to enhance the quality of life by any means beyond providing physical protection. Most social-contract theorists postulated that the physical harm people might do to each other in the absence of governmental restraint was caused not by innate viciousness but by a desire for property, whether the action prompted by the desire took the form of attempting to take someone else's property or of trying to protect property one already possessed. Thus the notion of private property and its importance was an integral feature of social contract philosophy. A corollary axiom was that a major part of the contract would be government's pledge not to interfere with private property or its owners' enjoyment of it.

Brandeis's political thought began at approximately that point. He initially accepted laissez-faire economics and believed in the value to society of small businessmen operating free of governmental constraints. His early life as the son of a successful businessman, the law that he learned at Harvard, and his clientele of other small businessmen when he was a young attorney predisposed him to believe that the social contract was in operation and that as a result the political system was functioning properly. Much of his later thought revolved around his answers to the question of whether the government had exercised the self-restraint implicit in both laissez-faire and the American Constitution.

His speeches and writings give no indication of whether he considered laissez-faire ever actually to have existed or to have been a viable policy. The historical development of the United States, and particularly industrialization, had rendered that question moot by the time he began addressing it. It was the prospect of even greater industrialization and the mass production of cheap consumer goods that accounted for the attractiveness of big business and the concentration of capital after the Civil War. The clock could not be turned back to the preindustrial age, and there is no reason to believe Brandeis thought that it would be a good idea to do so. He was concerned that the government had expanded well beyond its original powers in ways that he found unacceptable.

Governmental growth as such was not necessarily bad, but growth so extensive that it resulted in bureaucracy and bigness most certainly was. In Brandeis's sociological jurisprudence, the Constitution was a living entity that had to expand and contract in response to social needs. (Brandeis was never a state judge and did not write about state constitutions, but he considered his jurisprudence as applicable to state constitutions and judiciaries as to their federal counterparts: State judges were expected to view constitutions as dynamic and to permit as much governmental experimentation as possible.[8]) As life became more complicated, it was neither irrational nor out of keeping with the social contract to expect governmental involvement in it to become similarly complex. Yet the government had responded to new social circumstances by redefining itself in a way that had made people less free. It had damaged American liberty by permitting the growth of absolutism.

Brandeis made the unarticulated assumption that a social contract might not begin on a totally level playing field but was designed to create one that was reasonably even. The people who entered into the contract came from a world in which there were only individuals and small economic entities and were motivated to accept the contract in part by their fear of governmental absolutism as well as of each other. The Constitution was a step forward in the development of democracy. "One hundred years ago the civilized world did not believe that it was possible that the people could rule themselves," Brandeis told a group of workers, but "America in the last century proved that democracy is a success."[9] He did not say "America in the twentieth century" because his point was that democracy had been a success in the United States in the past and could work equally well in the future if given a chance. The people had the capacity to rule themselves, but "industrial absolutism"[10] made it impossible for them to do so, and that absolutism had been created with the assistance of the federal and state governments.

Social-contract theorists had postulated only two social forces: the people and the government. In the late nineteenth century, however, a third force, big business, had emerged and by doing so had altered the very nature of society. The Constitution said nothing about "industrial absolutism," a phenomenon that did not yet exist when it was written and could not have been anticipated. And yet if the objectives of the social contract were the negation of absolutism and the safeguarding of liberty, the social contract was not now working.[11] Brandeis's knowledge of the Massachusetts legislature and his experiences with Congress in the Pinchot-Ballinger affair had convinced him that the power of the corporations equaled that of government.[12] Corporate money could buy governmental policies, which, by the terms of the social contract, were to be created only by the people.

The chief villain of the piece was big business, but Brandeis also held the state and federal governments culpable (the word "government" without modifier in what follows is meant to apply to both). Government did not invent big business, but it became a coconspirator by abandoning what should have been its position of restraint and neutrality as industrialization increased the tensions between business and labor. Government had taken the side of capital in a multiplicity of ways, most significantly by turning corporations into constitutionally protected "persons" while simultaneously denying legal protection to the activities of labor unions.[13] It was governmental action that had permitted businesses to grow to the point where they had become massive concentrations of power unmatched by any entity outside the government itself and certainly not by labor. It was government, putting itself at the service of big business, that had created the version of "liberty of contract" enforced by the courts, a version that made impossible the natural growth of labor unions that could counteract the power of big business. Government thus had deprived workers of the right to participate in the democratic process that was at the heart of the social contract. To Brandeis, if government not only permitted but abetted the development of a power center that made democracy impossible, it had lost its legitimacy. He held no brief for those individuals who, sharing his awareness, reacted with violence or gave up on the system, but he understood and validated their frustration. "Lawless or arbitrary claims of organized labor should be resisted at whatever cost," he told a group of employers. But he added, "if labor unions are arbitrary or lawless, it is largely because employers have ignominiously submitted to arbitrariness or lawlessness."[14]

The social contract had been violated; the times were seriously out of joint. Government no longer kept one citizen from preying on another. Instead, through its protection of corporations, government enabled employers to prey on employees. It was not fulfilling its function of keeping people physically safe; typically, it had not protected the striking workers at Homestead from the guns of the Carnegie-hired Pinkertons. Locke had written of four "bounds" on government: It had to rule by established law that would be the same for rich and poor, it could enact only laws that were for "the good of the people," it could not raise property taxes without the people's consent, and the legislature could not transfer its powers to others.[15] Although there is no direct evidence that Brandeis read Locke, they were in clear agreement about the key duties of government and the equally crucial limitations on it. Brandeis examined government and found that its laws in the economic sphere were different for rich and poor, although not explicitly, and antithetical to the good of the people. Government was not impartially protecting the property of all people; it had in fact made true liberty of contract impossible, if liberty of contract was defined as the freedom of the individual to participate in a meaningful negotiating process. The result was a situation of "employer[s] so potent, so well organized, with such concentrated forces and with such extraordinary powers of reserve and the ability to endure against strikes and other efforts of a union, that the relatively loosely organized masses of even strong unions are unable to cope with the situation." Instead of liberty of contract, "you have necessarily a condition of inequality between the two contending forces."[16] What had emerged, "within the State," was another "state so powerful that the ordinary social and industrial forces existing are insufficient to cope with it."[17] Like Locke, Brandeis opposed extensive delegation of power by the federal legislature.[18] He was even more adamantly opposed to the government informally ceding its policymaking functions to big business.

Brandeis concluded that government had kept social problems from being solved in a manner that would have maintained individual freedom. Balancing the needs and desires of business and labor in the industrial era was a difficult problem. The government had acquiesced when big business stepped in and had given business virtual control of labor, so that long hours, low wages, poor working conditions, and child labor prevented the development of the informed citizenry necessary to a democratic state and thereby negated the possibility of true citizen-participation.[19]

To Brandeis, the very existence of the social contract — the Constitution — was predicated on the assumption of governmental responsiveness to the electorate and the active participation by all citizens in the democratic process. A true social contract, in other words, could exist only in a democratic state, and democracy was impossible without the ability of the people to make the government comply with the popular will. The social contract postulates the citizen as active participant, not as passive subject. But citizen-participation had become negligible, the corporations had monopolized power, and government was a major cause of the new and undemocratic situation.

Brandeis was not a theorist and did not speak or write like one. There is no record of his having read any of the social contract or other political theorists, although he occasionally referred to some;[20] certainly he did not comment on them as he frequently did when mentioning the works of history he seems to have preferred.[21] He knew De Quincey's *Plato's Republic*, did not like it much, and seems never to have bothered to look for the original.[22] Perhaps his opinion of at least some philosophers would have changed had he been familiar with John Dewey's statement that "the philosopher has received his problem from the world of action" and "must return his account there for auditing and liquidation."[23] As it was, after Brandeis had been told that Columbia University students were reading philosophy and that many of them had bought Will Durant's *Story of Philosophy*,[24] he wrote to Frankfurter, "I think some one should make clear to the public that this is a very bad sign." He elaborated, "Philosophy is rather the cyclone cellar for finer souls. As it was in the declining days of Greece, and as the monastery was in the so called Dark Ages." And he continued, "In our Democracy, the hopeful sign would be recognition of politics & government as the first of the sciences & of the arts."[25]

Facts and human beings rather than abstract analyses concerned Brandeis. He described life in the steel industry as "so inhuman. . . . The Steel Trust . . . looks on its slaves as something to be worked out and thrown aside. The result is physical and moral degeneracy — work, work, work, without recreation or any possibility of relief save that which dissipation brings. The men coming out of these steel mills move on pay day straight to the barroom. Think what such men transmit as a physical and moral heritage to their children and think of our American citizenship for men who live under such conditions."[26]

The severity of the perversion of the social contract and its horrendous effects on human beings had gone unnoticed by too many people. Now, however, "the awakened social sense of community" had begun to demand working conditions that would enable the citizenry to regain its rightful place in public affairs.[27] Brandeis, without using quite these words, proposed to use "the awakened social sense of community" to reinvigorate the old social contract between the people and the government and to create a new social contract in the workplace. In effect he argued that the social contract could not be confined to the political sphere because of the interaction between politics and economic life. Again speaking of the hard, demeaning lives and laboring conditions of steelworkers, he asked, "Must not this mean that the American who is brought up with the idea of political liberty must surrender what every citizen deems far more important, his industrial liberty? Can this contradiction—our grand political liberty and this industrial slavery—long coexist?"[28]

Because the country now faced the reality of a nongovernmental form of threatening institutional power, Brandeis considered resurrection of the original social contract to be necessary but insufficient. It was equally important to fashion a social contract between management and labor because a person cannot "be really free who is constantly in danger of becoming dependent for mere subsistence upon somebody and something else than his own exertion and conduct."[29] The labor unions had been attempting to negotiate a social contract within the world of work, and Brandeis continued to maintain that validation of unionism was a precondition of industrial democracy. The social contract that he ultimately came to favor, however, was quite different. It would make the unions unnecessary by turning workers into their own employers and would resemble the contract among citizens more than any agreement between labor and management. For the moment, however, one element of any revitalized contract between the electorate and the government would have to be the government's promise to recreate greater equality in the workplace. Only then would there be real "liberty of contract."

Brandeis was not arguing for the reimplementation either of an outmoded economic system or an irrelevant interpretation of the

Constitution. He was calling upon the government to undo its wrongs. That demand necessarily implied a more positive governmental role than the one included in the original social contract. Just as government had permitted the growth of industrial giantism at the expense of the worker, government now had to enact statutes that would destroy bigness. Governmental neutrality would no longer suffice, for neutrality was in effect maintenance of the unacceptable status quo. "Neutrality is at times a graver sin than belligerence," he declared,[30] and this was a time when it could not be countenanced.

Brandeis's conception of the social contract was largely similar to that of Locke and Jefferson in its notion of property. Locke insisted on the freedom to acquire and control property as necessary for individual protection. Jefferson's desire for an agrarian state reflected his similar belief that property was a necessary precondition for individual independence. Brandeis, too, placed the highest value on the liberty of the individual, as even a cursory reading of his opinion in *Whitney* v. *California* makes clear.[31] He described property as "only a means," not an end.[32] This belief is implicit in all his thought, but it is worth noting the specific formulation quoted by Ernest Poole:

> Property must be subject to that control . . . which is essential to the enjoyment by every man of a free individual life. And when property is used to interfere with that fundamental freedom of life for which property is only a means, then property must be controlled. This applies to . . . all the big industries that control the necessities of life. Laws regulating them, far from being infringements on liberty, are in reality protections against infringements on liberty.[33]

He regretted the "frequent error of our courts that they have made the means the end. Once correct that error, put property back into its right place, and the whole social-legal conception becomes at once consistent."[34] It was not the Constitution that needed amending. "Instead of amending the Constitution, I would amend men's economic and social ideals," he declared, calling the Constitution "perhaps the greatest of human experiments."[35] The fight for industrial democracy was in keeping with the gradual evolution of democracy in the United States: "First we had the struggle for independence, and the second great struggle in our history was to keep the nation whole and abolish slavery. The present struggle in which we are engaged is for social and industrial justice."[36] Brandeis's approach was essentially conservative, based on a conviction in the validity of the political system codified by the Constitution. He was nonetheless radical in his rejection of accepted wisdom, his insistence that many existing power relationships and institutions were neither good nor immutable, his vision of industrial liberty, his refusal to validate almost any limitations on speech, and his goal of a vibrant, egalitarian democracy.

Brandeis lambasted the acts of judges,[37] but in his calmer moments he retained his belief in the power of ideas and included his judicial colleagues in the category of redeemable humanity. "What we must do in America is not to attack our judges," he told Poole, "but to educate them." They had interfered with the will of the people. "They have no such right," but they could be instructed.[38] So, presumably, could officials in other branches of government. Brandeis's belief in the educational process surely surpassed that of most professional educators. He became exasperated with individuals but maintained his faith in secular redemption. Shown the proper path, government officials would understand the need to rectify past acts and get on with the business of undoing concentrations of power.

Governmental responsibility might well go beyond destruction of bigness. There were other effects of its wrongdoing that had to be rectified. "If the Government permits conditions to exist which make large classes of citizens financially dependent," Brandeis proclaimed, "the great evil of dependence should at least be minimized *by the State's assuming*, or causing to be assumed by others, in some form the burden incident to its own shortcomings."[39] Governmental ineptitude had contributed to the depression. If the way to alleviate the situation was to enact minimum-wage and maximum-hours laws, that was government's responsibility — as long as the enactment itself did not add to bigness, which meant that the appropriate enacting body was the states rather than the federal government. If one road out of the depression lay through a program of public works and public employment, then that road had to be taken — as long as it was taken primarily by the states. If another avenue was destructive taxation of corporations, it should be followed — as long as the taxes were not used to build up an overly large concentration of federal power.[40]

Brandeis's emphasis on education meant that the ideal state could not be viewed as a purely neutral, reactive body, even after some kind of equilibrium had been restored. It was clear that he favored public schools[41] — again, to be run by the states, not by the federal government, and presumably to be a key provision of the new social contracts that would be enacted within states. Equally, he saw health as an essential for both students and citizens.[42]

That did not necessarily mean that government had to provide health care, and certainly few voices were raised during his lifetime on behalf of public health insurance plans except as part of an overall social security system for the aged and the indigent.[43] Brandeis might have restated Jefferson's admonition, "That government is best that governs least," as "That government is best that undertakes only such socially necessary programs as are proved by experimentation to be unworkable when left to the private sector." He had designed a life insurance program that could be implemented by savings banks, for example, and so there was no reason for government to concentrate power by entering that sphere. The unions were his favored mechanism for ensuring fair working conditions, at least until the days of worker-participation. There were times, however, when cooperation between the public and the private spheres was necessary. It was legitimate in emergencies, whether as all-inclusive as the depression or simply when a group of people were being treated so unjustly that not only their physical well-being but their concomitant ability to participate in public life was impaired. This tenet presumably explained Brandeis's advocacy of an unemployment compensation plan that technically was voluntary but that included coercive state taxation of nonparticipating employers.[44] Private ownership of irreplaceable natural resources had proved too great a temptation for misuse, so Brandeis suggested a partnership of government and the private sector in Alaska, combining government ownership of land with a system of leasing all the land to those people who would work it.[45]

Brandeis believed the possibilities for human advancement to be unlimited but he did not think the same of human beings. Bigness and the overly great burden it placed on fallible humanity was still to be avoided. Responsibilities had to be shared and power had to be kept in check. The judiciary had to permit governmental experimentation, but it was also obligated to protect the rights of the people so that the democratic process would remain viable.

Above all, the United States had to find a formula for workplace democracy that would parallel the social contract underlying the political system. "The civilized world today believes that in the industrial world self-government is impossible," Brandeis declared to a group of workers. It was the opinion of the "civilized world" that "we must adhere to the system which we have known as the monarchical system, the system of master and servant, or, as now more politely called, employer and employee. It rests with this century and perhaps with America to prove that as we have in the political world shown what self-government can do, we are to pursue the same lines in the industrial world."[46]

When Brandeis first came to Boston, he kept notebooks filled with quotations that he particularly liked. Prominent among them were aphorisms from William James and Ralph Waldo Emerson. Brandeis thought the latter, whom he met at least once, to be especially impressive. The passages he copied from Emerson included, "They can conquer who believe they can," "It is easy in the world to live after the world's opinion . . . but the great man is he who in the midst of a crowd keeps with perfect sweetness the independence of solitude," and "A foolish consistency is the hobgoblin of small minds." He put into his notebook James's statement, "I am . . . in favor of the eternal forces of truth which always work in the individual and immediately unsuccessful way . . . till history comes, after they are long dead, and puts them on top."[47] He read other authors—Shakespeare, Swift, Walpole, Lowell, Arnold, Milton, Tennyson, Longfellow—but took even more notes on comments by his professors, jokes, and information about law and Boston. Nonetheless, it seems fair to say that if Brandeis can be classified with any particular school of theory, it is the pragmatists; certainly, pragmatism describes his approach to political life.

In spite of his distaste for what he considered the abstruseness and irrelevance of philosophy, the views Brandeis articulated fit social-contract theory and added important new elements to it. Brandeis's emphasis on individual rights, including privacy from governmental intrusion, is similar to Locke's statement that "every man has a property in his own person."[48] Brandeis also would have agreed with Locke that the highest civic virtue lies not in obedience to positive law, however important that may be, but to a higher law. This view is implicit in Brandeis's contempt for laws that violated individual liberty and permitted concentrations of power that would also harm liberty. Locke's conception of property as the creation of labor found its counterpart in Brandeis's delineation first of the inherent right of workers to share in a business' profits and, later, to become the managers of it through worker-participation.

Locke left open the question of the extent to which accumulation of property was legitimate. He argued that no one had a right to property he could not use and that would spoil but acknowledged that much property had evolved into money and nonperishable goods. Perceiving the relationship between property and power, Locke described property as protection against the power of others. Brandeis answered the question and consolidated these thoughts by asserting that the accumulation of property exceeded acceptable limits when the property resulted in a concentration of power that endangered liberty.

One of Brandeis's contributions to social-contract theory concerned the reason for entering into it. Democracy was not only the appropriate alternative to absolutism; it also possessed what might be called a psychological component. It was wise for the individual to be a member of a democratic community both because it would make policies helpful to the individual and because participation in public policymaking was a key element of individual growth. Even if a state performed only wise actions, the individual who was not continually involved in the formal community created by the social contract would be deprived of experiences necessary to individual self-fulfillment.[49]

Other elements of Brandeis's thought were reminiscent of John Stuart Mill, most obviously in the extent to which each would have provided both conscience and speech with the greatest possible leeway but not to the extreme of declaring speech an absolute right. Mill argued in *Political Economy* that capitalism and socialism had to be judged by the criterion of which system provided "the greatest amount of human liberty and spontaneity."[50] He added in his unfinished *Chapters on Socialism* that collective ownership should be tried first among "elite groups" and expressed doubt that a fully collectivized economy would contain sufficient "asylum" for true freedom of thought.[51]

Brandeis implicitly agreed. He distrusted state socialism, believing it would concentrate power in a governmental bureaucracy and inevitably interfere with freedom of speech. He preferred the experimental form of socialism practiced on the kibbutzim, which he thought compatible with liberty.

Brandeis would have agreed also with the theory of gender equality spelled out in Mill's *Subjection of Women*.[52] The man who spoke against suffrage early in his professional career went on to preside over a meeting of the Boston Equal Suffrage Association addressed by Jane Addams, joined Addams and suffragette Carrie Chapman Catt in judging designs for a women's suffrage symbol in a contest sponsored by Alice Stone Blackwell's *Women's Journal*, and spoke to Boston audiences along with his older daughter when she decided to spend a year after college working for the suffrage movement. When Franklin Roosevelt became president Brandeis admonished Frankfurter, who was advising Roosevelt about appointments, "There ought to be a woman Ass. Atty. [Assistant Attorney] General again." He commented about Roosevelt's choice of Frances Perkins as secretary of labor that she was "the best the U.S. affords; & it is a distinct advance to have selected a women for the Cabinet."[53] Typically, when he was asked what had made him a supporter of women's suffrage, Brandeis answered that he had learned from experience. In this case it was his "experience in various movements," where he had seen "the insight which women have shown into problems that men did not and perhaps could not understand." His pride in his older daughter's having become a lawyer and the younger an economist in the days when most "ladies" did not adopt professions is evidence of a commitment to gender equality that went beyond the vote.[54] He was not a feminist; but then, he had no experience of feminism.

He was seemingly unaware of possible defects in the concept of the social contract. Arising in largely agricultural, homogeneous societies, the contract was based on the assumption that its primary goals of security of person and property would be met once individual acts of violence or illegitimate use of government violence were condemned and punished. This of course made no provision for the situation of Native Americans or black slaves. Neither did it address the problem of private and public violence condemned in theory but encouraged by governmental practice. The first permitted the battering and intimidation of women of all races; the second, violence against the entire southern black population after the Civil War.

If it is questionable whether the American social contract ever included women and nonwhites, it is certainly clear that it was not fashioned to apply to an industrialized, urbanized society. Brandeis responded to the second problem but not to the first. His version of the social contract included creation of circumstances under which people could achieve self-fulfillment, and he recognized that the contract had to apply to nongovernmental entities. Neither the social contract in the political sphere nor his proposed economic contract was addressed to the problem of status, equality, and the possibility of self-fulfillment in a society whose governmental and private institutions reflected an ideology of racism and sexism. Brandeis seems to have assumed that suffrage would be a sufficient condition for true gender equality and that self-fulfillment for both sexes and for all races would follow workplace democracy. He did not deal with the issue, for example, of how or whether one got into the workplace in the first instance. In this respect he was far from a radical; he was very much a man of his time.

That element of Brandeis's truth-seeking should not be forgotten. Ultimately, however much or little his thinking may have drawn upon the ideas of social-contract theorists[55] and whatever his ideas may offer to those individuals still seeking to perfect their own, his thought was pragmatically derived from the American experience of industrialization and was focused primarily on the problems arising from it. He was a product of a particular historical moment as well as of a tradition based largely on the conception of individual freedom as a primary value. He made no claims to a systemic philosophy, and what he would have said about specific aspects of an otherwise apparently coherent ideological outline can only be inferred. As he commented about himself, "I have no general philosophy. All my life I have thought only in connection with the facts that came before me."[56] The only certainty is that if he addressed a problem, his solution would have been fashioned in ways that he believed would enhance liberty, democracy, and self-fulfillment.

The answer to workplace injustice was workplace democracy. The cure for bad speech was good speech, to be heard by as many people as possible. Donald Richberg was correct in saying that Brandeis's religion was democracy.[57] That being the case, Brandeis might well be thought of as one of democracy's proselytizers if not one of its high priests. Neither is an appellation that he would have appreciated, however accurate either might be. It is precisely because he was a democrat that he would no doubt have preferred to be called a good citizen. In that capacity he went beyond progressivism to begin sketching a new social contract that contained the outlines of industrial democracy. The outline remains incomplete. Perhaps other good citizens are needed to fill it in.

NOTES

Abbreviations used:

LDB   Louis Dembitz Brandeis
FF   Felix Frankfurter
BP   Brandeis Papers, University of Louisville
BP-HLS Brandeis Papers, Harvard Law School
FF-HLS Frankfurter Papers, Harvard Law School
FF-LC   Frankfurter Papers, Library of Congress
Letters   Melvin I. Urofsky and David W. Levy, eds., *Letters of Louis D. Brandeis*, 5 vols. (Albany: State University of New York Press, 1971–1978).

Introduction

1. LDB to FF, January 7, 1927, FF-HLS.

2. An important if not yet dominant school of political thought includes an attack upon the distinction between the public and the private spheres. This approach can be found most persuasively in works by feminist theorists; see, e.g., Judith Butler and Joan W. Scott, eds., *Feminists Theorize the Political* (New York: Routledge, 1992); Carol Gilligan, *In A Different Voice* (Cambridge: Harvard University Press, 1982); Catharine A. MacKinnon, *Feminism Unmodified* (Cambridge: Harvard University Press, 1987); Susan Moller Okin, *Women in Western Political Thought* (Princeton, N.J.: Princeton University Press, 1992); and Cass R. Sunstein, ed., *Feminism and Political Theory* (Chicago: University of Chicago Press, 1982).

167

3. Many of Brandeis's numerous magazine articles, speeches, and testimony before governmental bodies are collected in LDB, *Business — A Profession*, ed. Ernest Poole (Boston: Small, Maynard, 1914), hereafter *Business*; LDB, *Other People's Money and How the Bankers Use It* (New York: Stokes, 1914); LDB, *The Curse of Bigness*, ed. Osmond K. Fraenkel (New York: Viking Press, 1934), hereafter *Bigness*; Solomon Goldman, ed., *Brandeis on Zionism* (Washington, D.C.: Zionist Organization of America, 1942); Alfred Lief, ed., *The Brandeis Guide to the Modern World* (Boston: Little, Brown and Company, 1941). Most of his important letters are to be found in *Letters* and in Melvin I. Urofsky and David W. Levy, eds., *"Half Brother, Half Son": The Letters of Louis D. Brandeis to Felix Frankfurter* (Norman: University of Oklahoma Press, 1991). Some of his previously unpublished judicial opinions can be found in Alexander M. Bickel, ed., *The Unpublished Opinions of Mr. Justice Brandeis* (Cambridge: Harvard University Press, 1957), and Alfred Lief, ed., *The Social and Economic Views of Mr. Justice Brandeis* (New York: Vanguard Press, 1930). The best bibliographies of works by and about LDB are Roy M. Mersky, *Louis Dembitz Brandeis, 1856–1941, A Bibliography* (1958; reprint, New Haven, Conn.: Yale Law School, 1987), and Gene Teitlebaum, *Justice Louis D. Brandeis: A Bibliography of Writings and Other Materials on the Justice* (Littleton, Colo.: Fred B. Rothman and Company, 1988).

4. Gordon S. Wood, however, has argued that the Founding Fathers were threatened by the individualism and the new conception of equality that he considers to have been implicit in the ideology of the American Revolution and that the Constitution reflected an attempt to recreate the traditional hierarchy of patronage. He sees Jeffersonianism and the new entrepreneurialism as ultimately triumphant and as responsible for the nineteenth-century antislavery and women's rights movements; Wood, *The Creation of the American Republic, 1776–1787* (New York: Norton, 1972), and *The Radicalism of the American Revolution* (New York: Knopf, 1992). Cf. Helen Garfield, "Twentieth Century Jeffersonian: Brandeis, Freedom of Speech, and the Republican Revival," *Oregon Law Review* 69 (1990): 527–88.

5. Jean-Jacques Rousseau, *On the Social Contract*, ed. Roger D. Masters (New York: St. Martin's Press, 1978), bk. 1, chap. 8.

6. John Stuart Mill, *Considerations on Representative Government* (New York: Liberal Arts Press, 1958), pp. 53, 55.

7. Speech in Brighton, Mass., December 2, 1904; Typescript, BP, Clippings Box 1.

8. Mill, *Considerations on Representative Government*, p. 50.

9. Ibid., p. 55; LDB in *Whitney* v. *California*, 274 U.S. 357, 373 (1927) (concurring).

10. Doron P. Levin, "Experts Doubt Cutbacks Alone Will Save G.M.,"

New York Times, December 23, 1991, pp. A1, D5. For critics of LDB's approach, see, e.g., Peter Drucker, *The Concept of the Corporation* (New York: John Day Company, 1946), which lauds GM and criticizes LDB (p. 185). Adolf A. Berle, Jr., *Power without Property* (New York: Harcourt, Brace, 1959), argues that big business and big government are inevitable; see particularly pp. 11–15.

11. Poole, "Brandeis," *Business*, p. lii.

12. Ibid., p. xii.

13. See, e.g., "Great Men and Their Environment," in William James, *The Will to Believe and Other Essays in Popular Philosophy* (New York: Longmans, Green, 1911), pp. 216–54.

14. See, for example, William James, *Some Problems of Philosophy: A Beginning of an Introduction to Philosophy* (New York: Longmans, Green, 1911), and also *Essays in Radical Empiricism* (New York: Longmans, Green, 1912).

15. John Dewey, "Mr. Justice Brandeis," *Columbia Law Review* 33 (1933): 175–76, reviewing Felix Frankfurter, ed., *Mr. Justice Brandeis* (New Haven, Conn.: Yale University Press, 1932), on p. 175.

16. John Dewey, *Studies in Logical Theory* (Chicago: University of Chicago Press, 1903), *Reconstruction in Philosophy* (New York: Henry Holt and Company, 1920), and *The Quest for Certainty: A Study of the Relation of Knowledge and Action* (New York: Minton, Balch, 1929).

17. John Dewey, "Philosophy and Democracy" in Dewey, *Characters and Events: Popular Essays in Social and Political Philosophy*, ed. Joseph Ratner, 2 vols. (New York: Henry Holt and Company, 1929), 2:851.

18. Ibid., p. 852.

19. Gertrude Himmelfarb, *Poverty and Compassion: The Moral Imagination of the Late Victorians* (New York: Knopf, 1991), p. 359.

20. Himmelfarb, pp. 361, 369, 372–74.

21. John Dewey, "Philosophy and Democracy," in *Characters and Events*, 2:854.

22. Universal Declaration of Human Rights, GA Res. 217A (3), UN Doc. A/810, at 71 (1948); International Covenant on Economic, Social and Cultural Rights, GA Res. 2200, UN Doc. A/6316 (1966).

23. *Whitney* v. *California*, at 375.

24. John Stuart Mill, *On Liberty*, ed. Alburey Castell (Arlington Heights, Ill.: Harlan Davidson, 1947), pp. 3, 75–77, 104; cf. Mill, *Principles of Political Economy*, ed. W. J. Ashley (London: Longmans, Green, 1909), bk. 4, chap. 11, sec. 9.

25. The best analysis of LDB's notion of civic courage is Vincent Blasi, "The First Amendment and the Ideal of Civic Courage: The Brandeis

Opinion in *Whitney* v. *California*," *William and Mary Law Review* 29 (Summer 1988): 653–97.

26. Mill, *Considerations on Representative Government,* chap. 3.

27. LDB to Robert Bruere, February 25, 1922, FF–HLS.

28. LDB, "Hours of Labor," speech delivered to first annual meeting of the Civic Federation of New England, January 11, 1906, printed in *Business,* p. 29.

29. Quoted in Alpheus T. Mason, *Brandeis: A Free Man's Life* (New York: Viking, 1946), p. 78.

30. LDB to Walter Bond Douglas, January 31, 1878, *Letters,* 1: 21; to Alfred Brandeis, June 28, 1878, *Letters,* 1:23; Mary Kay Tachau, interview with author, June 12, 1980, Louisville, Ky.; Philippa Strum, *Louis D. Brandeis: Justice for the People* (Cambridge: Harvard University Press, 1984), p. 23. James Landis wrote in 1941 that Brandeis's grades were still the best on record; see Landis, "Mr. Justice Brandeis and the Harvard Law School," *Harvard Law Review* 55 (1941): 184–90, on p. 184. Eric F. Goldman asserts that Brandeis's record had been matched but not bettered by Thomas Corcoran, although he does not mention his source; see Goldman, *Rendezvous with Destiny: A History of Modern American Reform* (New York: Vintage, 1959), pp. 106, 283. The law school currently declines to disclose grades on the grounds of privacy.

31. *Whitney* v. *California,* at 374.

32. Strum, *Brandeis,* pp. 23, 29, 227; cf. Mason, *Brandeis,* p. 63; Elizabeth Glendower Evans, "Memoirs" (Evans Papers, Schlesinger Library, Radcliffe College, Cambridge, Mass.); and Warren F. Kellogg to LDB, December 3, 1891, BP, NMF 7-15a. For the view that LDB was the victim of anti-Semitism and not accepted by Boston society, see Allon Gal, *Brandeis of Boston* (Cambridge: Harvard University Press, 1980).

33. Mason, *Brandeis,* chaps. 12, 13, 17, 18, 22, 27, and Strum, *Brandeis,* chaps. 5, 7, 10. The best accounts of these aspects of LDB's career are Alpheus T. Mason and Henry Lee Staples, *The Fall of a Railroad Empire: Brandeis and the New Haven Merger Battle* (Syracuse, N.Y.: Syracuse University Press, 1947); Alpheus T. Mason, *Bureaucracy Convicts Itself: The Ballinger-Pinchot Controversy of 1910* (New York: Viking Press, 1941); and James Penick, Jr., *Progressive Politics and Conservation: The Ballinger-Pinchot Affair* (Chicago: University of Chicago Press, 1968).

34. LDB to Huston Thompson, June 23, 1934, *Letters,* 5:541.

Chapter 1. Early Ideas

1. LDB, "Industrial Cooperation," address to the Filene Co-operative

Association, Boston, May 1905, published in *Filene Association Echo*, May 1905, reprinted in LDB, *The Curse of Bigness,* ed. Osmond K. Fraenkel (New York: Viking Press, 1934), pp. 35–37, on p. 36 (hereafter *Bigness*).

2. Interview in the *New York Times Annalist,* January 27, 1913, p. 36, reprinted in *Bigness*, pp. 40–42, on p. 41.

3. Brandeis's father, out of the country when the revolution began, rushed home to participate in it but was prevented from doing so by an attack of typhoid. No member of the three families was directly involved, but they were concerned about the post-uprising antipathy toward people known to have been sympathetic to its aims, particularly those who were Jewish. See Josephine Goldmark, *Pilgrims of '48* (New Haven, Conn.: Yale University Press, 1930), pp. 195, 199.

4. Father's business: Alpheus T. Mason, *Brandeis: A Free Man's Life* (New York: Viking, 1946), p. 23; Adolph's immigration, family beliefs: Goldmark, *Pilgrims*, pp. 178–220, 227, 228, 284; and Bert Ford, "Boyhood of Brandeis," *Boston American*, June 4, 1916, pp. 3–6, BP, Clippings Box 2, citing an interview with Brandeis's secretary Alice Grady. On Brandeis's first memory, see quotation by LDB in Ernest Poole, "Brandeis: A Remarkable Record of Unselfish Work Done in the Public Interest," *American Magazine,* February 1911, p. 481; cf. Solomon Goldman, ed., *The Words of Justice Brandeis* (New York: Henry Schuman, 1953), p. 6. The phrase "peculiar institution" was commonly used in the antebellum years; cf. Kenneth M. Stampp, *The Peculiar Institution: Slavery in the Ante-Bellum South* (New York: Vintage Books, 1956).

5. Dembitz: John W. Petrie, "Lewis Naphtali Dembitz," *Louisville Courier Journal*, February 27, 1916, in Louisville Free Public Library, Kentucky Authors Scrapbook no. 21; untitled typescript in same collection; Philippa Strum, *Louis D. Brandeis: Justice for the People* (Cambridge: Harvard University Press, 1984), pp. 10–11; John J. Weisert, "Lewis N. Dembitz and Onkel Tom's Hutte," *American-German Review* 19 (February 1953): 7–8; and "Report of Proceedings of the 10th Annual Convention of the Federation of American Zionists," *Maccabean* 13 (August 1907): 63–64.

6. LDB to Stella and Emily Dembitz, April 22, 1926, BP, M 4-4.

7. For LDB's mother's beliefs, see Frederika Dembitz Brandeis, *Reminiscences*, pp. 8–9, 32–34. *Reminiscences*, upon which much of Goldmark's account of the family was based, was written in German at LDB's request during 1880–1886, translated by his wife Alice Goldmark Brandeis, and printed privately in 1944. There are copies in the libraries of Radcliffe College (Schlesinger Library) and Yale University. Dinner conversation: Alfred Lief, *Brandeis: The Personal History of an American Ideal* (New York: Stackpole, 1936), p. 15.

8. Annen-Realschule: Ford, "Boyhood of Brandeis," pp. 3–6; LDB, *Business — A Profession*, ed. Ernest Poole (Boston: Small, Maynard, 1914),

p. xi (hereafter *Business*); comment about ideas: LDB to Paul Freund, quoted in Mason, *Brandeis*, p. 31.

9. LDB at Harvard: LDB to his brother-in-law Otto A. Wehle, March 12, 1876, BP, M 1–2, and to Wehle, November 12, 1876, BP, Unmarked Folder; to Walter Bond Douglas, January 31, 1878, *Letters*, 1:21; practice in St. Louis: LDB to his brother Alfred, June 28, 1878, *Letters*, 1: 23–34; Burton C. Bernard, "Brandeis in St. Louis," *St. Louis Bar Journal* 11 (1964): 53–68; establishing law firm with Warren: LDB to Alfred, July 31, 1879, *Letters*, 1:44; representing small businessmen: Mason, *Brandeis*, p. 61; Allon Gal, *Brandeis of Boston* (Cambridge: Harvard University Press, 1980), pp. 5, 16, 17, 43–46; LDB to his sister Amy, January 2, 1881, BP, M 2–2; Strum, *Brandeis*, chap. 3; course at Harvard: Mason, *Brandeis*, p. 6; Lewis Dembitz to LDB, April 16, 1882; Frederika to LDB, April 2, 1882; and Adolph to LDB, April 2, 1882, the latter three quoted in Mason, *Brandeis*, p. 66.

10. The elder Brandeis's finances and the extent to which he was disturbed by the change in them are reflected in Adolph to LDB, October 7, 1877, and February 20, 1878, BP, Misc. 1; I am grateful to the late Marion Lorie for her translation of the letters from the German. Loan from Alfred, tutoring, and proctoring: Adolph to LDB, October 7, 1877, BP, M 1–4; Alfred to LDB, November 10, 1877, BP, Addendum, Box 1; LDB to Amy Brandeis Wehle, December 2, 1877, *Letters*, 1:19; Mason, *Brandeis*, pp. 42, 48; living frugally and investing: Mason, *Brandeis*, p. 48; Lief, *Brandeis*, p. 22; LDB to Alfred, June 18, 1878, and July 5, 1878, *Letters*, 1:23, 25; Adolph's regret: Adolph to LDB, April 2, 1881, BP, Misc. 1.

11. U.S. Congress, House, "Statement before House Committee on Ways and Means, January 11, 1897: Tariff Hearings," 54th Cong., 2d sess., pp. 2081–84.

12. Typescript of speech delivered in Brighton, Mass., December 2, 1904, BP, Clippings Box 1.

13. LDB, "The Opportunity in the Law," delivered at Phillips Brooks House on May 4, 1905, and reprinted in *Business*, pp. 314–31, on p. 321; "Life Insurance, the Abuses and the Remedies," address before the Commercial Club of Boston, October 26, 1905, published in pamphlet form by the Policy-Holders' Protective Committee, reprinted in *Business*, pp. 109–53, on p. 153.

14. For a more extensive discussion of LDB's view of the lawyer as counsel rather than as advocate, see chapter 3.

15. Poole, in *Business*, pp. l–li.

16. David W. Levy, "The Lawyer as Judge: Brandeis's View of the Legal Profession," *Oklahoma Law Review* 22 (1969): 374–95.

17. LDB, "Opportunity in the Law," pp. 314, 321.

18. LDB to Alfred, January 30, 1884, *Letters*, 1:66. On his later support for women's suffrage, see Strum, *Brandeis*, pp. 128–30, and chapter 7.

19. Elizabeth Brandeis Raushenbush, interview with author, September 23, 1980, Madison, Wis.; cf. LDB to Alfred, March 20, 1886, *Letters*, 1: 67–68. The case was *Train* v. *Boston Disinfecting Co.*, 144 Mass. 523 (1887).

20. Mason, *Brandeis*, pp. 89–90, draws upon Mason's interview with LDB, July 21, 1940.

21. LDB, *Statement to Massachusetts Joint Legislative Committee on Liquor Law*, Feb. 27, 1891, BP, Scrapbook 1; newspapers: Brandeis reported that his address was "printed as news in full in the Boston Evening Transcript and either in full or in large part in general in the Press"; LDB to George Weston Anderson, March 6, 1916, BP, NMF 77-1; to fiancée: LDB to Alice Goldmark, February 9, 1891, *Letters*, 1:99; on reason for fee: to Anderson, *Letters*, 1:99.

22. See chapter 3.

23. See LDB to Matthew Fleming, January 23, 1905, BP, I 1-1. The most complete account of the insurance battle is in Alpheus T. Mason, *The Brandeis Way* (Princeton, N.J.: Princeton University Press, 1938). See also LDB, "Wage-Earners' Life Insurance," *Collier's* 37 (September 15, 1906), reprinted in Mason, *Brandeis Way*, pp. 311–25; LDB, "Massachusetts' Old Age Annuities," *American Federationist* 15 (August 1908): 595–97; "Massachusetts' Substitute for Old Age Pensions," *The Independent* 65 (July 16, 1908): 125–28; and LDB, "Massachusetts Savings Insurance and Annuity Banks," *Banker's Magazine* 78 (August 1908): 186–88.

24. LDB's Address to New England Dry Goods Association, Boston, February 11, 1908, about the attempt of the New Haven and Hartford Railroad Company to take over the Boston and Maine Railroad, published as Anti-Merger League, "New England Transportation Monopoly (The Proposed Merger)," reprinted in *Business*, pp. 255–78, on p. 271.

25. LDB to W. H. McElwain, June 18, 1902, BP, NMF 4-2.

26. LDB to John L. Bates, November 24, 1902, BP, NMF 3-4, and Mason, *Brandeis*, p. 123.

27. Reported in the *Boston Post*, March 19, 1903, and in the *Boston Journal*, April 9, 1903.

28. Address to Unitarian Club, in *Boston Journal*, April 9, 1903.

29. Mason, *Brandeis*, pp. 117–18, and LDB to Charles S. Davis, January 12, 1905, BP, NMF 3-4.

30. Mason, *Brandeis*, p. 124.

31. See chapter 5.

32. U.S. Congress, Senate, *Hearings before Committee of Investigation of Interior*

Department and Bureau of Forestry, 61st Cong., 3d sess., 1910–1911, S. Doc. 719, vols. 8 and 9; Strum, *Brandeis*, pp. 132–45. For Brandeis's role in the Pinchot-Ballinger affair, see Alpheus T. Mason, *Bureaucracy Convicts Itself* (New York: Viking Press, 1941). Although LDB's immediate concern was more the sale of public lands to private interests and the subsequent cover-up than Ballinger's belief that commercial foresting could be combined with conservation (see, e.g., LDB to Amos Pinchot, BP, NMF 39–1), upon further study he adopted a somewhat similar approach to land development. See, e.g., LDB to Robert M. La Follette, July 29, 1911, BP, SC 1–2; to Gifford Pinchot, July 29, 1922, BP, NMF 39–1; to John E. Lathrop, August 2, 1911, BP, NMF 39–1; and to Amos Pinchot, August 2, 1911, BP, NMF 39–1. His continued interest in land and conservation is evident in these letters as well as in LDB to Norman Hapgood, June 9, 1911, NMF 46–3; to Herbert Putnam, August 2, 1911, BP, NMF 39–1 (requesting a bibliography about Alaska in addition to government publications on the subject); to Gifford Pinchot, November 11, 1912, BP, NMF 51–7; to Pinchot, December 5, 1912, BP, NMF 52–2; to Ernest Jose, January 21, 1913, BP, NMF 51–7; to Chaim Weizmann, January 13, 1918, *Letters*, 4:335; and points 2 through 4 of the "Pittsburgh Platform" for a Jewish state, in Strum, *Brandeis*, p. 274 (cf. Strum, p. 275); LDB to Paul Kellogg, June 9, 1924, *Letters*, 5:133; to Elizabeth Brandeis Raushenbush, November 19, 1933, *Letters*, 5:527–28; and to FF, January 30, 1933, February 6, 1933, Melvin I. Urofsky and David W. Levy, eds., *"Half Brother, Half Son": The Letters of Louis D. Brandeis to Felix Frankfurter* (Norman: University of Oklahoma Press, 1991), pp. 510–11.

33. John Dewey: *How We Think, A Restatement of the Relation of Reflective Thinking to the Educative Process* (Boston: D. C. Heath and Company, 1933), pp. 67–78.

34. LDB to father: LDB to Alice Goldmark, early November 1890, quoted in Mason, *Brandeis*, p. 75; right living: LDB to Goldmark, December 9, 1890, *Letters*, 1:96; character, Matthew Arnold: LDB to Goldmark, October 27, 1890, quoted in Mason, *Brandeis*, p. 94; corruption: LDB to Goldmark, February 26, 1891, *Letters*, 1:100.

35. William James, *Some Problems of Philosophy: A Beginning of an Introduction to Philosophy* (New York: Longmans, Green, 1911); *Essays in Radical Empiricism* (New York: Longmans, Green, 1912); and John Dewey, *Psychology* (New York: Harper and Brothers, 1890).

36. *Adair* v. *United States*, 208 U.S. 161 (1908); *Coppage* v. *Kansas*, 236 U.S. 1 (1915); and *Hitchman Coal and Coke Co.* v. *Mitchell*, 245 U.S. 229, 232 (1917).

37. See Sidney Fine, *Laissez Faire and the General-Welfare State: A Study of*

Conflict in American Thought, 1865–1901 (Ann Arbor: University of Michigan, 1964), chaps. 6–10.

38. John Dewey, *The Ethics of Democracy* (Ann Arbor: Andrews and Company, 1888), pp. 25–28; John Dewey and J. A. McLellan, *Applied Psychology* (Boston: Educational Publishing Company, 1889), p. 151; and John Dewey and James H. Tufts, *Ethics* (New York: Henry Holt, 1910), pp. 443–45, 461, 474–76, 481, 485, 540–41.

Chapter 2. From Laissez-Faire Capitalism to Worker-Management

1. LDB, address delivered to Boston Typothetae, April 21, 1904, printed as "The Employer and Trades Unions," in *Business — A Profession*, ed. Ernest Poole (Boston: Small, Maynard, 1914), pp. 13–27, on p. 16 (hereafter *Business*).

2. Impact of Homestead strike, course at MIT: Josephine Goldmark, *Impatient Crusader: Florence Kelley's Life Story* (Urbana: University of Illinois Press, 1953), p. 153, and Livy S. Richard, "Up from Aristocracy," interview with LDB in *The Independent*, July 27, 1914, BP, Clippings Box 2. Both sets of notes for the MIT lectures are in *The Public Papers of Louis Dembitz Brandeis in the Jacob and Bertha Goldfarb Library of Brandeis University*, comp. Abram L. Sachar and William M. Goldsmith (microfilm, Brandeis University, Waltham, Massachusetts).

3. Alfred Lief, *Brandeis: The Personal History of an American Ideal* (New York: Stackpole, 1936), pp. 39–40; Allon Gal, *Brandeis of Boston* (Cambridge: Harvard University Press, 1980), pp. 56–58; and Horace Kallen, *The Faith of Louis D. Brandeis, Zionist* (New York: Hadassah, n.d.), p. 7.

4. Edward A. Filene, "Louis D. Brandeis, As We Know Him," *Boston Post*, March 4, 1916; LDB interview, *New York Times Annalist*, January 27, 1913, p. 36; LDB, "Business — A Profession," address at Brown University Commencement, 1912, published in *System, the Magazine of Business* 11 (October 1912), reprinted as "Business — the New Profession," in *Business*, pp. 1, 6–9.

5. LDB, interview, in LDB, *The Curse of Bigness*, ed. Osmond K. Fraenkel (New York: Viking Press, 1934), p. 41 (hereafter *Bigness*); irregularity of employment: Elizabeth Glendower Evans, "Mr. Justice Brandeis, the People's Tribune," *Survey*, October 29, 1931; LDB to Clarence Darrow, December 10, December 12, and December 13, 1902, BP, NMF 5-1; to Henry Demarest Lloyd, November 24, 1902, December 20, 1902, January 2, 1903, and February 2, 1903, BP, NMF 5-1.

6. Contact with Tobin: LDB to Tobin, March 28, 1905, BP, NMF 8-3; "many things": interview in *New York Times Annalist*, January 27, 1913, p. 36, reprinted in *Bigness*, pp. 40–42, on p. 41.

7. John Stuart Mill, *Considerations on Representative Government* (New York: Liberal Arts Press, 1958), p. 43.

8. LDB, "Employer and Trades Unions," p. 17.

9. William James, *Talks to Teachers on Psychology: and to Students on Some of Life's Ideals* (New York: H. Holt and Company, 1908), pp. 297–98.

10. LDB, "Employer and Trades Unions," p. 19.

11. Philippa Strum, *Louis D. Brandeis: Justice for the People* (Cambridge: Harvard University Press, 1984), pp. 104–7.

12. James Madison, Federalist Paper no. 51; cf. Mill, *Considerations on Representative Government,* pp. 43–44: "Human beings are only secure from evil at the hands of others in proportion as they have the power of being, and are, self-*protecting*; and they only achieve a high degree of success in their struggle with nature in proportion as they are self-*dependent*, relying on what they themselves can do, either separately or in concert, rather than on what others do for them."

13. Closed shop: LDB, in *National Civic Federation Review,* May 11, 1905, quoted in Alpheus T. Mason, *Brandeis: A Free Man's Life* (New York: Viking, 1946), p. 150; conduct of negotiations: LDB, "Employer and Trades Unions"; trusts: LDB, testimony, U.S. Congress, Senate, Committee on Interstate Commerce, *Hearings on Control of Corporations, Persons, and Firms Engaged in Interstate Commerce,* 62d Cong., 2d sess., 1911, vol. 1, pt. 16, pp. 1146–1291; testimony, U.S. Congress, House, *Hearings before the Committee on Investigation of United States Steel Corp.,* 26th Cong., 3d sess., 1912, H. Rep. 1137, pp. 2835–72. Many of Brandeis's articles about the failings of trusts, originally published by *Collier's Weekly* and *Harper's,* are reprinted in *Business* and *Bigness.*

14. "Powers of the individual": LDB, "Employer and Trades Unions"; need for leisure: LDB to Alfred Brandeis, February 23, 1906, *Letters,* 1: 407–8; to Alfred, June 18, 1907, BP, M 2–4; to Alfred, February 22, 1906, *Letters,* 1: 407.

15. LDB, "Industrial Co-operation," address to the Filene Co-operative Association, Boston, May, 1905, published in *Filene Association Echo,* May 1905, reprinted in LDB, *Bigness,* pp. 35–37.

16. Development of character: LDB, "Employer and Trades Unions"; limits of development: LDB, "Hours of Labor," address before first annual meeting of the Civil Federation of New England, January 11, 1906, reprinted in *Business,* pp. 28–36, on p. 31; speech to the Central Labor Union, *Boston Post,* February 6, 1905, quoted in Mason, *Brandeis,* p. 151.

17. *Muller* v. *Oregon,* 208 U.S. 412 (1908); *Stettler* v. *O'Hara,* 69 Oregon 519 (1914); *Stettler* v. *O'Hara,* 243 U.S. 629 (1917). LDB's argument before the Supreme Court in *Stettler* was published as "The Constitution and the

Minimum Wage," in *Survey* 33 (February 7, 1915): 490–94, 521–24, and reprinted in *Bigness*, pp. 52–69.

18. LDB testimony, U.S. Congress, Senate, Commission on Industrial Relations, S. Doc. 415, 64th Cong., 1st sess., 1914, Serial 6936, pp. 7657–81, quotation on p. 7659 (hereafter *Commission*); portions reprinted as "On Industrial Relations" in *Bigness*, pp. 70–95. Cf. LDB to Elizabeth Glendower Evans, December 22, 1911, and to Mary McDowell, July 8, 1912, BP, NMF 69–2.

19. FF-LC, Box 128.

20. See Mason, *Brandeis*, p. 91, for LDB on paupers and the loss of human potential that their situation implied.

21. See, e.g., LDB to Lawrence Fraser Abbott, September 6, 1910, BP, NMF 33–5; to Jane Addams, November 26, 1910, BP, NMF 33–1; to Julius Cohen, November 30 and December 3, 1910, BP, NMF 33–1; to Florence Kelley, December 14, 1910, BP, NMF 33–3; to Charles Crane, February 17, 1911, BP, NMF 33–1; to Meyer Bloomfield, May 1, 1911, BP, NMF 48–3; to Myrta L. Jones, September 7, 1911, BP, NMF 31–1; to Henry Moskowitz, September 29, 1911, BP, NMF 33–1, and December 4, 1911, BP, NMF 42–2; to Norman Hapgood, February 23, 1912, BP, NMF 46–3; to Ray Stannard Baker, February 26, 1912, BP, NMF 55–1; to Henry Moskowitz, March 25 and April 16, 1912, BP, NMF 42–2; to Alfred Brandeis, July 28, 1912, M 3–3; and to Arthur Holcombe, October 3, 1912, BP, NMF 53–2. See also LDB to Meyer Bloomfield, July 6, 1908, *Letters*, 2:195.

22. LDB to Alfred, July 24, 1910, BP, M 3–3; Mason, *Brandeis*, pp. 291–93; Lief, *Brandeis*, pp. 183–86.

23. LDB, "The Spirit of Get-Together," *American Cloak and Suit Review*, January 1911, p. 159, reprinted in *Bigness*, p. 266; Edith F. Wyatt, "The New York Cloak-makers' Strike," *McClure's* 34 (April 1911): 708–11; John Bruce McPherson, "The New York Cloakmakers' Strike," *Journal of Political Economy* 19 (March 1911): 153–87; Henry Moskowitz, "An Experiment in Industrial Control," *La Follette's Weekly* 5 (April 19, 1913): 13–14; Mason, *Brandeis*, pp. 300–302; Lief, *Brandeis*, pp. 188–91.

24. In this respect, LDB was typical of Jews from German backgrounds. See William S. Berlin, *On the Edge of Politics: The Roots of Jewish Political Thought in America* (Westport, Conn.: Greenwood, 1978), pp. 21–45.

25. The worker was quoting from Isaiah 3:3. Milton R. Konvitz, "Louis D. Brandeis," in *Great Jewish Personalities in Modern Times*, ed. Simon Noveck (Washington, D.C.: B'nai Brith, 1960), p. 300; cf. Solomon Goldman, ed., *The Words of Justice Brandeis* (New York: Henry Schuman, 1953), p. 12, giving up alcohol: LDB to Alfred Brandeis, BP, Addendum, Box 1, folders 1–3

and folders 1910–1928; BP, M 2–4; Mary Kay Tachau, interview with author, June 12, 1980, Louisville, Ky.; drinking beer with the workers: Lief, *Brandeis*, p. 187.

26. LDB to Dix Smith, November 5, 1913, BP, NMF 47–2.

27. U.S. Senate, Committee on Interstate Commerce, *Hearings on Control of Corporations, Persons, and Firms Engaged in Interstate Commerce*, pp. 1146–1291.

28. The letter was printed as "The Preferential Shop: A Letter from Louis D. Brandeis," *Human Engineering*, August 1912, pp. 179–81.

29. LDB to Maurice Barnett, May 26, 1913, BP, NMF 47–2, and to Dix W. Smith, November 5, 1913, BP, NMF 47–2.

30. LDB, "Hours of Labor," in *Business*, pp. 28–29.

31. John Locke, *Second Treatise of Government*, ed. C. B. Macpherson (Indianapolis, Ind.: Hacket, 1980), chap. 5, paragraphs 7–16.

32. *Commission*, pp. 7658–59.

33. Ibid.

34. Ibid.

35. LDB, "The Democracy of Business," address to United States Chamber of Commerce, February 5, 1914, published as pamphlet and reprinted in *Bigness*, 137–42, on pp. 140–41.

36. *Commission*, p. 7660.

37. Ibid., pp. 7660, 7664; emphasis added.

38. Ibid., p. 7665.

39. Ibid., pp. 7660, 7664–66, 7669.

40. Ibid., p. 7663.

41. Progressivism as conservative: Samuel Haber, *Efficiency and Uplift: Scientific Management in the Progressive Era 1890–1920* (Chicago: University of Chicago Press, 1964), p. xi, and Melvin I. Urofsky, *Louis D. Brandeis and the Progressive Tradition* (Boston: Little, Brown, 1981), pp. 18, 21, 22.

42. Mary La Dame, *The Filene Store: A Study of Employees' Relation to Management in a Retail Store* (New York: Russell Sage Foundation, 1930), pp. 47, 164–88, 306–21, 441, 442, and LDB to Edward Filene, June 25, 1906, BP, NMF 7–2.

43. Beatrice Potter, *The Cooperative Movement in Great Britain* (London: Swan Sonnenschein, 1899), pp. 118, 127, 138, 139.

44. Interview, *Boston Post*, February 14, 1915, BP, Scrapbook II.

45. Ibid.

46. Sidney and Beatrice Webb, *The Consumer's Cooperative Movement* (London and New York: Longmans, Green, 1921), and *The Decay of Capitalist Civilization* (New York: Harcourt, Brace, 1923); LDB to Frankfurter, April 6, 1923, *Letters*, 5: 90; LDB to Elizabeth B. Raushenbush, August 7, 1923, *Letters*, 5:99.

47. See LDB to FF, September 30, 1922, in Melvin I. Urofsky and David W. Levy, eds., *"Half Brother, Half Son": The Letters of Louis D. Brandeis to Felix Frankfurter* (Norman: University of Oklahoma Press, 1991), pp. 114–15.

48. Denmark: LDB to Norman Hapgood, March 2, 1915, BP, NMF 62-1, and Alice Brandeis and Josephine Goldmark, *Democracy in Denmark* (Washington, D.C.: National Home Library Foundation, 1936).

49. Leadership of the Zionists and interest in kibbutzim: Strum, *Brandeis*, pp. 248–65, 273–76, 289; Melvin I. Urofsky, *American Zionism from Herzl to the Holocaust* (Garden City, N.Y.: Doubleday, 1975), pp. 119–21; Samuel Ben-Zvi, "Justice Brandeis and Ein Hashofet," *New Palestine*, November 14, 1941, p. 10.

50. LDB to Alfred Brandeis, July 28, 1904, BP, M 2-4.

51. Quoted in Alfred Lief, *The Brandeis Guide to the Modern World* (Boston: Little, Brown and Company, 1941), p. 116.

52. LDB to Alfred Brandeis, July 28, 1904, BP, M 2-4.

53. Lief, *Brandeis Guide*, p. 303.

54. Frederick W. Taylor, "Shop Management," in *Transactions of the American Society of Mechanical Engineers* (1903); cf. his *Principles of Scientific Management* (New York: Harper, 1911); meetings: LDB to Alice Brandeis, October 9, 16, 22, and 29, and November 3, 1910, Brandeis Family Letters, Goldfarb Library, Brandeis University, Waltham, Mass. LDB wrote the foreword to Frank B. Gilbreth's *Primer of Scientific Management* (London: Constable, 1912). LDB also read Harrington Emerson's articles on scientific management as applied to the Atchison, Topeka and Santa Fe Railroad in *American Engineer and Railroad Journal* (1906), Emerson's *Efficiency as a Basis for Operations and Wages* (New York: Engineering Magazine, 1909), and Henry L. Gantt's five-part series in *Engineering Magazine* 39 (January–June 1910). Communication with employers using scientific management: LDB, *Scientific Management and the Railroads* (New York: Engineering Magazine, 1911); Haber, *Efficiency and Uplift*, especially p. xi and chap. 5; Oscar Kraines, "Brandeis' Philosophy of Scientific Management," *Western Political Quarterly* 13 (March 1960): 191–201; meetings: Kraines, p. 192. Richard P. Adelstein, "'Islands of Conscious Power': Louis D. Brandeis and the Modern Corporation," *Business History Review* 63 (Autumn 1989): 614–56.

55. LDB, *Scientific Management and the Railroads*, incorporates about half of LDB's brief submitted to and some of the testimony in a hearing about proposed railroad freight rates before the Interstate Commerce Commission (ICC), *In the Matter of Proposed Advances in Freight Rates by Carriers*, 61st Cong., 3d sess., Doc. 725, January 3 and 11, 1911, and LDB, "Brief on Behalf of Traffic Committee of Commercial Organizations of the Atlantic Seaboard," ICC, *Freight Rates*, vol. 8, Briefs of Counsel, Docket No. 3400.

See also LDB, "Organized Labor and Efficiency," address to Boston Central Labor Union, April 2, 1911, published in *Survey*, April 22, 1911, pp. 148–51, and reprinted in *Business*, pp. 37–50.

56. LDB, "Organized Labor and Efficiency," pp. 39, 41, 42.

57. LDB, *Scientific Management and the Railroads*, pp. 8, 9, 12–15, 17–22, 35–36, 37–47, 48–50, 55, 57–60.

58. LDB, "Organized Labor and Efficiency," p. 49.

59. Quoted in Lief, *Brandeis*, p. 223. For a sense of the unions' reaction, see the exchange of letters between LDB and John Mitchell in *Letters*, 2: 394–95, 398.

60. LDB, "Organized Labor and Efficiency," pp. 41, 42–43, 48–49.

61. *Di Santo* v. *Pennsylvania*, 273 U.S. 34, 37 (1927) (dissenting), at 43.

62. FF, "Memorandum," July 9, 1922, BP-HLS Box 114-7, also in FF-LC, Box 224, p. 4. Brandeis's interest in worker-participation was confirmed by Roger Baldwin, whose merchant father was one of Brandeis's clients, in a telephone interview with the author (May 19, 1981). See Baldwin, "Affirmation of Democracy," *Jewish Frontier* 3 (November 1936): 10.

63. Norman Hapgood, *The Changing Years* (New York: Farrar and Rinehart, 1930), pp. 290–96, 393–94, and LDB to Hapgood, May 14, 1917, *Letters*, 4:292.

64. LDB to Robert Bruere, February 25, 1922, BP, NMF 15.

65. See John Dewey, "Mr. Justice Brandeis," *Columbia Law Review* 33 (1933): 175–76, reviewing Felix Frankfurter, ed., *Mr. Justice Brandeis* (New Haven, Conn.: Yale University Press, 1932), on p. 175. Dewey also believed that democracy necessarily included economic democracy; see Dewey, *The Ethics of Democracy* (Ann Arbor: Andrews and Company, 1888), pp. 25–28.

CHAPTER 3. LAW, LAWYER, AND JUDGE

1. Euripides, *The Suppliant Women*, trans. Gilbert Murray (London: Oxford University Press, 1936), 2.320–30.

2. According to Alpheus Mason, Brandeis "drew enduring inspiration" from the excerpt (Sam Warren to LDB, n.d., BP, Clippings Box 1, and Alpheus T. Mason, *Brandeis: A Free Man's Life* [New York: Viking, 1946], p. 95). Mason misidentified it as coming from Euripides' *Bacchae*; Blasi corrected the attribution (Vincent Blasi, "The First Amendment and the Ideal of Civil Courage: The Brandeis Opinion in *Whitney* v. *California*," *William and Mary Law Review* 29 [Summer 1988]: 653–97, on p. 682 n. 101).

3. LDB, "Some Objections to the Matthews-Livermore Terminal Subway Bill," February 17, 1902, typescript, BP, NMF 2-5; LDB, "The Experience of Massachusetts in Street Railways," speech to the National

Convention on Municipal Ownership and Public Franchise, February 25, 1903, printed in *Boston Transcript*, February 25, 1903, and reprinted in *Municipal Affairs* 6 (1903): 721, 727; LDB, "The Massachusetts System of Dealing with Public Franchises," address at Cooper Union, New York City, February 24, 1905, typescript BP, Clippings Box 1; Philippa Strum, *Louis D. Brandeis: Justice for the People* (Cambridge: Harvard University Press, 1984), pp. 57–61; and Alfred Lief, *Brandeis: The Personal History of an American Ideal* (New York: Stackpole, 1936), pp. 55–69.

4. Edward A. Filene, "Louis D. Brandeis as We Know Him," *Boston Post*, July 14, 1915.

5. Mason, *Brandeis*, p. 180; cf. LDB to Louise Malloch (his secretary), November 4, 1907, BP, NMF 1–H–1.

6. Edward F. McClennen (one of LDB's partners), "Louis D. Brandeis as a Lawyer," *Massachusetts Law Quarterly* 33 (1948): 24.

7. McClennen, "Brandeis as Lawyer," p. 24; LDB to Louise Malloch, November 4, 1907, BP, NMF 1–H–1; LDB interview in *American Cloak and Suit Review*, January 1911, p. 159, reprinted in LDB, *The Curse of Bigness*, ed. Osmond K. Fraenkel (New York: Viking Press, 1934), p. 266 (hereafter *Bigness*).

8. According to Jacob de Haas, LDB first became known as "the people's attorney" "in 1896 when he appeared without retainer for the citizens of Boston in the first big fight" over the Boston railway; see de Haas, *Louis D. Brandeis: A Biographical Sketch* (New York: Bloch Publishing Company, 1929), p. 42. Brandeis was publicly involved in the fight as early as 1893 (see Walter H. Reynolds to LDB, February 21, 1893, quoted in Mason, *Brandeis*, p. 106), so de Haas may not have had the date precisely right. The soubriquet was clearly in general use by the early years of the twentieth century.

9. LDB, "The Living Law," address before the Chicago Bar Association, January 3, 1916, published in *Illinois Law Review* 10 (February 1916): 461–71, and in *Harper's Weekly*, February 19 and 26, 1916, pp. 173–74, 201–2, and reprinted in *Bigness*, pp. 316–26, on p. 324.

10. LDB, address to Harvard Law Review Association, June 22, 1907, quoted in Alfred Lief, ed., *The Brandeis Guide to the Modern World* (Boston: Little, Brown and Company, 1941), p. 171.

11. Horace Kallen, *The Faith of Louis D. Brandeis, Zionist* (New York: Hadassah, n.d.), p. 7.

12. Alexis de Tocqueville, *Democracy in America*, 2 vols. (1835; reprint, New York: Knopf, 1945), 2:102–12.

13. For the change in law and lawyers, see David W. Levy, "The Lawyer as Judge: Brandeis's View of the Legal Profession," *Oklahoma Law Review*

22 (1969): 374–95, on pp. 376–80; Richard Hofstadter, *The Age of Reform: From Bryan to F.D.R.* (New York: Vintage, 1960), pp. 156–64.

14. See, e.g., *Allgeyer* v. *Louisiana*, 165 U.S. 578 (1897); *Powell* v. *Pennsylvania*, 127 U.S. 678 (1888); *Farmers' Loan & Trust* v. *Northern Pacific Railroad*, 60 Fed. 803 (1894); *Ritchie* v. *People*, 155 Ill. 98 (1895); and *People* v. *Williams*, 81 N. E. R. 778 (1907). On lawyers, see "Babbitry at the Bar," in Jerold S. Auerbach, *Unequal Justice: Lawyers and Social Change in Modern America* (New York: Oxford University Press), pp. 130–57, and on lawyers and judges, Arnold M. Paul, *Conservative Crisis and the Rule of Law: Attitudes of Bar and Bench, 1887–1895* (Ithaca, N.Y.: Cornell University Press, 1960).

15. Morton J. Horwitz, *The Transformation of American Law, 1780–1860* (Cambridge: Harvard University Press, 1977).

16. See the series of analyses by Jacobus ten Broek, "Use by the United States Supreme Court of Extrinsic Aids in Constitutional Construction," *California Law Review* 26 (1938): 287–308, 437–54, 664–81, and *California Law Review* 27 (1939): 157–81, 399–421.

17. Oliver Wendell Holmes, "The Path of the Law," in Holmes, *Collected Legal Papers* (1921; reprint, New York: Peter Smith, 1952), p. 187.

18. LDB, "The Practice of the Law," BP, NMF 85-3.

19. LDB to William H. Dunbar, February 2, 1893, FF-LC.

20. LDB, "Living Law," p. 324.

21. LDB to William H. Dunbar, August 19, 1896, *Letters*, 1: 124–26.

22. LDB to William H. Dunbar, February 2, 1893, FF-LC.

23. "Rather have clients": Ernest Poole in LDB, *Business — A Profession*, ed. Poole (Boston: Small, Maynard, 1914), pp. l–li; turning away clients: Mason, *Brandeis*, pp. 232–37; and McClennen, "Brandeis as Lawyer," p. 21.

24. According to Mason, Brandeis's income was approximately $50,000 a year in 1890; that of the average lawyer was $5,000. By the second decade of the twentieth century his income from investments alone was close to $100,000 (tax free, as Mason notes, until 1913), of which the frugal family spent only about $10,000 (Mason, *Brandeis*, p. 640).

25. Jacob de Haas, "The People's Attorney: Justice Louis D. Brandeis," *Jewish Tribune*, August 23, 1929, pp. 3, 9; Lief, *Brandeis: American Ideal*, pp. 56–57.

26. Laski to Holmes, August 12, 1933, in Mark A. DeWolfe Howe, ed., *The Holmes-Laski Letters* (Cambridge: Harvard University Press, 1953), p. 1448.

27. LDB, "Living Law," pp. 317–18, 319. LDB was of course not alone in attacking lawyers who served corporations and judges who ignored social realities; see Paul, *Conservative Crisis and the Rule of Law*, pp. 44, 50–60. It was he, however, who went from criticism to development of a new jurisprudence.

28. Life of the law: Oliver Wendell Holmes, *The Common Law* (Boston: Little, Brown, 1881), p. 5; "felt necessities": p. 1; cf. Holmes, "Path of the Law."

29. Mark De Wolfe Howe, ed., 2 vols. *The Holmes-Pollock Letters* (Cambridge: Harvard University Press, 1941), 1:163.

30. Roscoe Pound, "Liberty of Contract," *Yale Law Journal* 18 (1909): 454; *The Spirit of the Common Law* (Boston: Marshall Jones, 1921); *The History and System of the Common Law* (New York: Collier, 1939); *An Introduction to the Philosophy of Law* (New Haven, Conn.: Yale University Press, 1922); and other works cited in George A. Strait, *A Bibliography of the Writings of Roscoe Pound* (Cambridge: Harvard Law School Library, 1960). Cf. David Wigdor, *Roscoe Pound, Philosopher of Law* (Westport, Conn.: Greenwood Press, 1974).

31. *Cohens* v. *Virginia*, 19 U.S. (6 Wheat.) 264, 387 (1821).

32. Cf. H. N. Hirsch, *A Theory of Liberty: The Constitution and Minorities* (New York: Routledge, 1992).

33. *Lochner* v. *New York*, 198 U.S. 45, 74 (1905) (dissenting). Cf., e.g., *Adkins* v. *Children's Hospital*, 261 U.S. 525 (1923) (dissenting), at 567; *Hammer* v. *Dagenhart*, 247 U.S. 251 (1918) (dissenting), at 277; and *Bartels* v. *Iowa*, 262 U.S. 404 (1923) (dissenting), at 412.

34. See Samuel J. Konefsky, *The Legacy of Holmes and Brandeis* (New York: Macmillan, 1956), pp. 185-86, 188-89.

35. See, e.g., *Colegrove* v. *Green*, 328 U.S. 549, 554, 556 (1946), and *Baker* v. *Carr*, 364 U.S. 186, 267, 270 (1962) (dissenting); cf. Sanford V. Levinson, "The Democratic Faith of Felix Frankfurter," *Stanford Law Review* 25 (1973), who argues persuasively that much of Frankfurter's jurisprudence stemmed from his belief that "the United States is in fact an open polity, and there is therefore no need for an alert and active Court to further the development of greater openness" (p. 430). Cf. Melvin I. Urofsky, *Felix Frankfurter: Judicial Restraint and Individual Rights* (Boston: Twayne, 1991), chaps. 4, 5, and 7.

36. See, e.g., Justice Scalia in *Immigration and Naturalization Service* v. *Elias Zacharias* (no. 90-1342, January 22, 1992), and Robert Bork, "Original Intent and the Constitution," *Humanities* 7 (February 1986): 22.

37. *United States* v. *Butler*, 297 U.S. 1, 62, 63 (1936).

38. See, e.g., *Allgeyer* v. *Louisiana*, 163 U.S. 578 (1897), and *Lochner* v. *New York*, 198 U.S. 45 (1905).

39. The Brandeis brief was published as LDB, assisted by Josephine Goldmark, *Women in Industry* (New York: National Consumers' League, n.d.); the case was *Muller* v. *Oregon*, 208 U.S. 412 (1908). To give credit where it is due, it should be noted that three years earlier, a fact-filled brief was filed on behalf of New York by attorney Julius Mayer in *Lochner* v. *New York*.

It was used extensively in Justice Harlan's dissent, 298 U.S. 70–71, and LDB may well have been aware of it.

40. *Lochner* v. *New York*, at 63.

41. *Lochner* had said that hours could be limited only in occupations about which "there be some fair ground . . . to say that there is material danger to the public health or to the health of the employees, if the hours of labor are not curtailed" and that no such danger existed for the bakers covered by the New York law (*Lochner*, at 61). In *Holden* v. *Hardy*, 169 U.S. 366 (1898), the Court upheld a Utah law limiting miners' hours. See *People* v. *Williams*, 189 N.Y. 131 (1907), where the state court of appeals overturned a law prohibiting employment of women after 10:00 P.M., saying that "nothing in the language of the [law] . . . suggests the purpose of promoting health" (at 134).

42. Nancy Erickson has argued that the Brandeis brief was unnecessary, as the doctrine of liberty of contract had always been gender-based and there were sufficient examples of courts upholding state legislation protecting women in the absence of such a brief. See Erickson, "Muller v. Oregon Considered: The Origins of a Sex-Based Doctrine of Liberty of Contract," *Labor History* 30 (1989): 228–50. The importance of the Brandeis brief, however, lay not in what other writers have labeled its inherent sexism but in its approach to legal argumentation relying on social facts rather than on legal precedents or such stereotypes as the innate difference of women workers, thus opening the door for use of the approach for male workers and in other areas of the law. Ultimately, social facts about matters such as the roles of women in the mid-twentieth century, the comparative dangers of childbirth and abortions, and fetal viability were used to benefit women in cases establishing the constitutional rights of gender equality and of abortion; see, e.g., *Reed* v. *Reed*, 404 U.S. 71 (1971); *Frontiero* v. *Richardson*, 411 U.S. 677 (1973); and *Roe* v. *Wade*, 410 U.S. 113 (1973).

43. Josephine Goldmark, *Fatigue and Efficiency* (New York: Russell Sage Foundation, 1912); *Muller* applicable to men: LDB and Goldmark, *Women in Industry*, see, e.g., pp. 24–32, 35–36, 42–45, 56, 61–64; see LDB to John Mark Glenn, general director of Russell Sage, November 30, 1909, *Letters*, 2:297–98.

44. John E. Semonche has noted that the Supreme Court had upheld other statutes limiting hours in *Charting the Future: The Supreme Court Responds to a Changing Society, 1890–1920* (Westport, Conn.: Greenwood Press, 1978), pp. 94–95, 106–8, 115–16, 143–44, 165–69, 181–85. *Lochner*, however, raised the possibility that the Court would follow a different route after 1905, and as Semonche notes, *Muller* "was the first wedge hammered into *Lochner*" (p. 221).

45. *Muller* v. *Oregon* at 419, 419–20 n. 1.

46. Requests for briefs, reenactment of Illinois law: Josephine Goldmark, *Impatient Crusader* (Urbana: University of Illinois Press, 1953), pp. 158–63; *Ritchie* v. *People*, 155 Ill. 98 (1895); and *Ritchie* v. *Wyman*, 244 Ill. 509 (1910). LDB expressed his anger at the earlier Illinois decision in "Living Law," pp. 319–20. He told Goldmark he had wanted to list her as his assistant in *Muller* but was too worried about the substantive unconventionality of the brief to do so. See Goldmark, *Impatient Crusader*, pp. 158–64. Following cases: Goldmark, pp. 162–79, and Strum, *Brandeis*, p. 123. For LDB's defense of the concept of minimum-wage laws, see his argument before the Supreme Court in *Stettler* v. *O'Hara*, 243 U.S. 629 (1917), published in *Survey*, February 6, 1915, pp. 490–94, 521–24, as "The Constitution and the Minimum Wage," and reprinted in *Bigness*, pp. 52–69.

47. Goldmark describes the way the briefs were put together in *Impatient Crusader*, chaps. 13 and 14. Brandeis and Goldmark prepared a 960-page brief for the case of *Bunting* v. *Oregon*, 243 U.S. 426 (1917), which was taken over by Felix Frankfurter when LDB was appointed to the Court. Frankfurter apparently added only appendices. It was printed as Felix Frankfurter, assisted by Josephine Goldmark, *The Case for the Shorter Work Day* (New York: National Consumers' League, 1915).

48. William Hitz to FF, December 17, 1914, BP, Addendum, Scrapbook 2.

49. "Babbit's Column," *Boston Herald*, January 3, 1915, BP, Addendum, Scrapbook 2.

50. McClennen, "Brandeis as Lawyer," pp. 3, 4, 17.

51. Quoted in Konefsky, *Legacy of Holmes and Brandeis*, p. 305 n. 54.

52. Roscoe Pound to Sen. William E. Chilton, 1916, FF–LC Box 127.

53. Kelley and Goldmark chose LDB as the attorney in the case because they wanted a lawyer "who believed in the law and was . . . prepared to show the court why it was needed to protect women's health" (Goldmark, *Impatient Crusader*, pp. 149–50).

54. Laski to Holmes, August 12, 1933, in Howe, *Holmes-Laski Letters*, p. 1448.

55. LDB, "Living Law," p. 325.

56. Holmes, "Path of the Law," p. 166.

57. LDB, *Statement to Massachusetts Joint Legislative Committee on Liquor Law*, February 27, 1891, BP, Scrapbook 1.

58. Mason, *Brandeis*, pp. 248–49, 38.

59. LDB, interview with Ernest Poole, quoted in "A Great American," *Philadelphia North American*, February 11, 1911, BP, Addendum, Clippings Box 1.

60. John Dewey, *Reconstruction in Philosophy* (New York: Henry Holt and Company, 1920), pp. 26, 124.

61. Super-legislature: *Jay Burns Baking Co.* v. *Bryan*, 264 U.S. 504 (1924), at 534, and *Di Santo* v. *Pennsylvania*, 273 U.S. 34, 42, 47 (1927).

62. John Stuart Mill, *Considerations on Representative Government* (New York: Liberal Arts Press, 1958), p. 6.

63. Ibid., p. 4.

64. *Truax* v. *Corrigan*, 257 U.S. 312, 378 (1921).

65. *New State Ice Co.* v. *Liebmann*, 285 U.S. 262 (1932); consideration of conditions: *Truax* v. *Corrigan*, 257 U.S. 312, 355–57 (1921) (dissenting). Clerks and research: interviews, Thomas H. Austern, October 22, 1978, Washington, D.C.; Willard H. Hurst, September 24, 1980, Madison, Wis.; and David Riesman, December 4, 1977, Cambridge, Mass.; LDB to William F. McCurdy, June 26, July 19, and August 18, 1923, BP-HLS; letters to and from James Landis, BP-HLS, 38-7; Landis notes for the case of *Myers* v. *United States*, 272 U.S. 52 (1926), BP-HLS, 39-10; memorandum by Warren Ege, BP-HLS, 38-9; Paul A. Freund, "Justice Brandeis: A Law Clerk's Remembrance," *American Jewish History* 68 (1978): 7–18, on p. 9.

66. *New State Ice Co.*, 287–300, 287–90 n. 8–17, 306–10.

67. Ibid., at 310–11.

68. *Liggett* v. *Lee*, 288 U.S. 517, 533 (1933) (dissenting), at 548–49.

69. Ibid., at 564n, 50–569 n. 61, 573 n. 65, 565–67.

70. Ibid., at 566–68.

71. *Jay Burns Baking Co.* v. *Bryan*, 264 U.S. 504, 517 (1924) (dissenting), at 520.

72. Ibid., at 520–34. For LDB's use of facts in a similar way, see, e.g., *Truax* v. *Corrigan*, 257 U.S. 312, 355 (1921) (dissenting); *Southwestern Bell Telephone Co.* v. *Public Service Commission*, 262 U.S. 276, 290 (1923) (dissenting); *Frost* v. *Corporations Comm.*, 278 U.S. 515, 528 (1929) (dissenting); *St. Louis & O'Fallon Railway* v. *United States*, 279 U.S. 461, 488 (1929) (dissenting); and *United Railways* v. *West*, 280 U.S. 234, 255 (1939) (dissenting).

73. Felix Frankfurter, "Mr. Justice Brandeis and the Constitution," in Frankfurter, ed., *Mr. Justice Brandeis* (New Haven, Conn.: Yale University Press, 1932), pp. 47–125, on p. 124.

74. I am grateful to Prof. Vincent Blasi for pointing out that Holmes's social Darwinism lay in his belief that progress or the lack of it was as much a matter of chance as was evolution and that he scorned Spencer's and Sumner's attempt to transform Darwinism into a moral justification of domination by supposedly superior races.

75. Holmes to LDB, April 20, 1919, BP, SC 4–2, and Holmes to Pollock, May 26, 1919, in Howe, *Holmes-Pollock Letters*, 2:13–14. Holmes sent a similar account of his and LDB's differing views about the importance of facts to Harold Laski on June 16, 1919; see Howe, *Holmes-Laski Letters*, 1: 212. Eric F. Goldman delineates this side of Holmes thoroughly in *Rendezvous with Destiny: A History of Modern American Reform*, rev. ed. (New York: Vintage Books, 1959), chap. 7.

76. David Riesman, "Notes for an Essay on Justice Brandeis," sent to FF, May 22, 1936, FF-LC, Box 127, pp. 1–2.

77. Freund, "Justice Brandeis," p. 11; cf. Paul Freund, "Driven by Passion," in *Sunday Herald*, November 11, 1956, p. 3, FF-LC, Box 128, which recounts LDB's question in slightly different words. Although Freund does not name the case, it seems clear from his description that it was *National Surety Company* v. *Corielli*, 289 U.S. 426 (1933). See Dean Acheson, *Morning and Noon* (Boston: Houghton Mifflin, 1965), p. 94; cf. p. 103. Acheson was directed to collect what proved to be fifteen pages of footnotes for a minor case (p. 80). Austern, in an interview with the author, claimed to have had the same experience. Other clerks: Willard Hurst, letter to author, November 18, 1977; Calvert Magruder, speech at memorial meeting for LDB, Temple Israel, Boston, October 31, 1941, Harvard Law School, Magruder Papers 33–9, pp. 11–13; sixty changes: author's interview with Austern.

78. Acheson, *Morning and Noon*, p. 94.

79. See, e.g., LDB's dissents in *Adams* v. *Tanner*, 244 U.S. 590, 597 (1917); *Schaefer* v. *United States*, 251 U.S. 466, 482 (1920); *Pierce* v. *United States*, 252 U.S. 239, 253 (1920); *Gilbert* v. *Minnesota*, 254 U.S. 325, 334 (1920); *Milwaukee Publishing Co.* v. *Burleson*, 255 U.S. 407, 417 (1921); *Duplex Printing Co.* v. *Deering*, 254 U.S. 443, 479 (1921); *Pennsylvania Coal Co.* v. *Mahon*, 260 U.S. 393, 416 (1922); *Myers* v. *United States*, 272 U.S. 52, 240 (1926); *Olmstead* v. *United States*, 277 U.S. 438, 471 (1928); and *Whitney* v. *California*, 274 U.S. 357, 372 (1927) (concurring).

80. *Adams* v. *Tanner*, 244 U.S. 590, 597, 603 n. 3, 613 nn. 1–3, 615 n. 1 (1917) (dissenting).

81. See, e.g., LDB's opinion for the Court in *Erie Railroad* v. *Tompkins*, 304 U.S. 64 (1938), at 72 nn. 3, 4; 73 nn. 5, 6; 74 n. 7; 75 nn. 9, 10; 77 nn. 20–22, citing twenty-eight law review articles.

82. Cf. Strum, *Brandeis*, pp. 363–64. LDB completed the circle by suggesting law review articles to a variety of law school professors, particularly FF. Although not all of his suggestions were taken, many were, and articles and notes in the *Harvard Law Review* followed. See Philippa Strum, "Brandeis: People's Attorney," *American Jewish History*, Centennial Issue no. 4, 81:4

(forthcoming); Melvin I. Urofsky and David W. Levy, eds, *"Half Brother, Half Son": The Letters of Louis D. Brandeis to Felix Frankfurter* (Norman: University of Oklahoma, 1991), passim.

83. Frankfurter, "Mr. Justice Brandeis and the Constitution," p. 51.

84. See chapter 6.

CHAPTER 4. THE CURSE OF BIGNESS

1. LDB, testimony, U.S. Congress, Senate, Committee on Interstate Commerce, *Hearings on Control of Corporations, Persons, and Firms Engaged in Interstate Commerce,* 62d Cong., 2d sess., 1911, pt. 16, pp. 1146–1291, on p. 1170 (hereafter *Hearings*).

2. LDB, "The Employer and Trades Unions," address to the Boston Typothetae, April 21, 1904, reprinted in LDB, *Business — A Profession,* ed. Ernest Poole (Boston: Small, Maynard, 1914), pp. 13–27, on p. 17 (hereafter *Business*).

3. The case was *Schechter* v. *U.S.*, 295 U.S. 495 (1935). For FDR's comment, see Melvin I. Urofsky, *Louis D. Brandeis and the Progressive Tradition* (Boston: Little, Brown, 1981), p. 162.

4. See Arthur Schlesinger, Jr., *The Politics of Upheaval* (Boston: Houghton Mifflin, 1960), p. 280.

5. LDB dismissed the NRA and the Agricultural Adjustment Act as *Kunststücke* ("clever tricks"); see LDB to FF, February 27, 1934, Melvin I. Urofsky and David W. Levy, eds., *"Half Brother, Half Son": The Letters of Louis D. Brandeis to Felix Frankfurter* (Norman: University of Oklahoma Press, 1991), p. 541.

6. LDB, "Organized Labor and Efficiency," address before the Boston Central Labor Union, April 2, 1911, published in *Survey,* April 22, 1911, and reprinted in *Business,* pp. 38–50, on pp. 37–38.

7. LDB, *The Curse of Bigness,* ed. Osmond K. Fraenkel (New York: Viking, 1934), hereafter *Bigness*.

8. LDB, *Other People's Money,* a collection of his articles in 1913 and 1914 for *Harper's Weekly,* was first published by Frederick A. Stokes (New York, 1914), with a foreword by Norman Hapgood, and reprinted by the National Home Library Foundation in 1933; see also LDB, *The Social and Economic Views of Mr. Justice Brandeis,* ed. Alfred Lief (New York: Vanguard, 1930), and *Business.* Jacob de Haas, *Louis D. Brandeis: A Biographical Sketch* (New York: Bloch Publishing Company, 1929), reprints a number of speeches dealing primarily with Zionism.

9. Elizabeth Brandeis Raushenbush, interview with author, September 23, 1980, Madison, Wis.; cf. LDB to Alfred Brandeis, March 20, 1886,

Letters, 1:67-68. The case was *Train* v. *Boston Disinfecting Co.*, 144 Mass. 523 (1887).

10. LDB, *The Public Papers of Louis Dembitz Brandeis in the Jacob and Bertha Goldfarb Library of Brandeis University* (microfilm), Document 9, lecture notes, pp. 321-34.

11. LDB to Matthew Fleming, January 23, 1905, BP, I 1-1. For the story of the insurance fight, see Alpheus T. Mason, *The Brandeis Way* (Princeton, N.J.: Princeton University Press, 1938). Cf. LDB, "Life Insurance: The Abuses and the Remedies," address to the Commercial Club of Boston, October 26, 1905, reprinted in *Business*, pp. 109-53; "Savings Bank Insurance," published in *Collier's Weekly*, September 15, 1906, reprinted in *Business*, pp. 154-81.

12. LDB to Louise Malloch (his secretary), November 4, 1907, BP, NMF 1-H-1; Edward F. McClennen, "Louis D. Brandeis as a Lawyer," *Massachusetts Law Quarterly* 33 (1948): 24.

13. The story of the New Haven battle is told in Henry Lee Staples and Alpheus T. Mason, *The Fall of a Railroad Empire* (Syracuse, N.Y.: Syracuse University Press, 1947). Cf. U.S. Congress, Senate, *Financial Transactions of the New York and Hartford Railroad*, 63d Cong., 2d sess., 1914, S. Doc. 543, pp. 37-38.

14. Quoted in LDB, *The Brandeis Guide to the Modern World*, ed. Alfred Lief (Boston: Little, Brown and Company, 1941), p. 22; LDB to Harold Laski, quoted in *Unpublished Opinions of Mr. Justice Brandeis*, ed. Alexander M. Bickel (Cambridge: Harvard University Press, 1957), p. 120; LDB, "Trusts, Efficiency and the New Party," *Collier's Weekly* 49 (September 14, 1912), reprinted in *Business*, pp. 198-217, on pp. 216-17.

15. Unnaturalness of trusts: LDB, "Competition," in *American Legal News* 44 (January 1913): 5-14, reprinted in *Bigness*, pp. 112-24, on pp. 115-16, and Supreme Court: *Santa Clara County* v. *Southern Pacific Railroad Co.*, 118 U.S. 394 (1886). See Morton J. Horwitz, "Santa Clara Revisited: The Development of Corporate Theory," *West Virginia Law Review* 88 (1985): 173-224; cf. Willard Hurst, *The Legitimacy of the Business Corporation in the Law of the United States, 1780-1970* (Charlottesville: University Press of Virginia, 1970). State governments: see LDB in *New State Ice Co.* v. *Liebmann*, 285 U.S. 262, 280 (1932) (dissenting); federal government: see, e.g., LDB, "Shall We Abandon the Policy of Competition?" *Case and Comment* 18 (1912): 494-96, reprinted in *Bigness*, 104-8, on 104-6; LDB, "The Regulation of Competition against the Regulation of Monopoly," address to the Economic Club, November 1, 1912, reported in *New York Times*, November 2, 1912, reprinted in *Bigness*, 109-11, on p. 109.

16. La Follette to LDB, December 30, 1910, with accompanying transcript, BP, SC 1-2.

17. Mason, *Brandeis Way*, p. 368; LDB, "Interview," *New York Times Annalist*, January 27, 1913, p. 36, reprinted in *Bigness*, p. 41. LDB told Alfred Lief in 1934, "I was always a conservative. Of course, I did not want to conserve the things that were bad. I believed in conserving for the many, not for the few" (Lief, *Brandeis Guide*, p. 211, quoting a conversation with LDB on May 20, 1934).

18. See the discussion of center and periphery enterprises in Thomas K. McCraw, *Prophets of Regulation* (Cambridge: Harvard University Press, 1984), chap. 3.

19. See, e.g., Albro Martin, *Enterprise Denied: Origins of the Decline of American Railroads, 1897–1917* (New York: Columbia University Press, 1970); Thomas K. McCraw, "Rethinking the Trust Question" in McCraw, ed., *Regulation in Perspective: Historical Essays* (Cambridge: Harvard University Press), pp. 1–55; McCraw, *Prophets of Regulation*, chap. 3; and Thomas K. McCraw, "Louis D. Brandeis Reappraised," *American Scholar* 54 (1985): 525–33.

20. McCraw, *Prophets of Regulation*, chap. 3.

21. See LDB, *Other People's Money*, pp. viii–ix.

22. *Standard Oil* v. *United States*, 22 U.S. 1 (1911), LDB to Moses Clapp, June 22, 1911, BP, NMF 43-4.

23. LDB privately called Perkins's testimony "the weakest rot man ever uttered" and said, "I should rejoice to go through the Country on joint debate with him" (LDB to Alice Brandeis, December 14, 1911, Brandeis Family Letters).

24. LDB, "Competition," p. 115.

25. Ibid., pp. 116–17.

26. U.S. Congress, Senate, Committee on Interstate Commerce, *Hearings*, pp. 1146–1291; LDB, "Competition," pp. 112–24; LDB, "Trusts and Efficiency," pp. 198–217; LDB, "Trusts, the Export Trade, and the New Party," *Collier's Weekly* 50 (September 21, 1912), reprinted in *Business*, pp. 218–35; LDB, "The Solution of the Trust Problem," *Harper's*, November 8, 1913, reprinted in *Bigness*, pp. 128–36; and LDB, "Competition That Kills," *Harper's*, November 15, 1913, reprinted in *Business*, pp. 236–54.

27. *Bigness*, p. 116.

28. *Hearings*, and LDB to the editor of the *Boston Globe*, December 2, 1911, BP, NMF 803.

29. LDB to Charles Amidon, July 3, 1912, BP, NMF 40-1, and to Norman Hapgood, July 3, 1912, BP, NMF 53-2. For the Democratic platform, see Arthur Link, *Wilson: The Road to the White House* (Princeton, N.J.: Princeton University Press, 1968), chap. 13.

30. Arthur S. Link, *Woodrow Wilson and the Progressive Era* (New York: Harper and Brothers, 1954), pp. 20–21, 28, 48.

31. LDB to WW, September 30, 1912, *Letters*, 2: 686–94, and Link on memo: Link, *Road*, pp. 491–92. The memo also became the basis for articles by LDB and for editorials in *Collier's*; see LDB, "Trusts and Efficiency," p. 14, and "Trusts and the Export Trade," p. 10. Editorials: LDB to Hapgood, September 4, 1912, BP, NMF 46–3, September 25, 1912, BP, NMF 50–3, and October 2, 1912, BP, NMF 52–2.

32. LDB to Elizabeth Brandeis Raushenbush, April 8, 1926: "It is my hope . . . that *no* other state will try anything very like Savings Bank Insurance for some years to come. It will be better for all that Mass. should have become thoroughly permeated with S.B.I. before it is tried anywhere else" (*Letters*, 5:216).

33. Wilson is quoted in John Milton Cooper, Jr., *The Warrior and the Priest: Woodrow Wilson and Theodore Roosevelt* (Cambridge: Harvard University Press, 1983), p. 120. Wilson's thinking is analyzed and contrasted with that of Roosevelt throughout the volume, but see particularly chapter 14, "The New Nationalism versus the New Freedom." For Wilson's thought generally, see, e.g., Link, *Progressive Era*, and William Diamond, *The Economic Thought of Woodrow Wilson* (Baltimore: Johns Hopkins University Press, 1943).

34. Woodrow Wilson, 6 vols. *A History of the American People* (New York and London: Harper and Brothers, 1922), 5:267–68, and Norman Thomas, "Mr. Wilson's Tragedy and Ours," *World Tomorrow*, March 1921, p. 82; cf. Link, *Road*, pp. 24, 27.

35. Woodrow Wilson, *Congressional Government* (Boston: Houghton, Mifflin, 1885).

36. Woodrow Wilson, *Constitutional Government in the United States* (New York: Columbia University Press, 1908), pp. 68, 82–111, 128, 191.

37. Link, *Progressive Era*, p. 48.

38. LDB on money trust: *Other People's Money*, passim; LDB to WW, June 14, 1913, *Letters*, 3:113–15; Federal Reserve bill: Melvin I. Urofsky, "Wilson, Brandeis and the Trust Issue, 1912–1914," *Mid-America* 49 (1967): 3–28, on p. 18; H. Parker Willis, *The Federal Reserve System* (New York: Ronald Press, 1923), passim; and Link, *Progressive Era*, p. 48.

39. LDB to Franklin K. Lane, December 12, 1913, *Letters*, 3:210–11; on price maintenance: LDB to John Commons, May 27, 1913, BP, NMF 58–1; to William Cox Redfield, May 27, 1913, BP, NMF 58–1; and LDB, testimony, U.S. Congress, House, Committee on Patents, *Hearings*, 62d Cong., 2d sess., 1912, No. 18, pp. 3–25, reprinted in part in LDB, *Social and Economic Views*, pp. 400–403.

40. LDB, *Other People's Money*, pp. 36–37.

41. LDB to Alfred Brandeis, January 23, 1913, BP, M 4–1.

42. Testimony and lobbying: Melvin I. Urofsky, *A Mind of One Piece:*

Brandeis and American Reform (New York: Scribner, 1971), pp. 24–25, 27; Alpheus T. Mason, *Brandeis: A Free Man's Life* (New York: Viking, 1946), p. 402; Link, *Progressive Era*, pp. 71–72; disappointments at FTC and Federal Reserve Board appointments: LDB to Henry French Hollis, November 4, 1914, BP, NMF 68-2; to Charles McCarthy, December 2, 1914, BP, NMF 66-3; to WW, March 6, 1915, BP, NMF 68-2; to George Rublee, March 20 and 29, 1915, BP, NMF 66-3; to Gilson Gardner, September 7, 1915, BP, NMF 66-3; to William Smyth, September 22, 1915, BP, NMF 66-3; and to Charles Crane, October 9, 1915, BP, NMF 66-3.

43. *Hitchman Coal and Coke Co.* v. *Mitchell*, 245 U.S. 229, 263, 271 (1917) (dissenting). Cf. *Duplex Printing Co.* v. *Deering*, 254 U.S. 443, 479 (1921) (dissenting); *Truax* v. *Corrigan*, 257 U.S. 312, 354 (1921) (dissenting); *Bedford Cut Stone* v. *Journeymen Cutter's Association*, 274 U.S. 37, 64 (1927) (dissenting).

44. *Quaker City Cab Co.* v. *Pennsylvania*, 277 U.S. 289, 403, 410–11 (1928) (dissenting).

45. See, e.g., *Pennsylvania Coal Co.* v. *Mahon*, 260 U.S. 393, 416 (1922) (dissenting); *New State Ice Co.* v. *Liebmann*, 285 U.S. 262, 279 (1932) (dissenting); *Liggett* v. *Lee*, 288 U.S. 517, 533 (1933) (dissenting).

46. *Swift* v. *Tyson*, 16 Pet. 1 (1842).

47. *Erie Railroad Co.* v. *Tompkins*, 340 U.S. 64 (1938). Cf. Holmes, dissenting with LDB and Justice Harlan Fiske Stone, in *Black & White Taxi Co.* v. *Brown & Yellow Taxi Co.*, 276 U.S. 518 (1928), at 533.

48. W. Graham Claytor, quoted in Helen Garfield, "Twentieth Century Jeffersonian: Brandeis, Freedom of Speech, and the Republican Revival," *Oregon Law Review* 69 (1990): 527–88, on p. 579. Cf. Henry J. Friendly, "In Praise of *Erie*—and of the New Federal Common Law," *New York University Law Review* 39 (1964): 383–422.

49. See *Ashwander* v. *TVA*, 297 U.S. 288, 341–48 (1936).

50. See, e.g., G. Edward White, *The American Judicial Tradition* (New York: Oxford University Press, 1976), pp. 168–69, 176.

51. *New State Ice Co.* v. *Liebmann*, 285 U.S. 262, 280 (1932) (dissenting).

52. *Hammer* v. *Dagenhart*, 247 U.S. 251, 177 (1918) (dissenting). LDB joined the majority of the Court in striking down a subsequent congressional attempt to use its taxing power to regulate child labor (*Bailey* v. *Drexel Furniture Co.*, 259 U.S. 20 [1922]). It is possible that LDB considered the case to be trumped-up, as his unpublished memorandum in the similar case of *Atherton Mills* v. *Johnston* (295 U.S. 13 [1922]) suggested. See Bickel, *Unpublished Opinions of Mr. Justice Brandeis*, chap. 1. For an interesting critique of this explanation, see Clyde Spillinger, "Reading the Judicial Canon: Alexander Bickel and the Book of Brandeis," *Journal of American History* 79 (June 1992): 125–51.

53. *United States* v. *Constantine*, 296 U.S. 287, 297 (1934) (concurring in the dissent of Cardozo, J.); *Railroad Retirement Board* v. *Alton R.R. Co.*, 295 U.S. 330, 374 (1935) (concurring in the dissent of Hughes, J.); *United States* v. *Butler*, 297 U.S. 1, 78 (1936) (concurring in the dissent of Stone, J.); *Carter* v. *Carter Coal Co.*, 298 U.S. 238 (1936) (concurring in the dissent of Cardozo, J.).

54. First FDR–LDB conversation: Harlan B. Phillips, ed., *Felix Frankfurter Reminisces* (New York: Reynal, 1960), pp. 239–40, and LDB to FF, November 24, 1932, FF–LC, Box 98. For later meetings of the two, see Frances Perkins to FF, April 5, 1933, quoted in Nelson Lloyd Dawson, *Louis D. Brandeis, Felix Frankfurter, and the New Deal* (Hamden, Conn.: Archon Books, 1980), p. 52, and see also pp. 53, 65, 91, 96; LDB to FF, March 13, 1933, FF–LC, Box 28; LDB to FF, April 12, 1933, Urofsky and Levy, *"Half Brother,"* p. 518; to Elizabeth Brandeis Raushenbush, November 17, 1933, *Letters*, 5:526–27; to FF, September 22, 1935, FF–LC, Box 28; Raymond Moley to FF, October 31, 1935, FF–HLS, Box 20; and Arthur M. Schlesinger, Jr., *The Coming of the New Deal* (Boston: Houghton Mifflin, 1958), pp. 236, 328.

55. Bruce Murphy gained an unfortunate measure of publicity by alleging improper behavior on LDB's part because, while he was a judge, he gave FF a regular and supposedly secret "allowance" so that the Harvard Law School professor with a relatively small income could undertake the same kind of public interest activities LDB had enjoyed. See Bruce Allen Murphy, *The Brandeis/Frankfurter Connection* (New York: Oxford University Press, 1982). In fact, there was nothing secret about the arrangement, which FF had mentioned to his Harvard seminars and to various correspondents; see Philippa Strum, *Louis D. Brandeis: Justice for the People* (Cambridge: Harvard University Press, 1984), pp. 373–75, 474–75 nn. 5, 7, 8; Leonard Baker, *Brandeis and Frankfurter: A Dual Biography* (New York: New York University Press, 1984), pp. 242–43; and Lewis J. Paper, "The Not So Sinister Brandeis-Frankfurter Connection," *American Bar Association Journal* 69 (1983): 1860–64. Other scholars had noted the arrangement before Murphy (see, e.g., H. N. Hirsch, *The Enigma of Felix Frankfurter* [New York: Basic Books, 1981], p. 44), and it was in keeping with LDB's similar subsidies to other people, foremost among them Hadassah leader Henrietta Szold. I have suggested that if LDB was guilty of any judicial impropriety, it was his participation in discussions of potential statutes with their authors. Given his admiration for Franklin Roosevelt and what the seventy-six-year-old LDB must have seen as his last chance to affect public policy, Brandeis "may have convinced himself that it was his duty as a citizen to give the state full use of his energy and talents. . . . Nonetheless, one must sadly conclude that, as

Brandeis said in the *Myers* case, dispersion of power is more important to a democracy than is efficiency" (Strum, *Brandeis*, pp. 402-4).

56. Impact on legislation: Thomas Corcoran to FF, October 10, 1933, quoted in Dawson, *Brandeis, Frankfurter, and the New Deal*, pp. 95-96, and see also 94-98; Corcoran to FF, December 30, 1933, LDB to FF, December 30, 1933, LDB to FF, January 10, 1934, cited in ibid., p. 96; Corcoran to FF, November 16, 1933, and December 30, 1933, FF-LC, Box 116; LDB to FF, December 17, 1933, FF-LC, Box 115; LDB to FF, July 26, 1934, Urofsky and Levy, *"Half Brother,"* p. 548; Schlesinger, *New Deal*, pp. 442, 456-57, 466; and Rexford Tugwell, *The Art of Politics as Practiced by Three Great Americans* (New York: Doubleday, 1958), pp. 247-48.

57. He also sent shorter letters to FF containing some of the ideas mentioned in the two statements. See, e.g., LDB to FF, August 3, 1933, and August 3, 1934, Urofsky and Levy, *"Half Brother,"* pp. 526, 550.

58. The Federal Trade Commission was an obvious exception.

59. Shulman memorandum, FF-HLS, 188-8. I am grateful to Prof. H. N. Hirsch for bringing this memorandum to my attention.

60. Laski to Holmes, August 12, 1933, Mark DeWolfe Howe, ed., *The Holmes-Laski Letters* (Cambridge: Harvard University Press, 1953), p. 1448.

61. Shulman memorandum.

62. Ibid. See Elizabeth Raushenbush, "Labor Legislation," in John R. Commons, *History of Labor in the United States*, 4 vols. (New York: A. M. Kelley, 1966), 3:399-700; Paul A. Raushenbush, *The Wisconsin Unemployment Reserve Law* (New York: New York House of Refuge, 1933); and Paul A. Raushenbush, *Unemployment Compensation: Federal-State Cooperation* (Madison: Industrial Commission of Wisconsin, 1943).

63. LDB to FF, August 3, 1933, Urofsky and Levy, *"Half Brother,"* p. 526; Joseph P. Lash, *From the Diaries of Felix Frankfurter* (New York: Norton, 1975), pp. 134, 135; Schlesinger, *Politics of Upheaval*, p. 236; LDB to FF, January 30, 1933, FF-LC, Box 28; LDB to FF, August 3, 1934, Urofsky and Levy, *"Half-Brother,"* p. 550; FF to LDB, August 31, 1934, BP, G 9-2; Dawson, *Brandeis, Frankfurter, and the New Deal*, pp. 30-31, 72, 91; and LDB, "Interlocking Directorates," address to American Academy of Political and Social Sciences, printed in its *Annals* 57 (January 1915): 45-49, and reprinted in *Business*, pp. 320-28.

64. LDB to Elizabeth Brandeis Raushenbush, November 19, 1933, *Letters*, 5:525-28. LDB had been interested in conservation at least since his involvement in the Pinchot-Ballinger hearings of 1910. See chapter 1.

65. See n. 5, this chapter. When LDB wanted to tell FF how little he thought FDR's move to take the United States off the gold standard would do to stop the deflation of American currency, he called it *Kunststücke*. LDB

to FF, April 26, 1933, Urofsky and Levy, *"Half Brother,"* p. 519; cf. to FF, June 13, 1933, October 24, 1933, May 11, 1934, ibid., pp. 523, 532, 545. He added further about the inflation move, "I am at times reminded of the Uncle from India's answer to the private Secretary. When asked by his housekeeper 'Do you believe in spirits?' 'Yes,' said he, 'in moderation.'" LDB to FF, May 14, 1933, ibid., p. 521.

66. Experimentation in states: LDB to Mary McDowell, July 8, 1912, BP, NMF 69-2; savings bank life insurance: LDB to Elizabeth Brandeis Raushenbush, April 8, 1926, *Letters*, 5:216; constitutionality of federal wage laws: speech to Massachusetts American Federation of Labor, printed in *La Follette's Weekly*, October 12, 1912; LDB to John J. Chapman, September 17, 1911, BP, NMF 50-3.

67. Wage law for men: LDB to John C. Barrett, February 24, 1915, BP, NMF, 69-2; wage law for women: LDB, testimony, U.S. Congress, Senate, Commission on Industrial Relations, S. Doc. 415, 64th Cong., 1st sess., 1914, Serial 6936, pp. 7657–81, esp. 7659 (hereafter *Commission*); portions reprinted as "On Industrial Relations" in *Bigness*, pp. 70–95.

68. *Morehead* v. *New York ex rel. Tipaldo*, 298 U.S. 587, 618, 631 (1936) (concurring with Hughes, J., dissenting, and with Stone, J., dissenting). For his defense of the concept of minimum-wage laws, see his argument before the Supreme Court in *Stettler* v. *O'Hara*, 243 U.S. 629 (1914), published in *Survey*, February 6, 1915, pp. 490–94, 521–24, as "The Constitution and the Minimum Wage" and reprinted in *Bigness*, pp. 52–69.

69. *Panama Refining Co.* v. *Ryan*, 293 U.S. 388 (1935); *Schecter* v. *United States*, 295 U.S. 495 (1935); *Louisville* v. *Radford*, 295 U.S. 555 (1935).

70. LDB to FF, November 9 and November 16, 1933, Urofsky and Levy, *"Half Brother,"* pp. 534, 535.

71. *Myers* v. *U.S.*, 272 U.S. 50, 250, 293 (1927) (dissenting).

72. Mason, *Brandeis: Free Man*, pp. 620–21.

73. *McCulloch* v. *Maryland*, 17 U.S. (4 Wheat.) 316 (1819), at 427.

74. Conversation, December 7, 1940, quoted in Lief, *Brandeis Guide*, p. 20.

75. Schlesinger, *Politics of Upheaval*, p. 222, and Nathaniel L. Nathanson, "Mr. Justice Brandeis: A Law Clerk's Recollections of the October Term, 1934," *American Jewish Archives* 15 (1963): 13.

76. Felix Frankfurter, "The Constitution," in Frankfurter, ed., *Mr. Justice Brandeis* (New Haven, Conn.: Yale University Press, 1932), p. 123; Paul A. Freund: "Mr. Justice Brandeis," in Allison Dunham and Philip B. Kurland, eds., *Mr. Justice* (Chicago: University of Chicago, 1956), p. 118; C. Herman Pritchett, *The Roosevelt Court* (New York: Macmillan, 1948), p. 265; James MacGregor Burns, *Roosevelt: The Lion and the Fox* (New York: Harcourt, Brace, 1956), p. 334; and Schlesinger, *Politics of Upheaval*, p. 561.

77. See clipping about television in one of LDB's working folders for *Olmstead*, BP-HLS, 48-7.

Chapter 5. Zionism and the Ideal State

1. LDB, "The Jewish Problem, How to Solve It," address to Conference of Eastern Council of Reform Rabbis, June 1915, New York City, reprinted in Solomon Goldman, ed., *Brandeis on Zionism* (Washington, D.C.: Zionist Organization of America, 1942), pp. 12-35, quotation on p. 34.

2. *Hadashot Haaretz*, July 10, July 11, July 15, July 17, July 20, July 22, July 27, 1919 (I am grateful to Prof. Asher Arian of City University of New York and Haifa University for locating the *Hadashot Haaretz* articles and having them translated); LDB to Alice Brandeis, June 27, July 10, 1919, BP, M 4-3; LDB to Chaim Weizmann, July 20, 1919, *Letters*, 4:418-19; cf. Jacob de Haas, *Louis D. Brandeis: A Biographical Sketch* (New York: Bloch Publishing Company, 1929), pp. 115-17.

3. LDB, in *Jewish Advocate*, December 9, 1910, reprinted as "Jews as a Priest People," in de Haas, *Brandeis*, pp. 151-52.

4. Elizabeth Glendower Evans, "Louis Dembitz Brandeis, Tribune of the People," *Springfield Daily Republican*, May 13, 1931; Benjamin V. Cohen, "Faith in Common Man," *New Palestine*, November 14, 1941, p. 14; Henry Moskowitz, "An Army of Striking Cloakmakers," *Jewish Frontier* 3 (November 1936): 16; and Michael M. Hammer and Samuel Stickles, "An Interview with Louis D. Brandeis," *The Invincible Ideal* 1 (June 1915): 7.

5. Alpheus T. Mason, *Brandeis: A Free Man's Life* (New York: Viking, 1946), p. 443; de Haas, *Brandeis*, pp. 51-52; Alfred Lief, *Brandeis: The Personal History of an American Ideal* (New York: Stackpole, 1936), pp. 278-79; LDB, quoted in Rose G. Jacobs, "Justice Brandeis and Hadassah," *New Palestine*, November 14, 1941, p. 17.

6. Joining organizations, Sokolow, making speeches: Mason, *Brandeis*, pp. 443-44; de Haas, *Brandeis*, pp. 54-55; Lief, *Brandeis*, pp. 279-80; Melvin I. Urofsky, *American Zionism from Herzl to the Holocaust* (Garden City, N.Y.: Doubleday,1975), pp. 62, 67-68.

7. Disheartened by Wilson; reading: LDB to Edwin Alderman, December 15, 1924, Alderman Manuscripts, University of Virginia Library; LDB to Charles McCarthy, November 18, 1914, BP, NMF 11-2; Arthur S. Link, *Wilson: The New Freedom* (Princeton, N.J.: Princeton University Press, 1956), pp. 445-60; Mason, *Brandeis*, pp. 444-45; de Haas, *Brandeis*, p. 53; Lief, *Brandeis*, p. 279; conference: Lief, *Brandeis*, p. 322; de Haas, *Brandeis*, pp. 57-61; Urofsky, *American Zionism*, pp. 119-20; and Elizabeth Brandeis Raushenbush, interview with author, September 23, 1980, Madison, Wis.

8. Philippa Strum, *Louis D. Brandeis: Justice for the People* (Cambridge: Harvard University Press, 1984), chaps. 13–14.

9. Alfred Zimmern, *The Greek Commonwealth* (1912; reprint, Oxford: Clarendon Press, 1931).

10. LDB, remarks accepting the Provisional Executive Committee chairmanship, August 30, 1914, in Goldman, *Brandeis on Zionism*, p. 44.

11. LDB to Stella and Emily Dembitz, May 17, 1926, quoted in Bernard Flexner, *Mr. Justice Brandeis and the University of Louisville* (Louisville, Ky.: University of Louisville Press, 1938), pp. 36–37. The line in *Whitney* is identified by Paul Freund in "Mr. Justice Brandeis: A Centennial Memoir," *Harvard Law Review* 70 (1957): 769, 789. Pnina Lahav, "Holmes and Brandeis: Libertarian and Republican Justifications for Free Speech," *Journal of Law and Politics* 4 (1988): 451–82, on pp. 462–64; William Hard, "Brandeis the Conservative or a 'Dangerous Radical'?" *Philadelphia Public Leader*, May 12, 1916, BP, Clippings Box 2.

12. LDB to Alfred Zimmern, July 21, 1917, Oxford University, Bodleian Library, Zimmern Manuscript Collection, Box 15, no. 73. My gratitude to attorney Burton C. Bernard, who brought the letter to my attention. See also LDB to Alice Brandeis, March 10, 25, and 28, and July 11, 1914, Brandeis Family Letters.

13. Guglielmo Ferrero, *The Greatness and Decline of Rome*, trans. A. Zimmern and H. J. Chaytor, 5 vols. (New York: Putnam, 1914). Cf. LDB to FF, September 1, 1925, *Letters*, 5:185, in which he writes, "In the Roman survey . . . Ferrero (Zimmern's translation) was my entree." Referring to Zimmern: Paul Freund, interview with author, October 28, 1977, Cambridge, Mass.; Mary Kay Tachau, interview with author, June 12, 1980, Louisville, Ky., and Elizabeth Brandeis Raushenbush, interview with author, September 23, 1980. Cf. Dean Acheson, *Morning and Noon* (Boston: Houghton Mifflin, 1965), pp. 50, 96.

14. Urofsky, *American Zionism*, pp. 136–37, 273–74; de Haas, *Brandeis*, p. 113; LDB to Alice, June 27, July 1, 4, 6, and August 1, 1919, BP, M 4–3.

15. Alfred Zimmern, "The Meaning of Nationality," *New Republic*, January 1, 1916, pp. 215–17.

16. LDB, "What Loyalty Demands," November 28, 1905, BP, Misc.; Urofsky, *American Zionism*, pp. 173–94; Yonathan Shapiro, *Leadership of the American Zionist Organization, 1897–1930* (Urbana: University of Illinois Press, 1971), pp. 55–57.

17. Zimmern, *Greek Commonwealth*, p. 432.

18. Ibid., pp. 67, 107, 166, 135, 144, 160.

19. LDB, testimony, Commission on Industrial Relations, p. 7663, reprinted in LDB, *The Curse of Bigness*, ed. Osmond K. Fraenkel (New York:

Viking Press, 1934), p. 81 (hereafter *Bigness*); Zimmern, *Greek Commonwealth*, pp. 260, 387.

20. Zimmern, *Greek Commonwealth*, pp. 19, 39, 43–44 n. 2, 298, 431–34; malaria in Louisville: de Haas, *Brandeis*, p. 116; Goldman, *Brandeis on Zionism*, p. 146; malaria in Palestine: Goldman, *Brandeis on Zionism*, pp. 124, 138.

21. Zimmern, *Greek Commonwealth*, pp. 71, 76–77, 91, 106, 120 n. 1, 122, 123–34, 181–82 n. 1, 258, 280, 298, 309 n. 1, 66.

22. LDB, "Jewish Problem," in Goldman, *Brandeis on Zionism*, p. 28; "To Be a Jew," speech to the Young Men's Hebrew Association of Chelsea, Mass., May 18, 1913, ibid., p. 39; "The Fruits of Zionism," ibid., pp. 50, 57–58; "Palestine Has Developed Jewish Character," address to emergency Palestine economic conference in Washington, D.C., November 24, 1929, ibid., pp. 144–45; Julian Hawthorne, "Brandeis Explains Zionist Plan," *Boston American*, July 1, 1915, BP Scrapbook 2.

23. LDB, "A Call to the Educated Jew," address to conference of the Intercollegiate Menorah Association, published in *Menorah Journal* 1 (1915), in Goldman, *Brandeis on Zionism*, p. 64.

24. Ibid., pp. 64–65, and LDB, "The Pilgrims Had Faith," address to the Second Annual Conference of the Palestine Land Development Council, May 1923, ibid., p. 132.

25. LDB, "Call to the Educated Jew," p. 63.

26. Brandeis has been accused of sexism on the basis of his brief in *Muller v. Oregon* (208 U.S. 412 [1908]), which depicts women as weak, dependent, subordinate, and in special need of protection by the state. In fact, that depiction was a tactical move, and by the time of *Muller* he was a suffragist. Speaking of women and the goal of industrial democracy, he said, "I learned much from them in my work. So from having been of the opinion that we would advance best by leaving voting to the men, I became convinced that we needed all the forces of the community to bring about this advance" (Lief, *Brandeis*, p. 256). He had not grown up believing in the vote for women, but, he said, "My own experience in various movements . . . converted me," and he was convinced that women and men shared a "duty of taking part in public affairs" (LDB to Mrs. F. W. Wile, June 19, 1915, BP, NMF 47-3). Brandeis told audiences at Boston's Tremont Temple and Fanueil Hall that women had to be given the vote, emphasizing that his support resulted from his experiences with the political talent demonstrated by women involved in causes he shared (Lief, *Brandeis*, pp. 340–41, and LDB to Alfred Brandeis, October 22, 1915, BP, M 4-1). See Conclusion of this book.

27. Horace Kallen, "The Faith of Louis Brandeis," *New Palestine*, November 14, 1941, pp. 24–25.

28. Ibid., p. 22.

29. LDB to La Follette, July 29, 1911, BP, NMF 31–1.

30. Ibid.; cf. LDB to Alice Brandeis, July 28, 1911, Brandeis Family Letters.

31. LDB to La Follette, July 29, 1911, BP, NMF 31–1; cf. LDB to Gifford Pinchot, July 29, 1911, BP, NMF 31–1.

32. See de Haas, *Brandeis*, pp. 96–97.

33. By 1930 he was writing about possible urbanization in Palestine and the existence of over 3,000 small factories; LDB to Maurice Beck Hexter, September 7, 1930, BP, Z 42–1.

34. See de Haas, *Brandeis*, pp. 96–97.

35. See, e.g., Shabtai Teveth, *Ben-Gurion and the Palestinian Arabs* (Oxford: Oxford University Press, 1985), pp. 46–85; John Ruedy, "Dynamics of Land Alienation," and David Waines, "The Failure of the National Resistance" in *The Transformation of Palestine*, ed. Ibrahim Abu-Lughod, 2d ed. (Evanston, Ill.: Northwestern University Press, 1987); and Michael J. Cohen, *The Origins and Evolution of the Arab-Zionist Conflict* (Berkeley: University of California Press, 1987), pp. 67–78.

36. See, e.g., LDB, "Jews and Arabs," address to the emergency Palestine economic conference in Washington, D.C., November 24, 1929, printed in Goldman, *Brandeis on Zionism*, pp. 150–53; LDB to Alfred Brandeis, May 2, 1926, BP, M 4–4, and to Stephen Wise, June 2, 1936, *Letters*, 5:571.

37. LDB to various Zionist leaders, 1929, FF–LC, Boxes 161, 162; LDB to Robert Szold, August 19, 1930, and November 11, 1938, *Letters*, 5:449, 604; to Zip Szold, September 16, 1930, BP, Z 42–1; and to Bernard Flexner, April 8, 1940, *Letters*, 5:637.

38. Louis E. Levinthal, *Louis Dembitz Brandeis* (Washington, D.C.: Zionist Organization of America, n.d.), p. 12.

39. The scholars who trace Brandeis's Zionism to his experiences of anti-Semitism are mistaken. He was fortunate in reaching Boston before its xenophobic stage began toward the end of the nineteenth century and was quickly accepted by Boston Brahmin society, both during his Harvard days and the period of his early practice. He gradually moved away from much of Boston society, and it from him, as his interests developed and he began challenging the large-scale concentrated economic wealth upon which much of it depended. Anti-Semitism emerged as no more than a minor theme during the battle over his nomination to the Supreme Court, with most opposition centering upon fear of Brandeis the Progressive Reformer rather than upon Brandeis the Jew. See Alden L. Todd, *Justice on Trial* (New York: McGraw-Hill, 1964). There is every indication that he felt fully accepted by the only parts of society that mattered to him: much of the legal profession,

the press, intellectual circles, the world of the Progressives, and political figures such as Presidents Woodrow Wilson and Franklin Roosevelt. See Strum, *Brandeis*, pp. 225–29; for differing views, however, see Allon Gal, *Brandeis of Boston* (Cambridge: Harvard University Press, 1980), and Robert Burt, *Two Jewish Justices* (Berkeley: University of California Press, 1988).

40. LDB to Alfred Brandeis, December 8 and 12, 1914, BP, M 4-1.

41. Horace Kallen, *Culture and Democracy in the United States* (New York: Boni and Liveright, 1924), p. 30. Asserting that the issue was one of democracy, LDB organized the American Jewish Congress as a Zionist body representative of the American Jewish community. It was created as an alternative and a balance to the largely anti-Zionist, elitist American Jewish Committee. The real issue was perceived by many people, however, as a power struggle between the American Jewish working masses with family backgrounds in Eastern Europe and the comparatively few wealthy American Jews whose origins were in Germany. See Shapiro, *Leadership of the American Zionist Organization*, chap. 4, and Urofsky, *American Zionism*, pp. 171–88.

42. LDB, "Jewish Problem," pp. 24–25.

43. Urofsky, *American Zionism*, p. 267.

44. LDB, "Jewish Problem," p. 25.

45. Ibid., p. 21, quoting W. Allison Philips, "Europe and the Problem of Nationality," *Edinburgh Review*, January 1915, pp. 27–29, and internationalism: LDB, "True Americanism," speech in Faneuil Hall, Boston, July 4, 1915, printed in Goldman, *Brandeis on Zionism*, pp. 3–11, on p. 11.

46. LDB, "An Essential of Lasting Peace," address to the Economic Club of Boston, February 8, 1915, published in *Harper's Weekly*, March 13, 1915, and reprinted in *Bigness*, pp. 267–69.

47. LDB, "Jewish Problem," pp. 13–14.

48. LDB, "The Jewish Problem-How to Solve It," in de Haas, *Brandeis*, p. 177. This paragraph has been omitted in Goldman's *Brandeis on Zionism*.

49. LDB, "Jewish Problem," in Goldman, *Brandeis on Zionism*, p. 18.

50. Ibid., pp. 19–20.

51. Ibid., p. 20.

52. Ibid., p. 19.

53. Ibid., p. 22.

54. Ibid., p. 34.

55. Quoted in Solomon Goldman, ed., *The Words of Justice Brandeis* (New York: Henry Schuman, 1953), pp. 50–51.

56. LDB, "Jewish Problem," in Goldman, *Brandeis on Zionism*, pp. 12–13.

57. LDB, "The Rebirth of the Jewish Nation," address on behalf of the Zionist Provisional Emergency Committee, fall or winter 1914–1915, printed in de Haas, *Brandeis*, p. 163.

Chapter 6. Civil and Economic Liberties

1. *Gilbert v. Minnesota*, 254 U.S. 325, 335 (1920) (dissenting), at 338.

2. See, e.g., Mark A. Graber, *Transforming Free Speech: The Ambiguous Legacy of Civil Libertarianism* (Berkeley: University of California Press, 1991), pp. 90–112.

3. LDB, *The Brandeis Guide to the Modern World*, ed. Alfred Lief (Boston: Little, Brown and Company, 1941), p. 36.

4. *Gilbert v. Minnesota*, 254 U.S. 325, 335 (1920) (dissenting), at 338.

5. Marketplace of ideas: *Abrams v. United States*, 250 U.S. 616, 630–31 (1919) (dissenting); early Holmes: see, e.g., *Commonwealth v. Davis*, 162 Mass. 510 (1895); *Patterson v. Colorado*, 205 U.S. 454 (1907); *Fox v. Washington*, 236 U.S. 273 (1915); cf. Samuel J. Konefsky, *The Legacy of Holmes and Brandeis* (New York: Macmillan, 1956), pp. 185–86, 188–89, and the articles cited in Gerald Gunther, "Learned Hand and the Origins of Modern First Amendment Doctrine: Some Fragments of History," *Stanford Law Review* 27 (1975): 719–73, on p. 720 n. 4.

6. LDB, "Jewish Unity and the Congress," address delivered in Baltimore, Maryland, September 27, 1915, published as a pamphlet by Jewish Congress Organization Committee, reprinted in LDB, *The Curse of Bigness*, ed. Osmond K. Fraenkel (New York: Viking Press, 1934), p. 233 (hereafter *Bigness*); Lief, *Brandeis Guide*, p. 36.

7. *Gilbert v. Minnesota*, at 338.

8. Robert M. Cover, "The Left, the Right and the First Amendment: 1918–1928," *Maryland Law Review* 40 (1981): 377–79.

9. David Riesman, "Notes for an Essay on Justice Brandeis," May 22, 1936, FF-LC, Box 127, p. 2.

10. See Sheldon Novick, *Honorable Justice* (New York: Dell Publishing, 1989), pp. 39–89, and Max Lerner, *The Mind and Faith of Justice Holmes: His Speeches, Essays, Letters, and Judicial Opinions* (New Brunswick, N.J.: Transaction Publishers, 1989), pp. 5–27, including both Lerner's comments and Holmes's writings and speeches about the war. Pnina Lahav has explored the different premises and conclusions embodied in Holmes's and Brandeis's approaches to speech, likening Holmes to Ecclesiastes and Brandeis to Isaiah, in "Holmes and Brandeis: Libertarian and Republic Justifications for Free Speech," *Journal of Law and Politics* 4 (1988): 451–82, on pp. 466–70.

11. Espionage Act of June 15, 1917, c. 30, sec. 3, 40 Stat. 217, 219; *Schenck v. United States*, 249 U.S. 47, 52 (1919).

12. *Frohwerk v. United States*, 249 U.S. 204, 206 (1919).

13. *Schenck v. United States*, at 52.

14. Holmes to Judge Learned Hand, in Gunther, "Origins," p. 757.

15. *Abrams* v. *United States*, 250 U.S. 616, 630 (1919) (dissenting).

16. A complete account of the case, its background, and its impact on free speech litigation is in Richard Polenberg, *Fighting Faiths: The Abrams Case, the Supreme Court, and Free Speech* (New York: Viking, 1987).

17. LDB on *Schenck*: FF, "Memorandum," FF-LC, Box 224, p. 23. The "Memorandum" is a typescript, put together by or for Alexander Bickel, of handwritten notes made by Frankfurter after talks with LDB during the summers of 1922–1926. The originals, mostly in notebooks and difficult to read because of Frankfurter's handwriting, are in BP-HLS, 114–7 and 114–8. For a transcript of them, see Melvin I. Urofsky, "The Brandeis-Frankfurter Conversations," *Supreme Court Review* (1985): 299–339.

18. *Schaefer* v. *United States*, 251 U.S. 466 (1920) (dissenting), at 482, 483, 484–85, 487–92, 494, 495.

19. *Pierce* v. *United States*, 252 U.S. 239 (1920) (dissenting), at 256–63, 264, 272–73.

20. LDB on *Schaefer* and *Pierce*: FF, "Memorandum," pp. 22–23; LDB on *Debs* v. *United States*, 249 U.S. 211 (1919): FF, "Memorandum," p. 23.

21. *Gilbert* v. *Minnesota*, 254 U.S. 325 (1920).

22. Ibid., at 334, 335–36, 342, 343; Holmes's concurrence is at 334.

23. See Mark A. DeWolfe Howe, ed., 2 vols. *The Holmes-Pollock Letters* (Cambridge: Harvard University Press, 1941), January 23, 1921, 2:61. Justice White's dissent in *Gilbert* is at 334. Holmes's disagreement with the Court's use of the clause to negate state legislation can be found in, e.g., *Lochner* v. *New York*, 198 U.S. 45, 74 (1905) (dissenting); *Coppage* v. *Kansas*, 236 U.S. 1, 28 (1915) (dissenting); *Weaver* v. *Palmer Brothers Co.*, 270 U.S. 402, 415 (1926) (dissenting); *Tyson Brothers* v. *Banton*, 273 U.S. 418, 445 (1927) (dissenting); and *Liggett* v. *Baldridge*, 271 U.S. 105, 114 (1928). His willingness to go along with it is evident in *Pennsylvania Coal Co.* v. *Mahon*, in which Holmes wrote for the Court, striking down a state law that he regarded as a violation of a state contract with a mining company, and Brandeis wrote as the sole dissenter, arguing that the law at issue was a legitimate use of the state's police power (*Pennsylvania Coal Co.* v. *Mahon*, 260 U.S. 393 [1922]; LDB's dissent is at 416). On the disputes over property rights and due process, cf. the discussion of *Bullock* v. *Florida*, 254 U.S. 513 (1921) in Alexander M. Bickel, ed., *The Unpublished Opinions of Mr. Justice Brandeis* (Cambridge: Harvard University Press, 1957), chap. 10.

24. *Gilbert* v. *Minnesota* (dissenting), at 343.

25. Walton H. Hamilton, "The Jurist's Art," in Felix Frankfurter, ed., *Mr. Justice Brandeis* (New Haven, Conn.: Yale University Press, 1932), 170–92, on p. 185.

26. *Meyer* v. *Nebraska*, 262 U.S. 390 (1923); Holmes's dissent is in the companion case of *Bartels* v. *Iowa*, 262 U.S. 404 (1923), at 412.

27. FF, "Memorandum," pp. 19, 20–21.

28. Ibid., p. 20.

29. *Gitlow* v. *New York*, 268 U.S. 652 (1925), at 666.

30. See, e.g., *Near* v. *Minnesota*, 284 U.S. 697 (1931); *DeJonge* v. *Oregon*, 299 U.S. 353 (1937); *Cantwell* v. *Connecticut*, 310 U.S. 296 (1940); *Adamson* v. *California*, 332 U.S. 46 (1947); *NAACP* v. *Alabama*, 357 U.S. 449 (1958); *Mapp* v. *Ohio*, 367 U.S. 643 (1961); *Gideon* v. *Wainright*, 372 U.S. 335 (1963); and *Argersinger* v. *Hamlin*, 407 U.S. 25 (1972), 314.

31. *Gitlow* v. *New York*, 268 U.S. 652, 673 (1925) (dissenting).

32. *Whitney* v. *California*, 274 U.S. 357, 372 (1927) (concurring).

33. See Vincent Blasi, "The First Amendment and the Ideal of Civil Courage: The Brandeis Opinion in *Whitney v. California*," *William and Mary Law Review* 29 (Summer 1988): 653–97, on pp. 656–57.

34. *Whitney* v. *California*, 274 U.S. 357 (1927).

35. Ibid., at 371–72; overruled in *Brandenburg* v. *Ohio*, 395 U.S. 444, 449 (1969).

36. Attorneys Walter Nelles and Walter Pollak, who had unsuccessfully argued the *Gitlow* case, made different constitutional arguments in *Whitney*: that the law did not provide a standard of guilt and therefore was void for vagueness, that it violated the equal protection clause by penalizing advocacy of violence to change industrial ownership but not advocacy of violence to maintain it in its current form, and that although *Gitlow* had upheld prohibitions on advocacy of violence, the New York statute involved in that case had not made criminally liable people such as Ms. Whitney who merely associated with those advocating violence. See *Whitney*, at 368–70.

37. *Whitney*, at 373.

38. In fact, she was released on bail after ten days' imprisonment, when three physicians testified about her poor physical condition; see Blasi, "First Amendment," p. 659.

39. Ibid., pp. 696–97.

40. *Whitney*, at 373.

41. Charles A. Miller, *The Supreme Court and the Uses of History* (Cambridge: Belknap Press of Harvard University, 1969), p. 99.

42. See Blasi, "First Amendment," pp. 679–96. The entire article should be read by anyone interested in Brandeis's thought or in his impact on free speech jurisprudence.

43. *Whitney*, at 376.

44. *Whitney*, at 374.

45. Ibid., and *Gilbert* v. *Minnesota*, at 338.

46. For the courts' reliance upon Brandeis's *Whitney* concurrence, however, see Blasi, "First Amendment," pp. 682–83.

47. *Ruthenberg* v. *Michigan*, 273 U.S. 782 (1927); LDB's notes for the case are in FF–HLS, 44–5. Cf. Cover, "The Left, the Right and the First Amendment," pp. 384–85.

48. Alvin Johnson, quoted in Bickel, *Unpublished Opinions*, p. 163, and Donald Richberg, "The Industrial Liberalism of Mr. Justice Brandeis," in Frankfurter, *Mr. Justice Brandeis*, 130–40, on p. 137.

49. Saul K. Padover, *Jefferson* (New York: New American Library, 1952), p. 186; John Dewey, *How We Think, A Restatement of the Relation of Reflective Thinking to the Educative Process* (Boston: D.C. Heath, 1933); Dewey, *Reconstruction in Philosophy* (New York: Henry Holt and Company, 1920), pp. 186, 209; Dewey, *Education Today*, ed. Joseph Ratner (New York: Greenwood Press, 1940), pp. 104–5, 157–63, 258–59, 359–70; and William H. Kilpatrick, John Dewey et al., *The Educational Frontier* (New York: Century Company, 1933), pp. 318–19.

50. Richard P. Adelstein, "Deciding for Bigness: Constitutional Choice and the Growth of Firms," *Constitutional Political Economy* 2 (1991): 7–30, on pp. 23–27.

51. LDB, "Hours of Labor," address to first annual meeting of the Civil Federation of New England, January 11, 1906, reprinted in LDB, *Business — A Profession*, ed. Ernest Poole (Boston: Small, Maynard, 1914), pp. 28–36, on pp. 32–33 (hereafter *Business*). "Democratic methods": LDB to Norman Hapgood, quoted in Alpheus T. Mason, *Brandeis: A Free Man's Life* (New York: Viking, 1946), p. 520.

52. LDB to Edward Filene, June 1, 1901, BP, NMF 2–5.

53. Letters to supporters: see, e.g., LDB to James R. Carter, March 24, 1900; to Laurence Minot, April 16, 1900; to Morton Prince, May 18, 1900; to Carter, January 28, 1901; to Minot, February 15, 1901; to Charles R. Saunders, June 4, 1901; to Morton Prince, June 6, 1901; asking others for support: to Jerome Jones, March 24, 1900; to Edward A. Clement, April 18, 1900; to Arthur A. Maxwell, April 24, 1900; to John E. Parry, May 6, 1901; to William Schofield, May 27, 1901; and to Guy W. Currier, June 8, 1901, BP, NMF 2–5.

54. LDB to Alfred Brandeis, November 30, 1906, *Letters*, 1:499, and to Alfred, January 3, 1907, BP, M 2–4.

55. LDB to Norman Hapgood, January 10, 1906, BP, NMF 10–5, and May 28, 1906, BP, NMF 10–1; to Hapgood, July 14, 1906, and June 25, 1906, *Letters*, 1:453, 448–49.

56. See Mason, *Brandeis*, pp. 240, 280–81; Alfred Lief, *Brandeis: The Personal History of an American Ideal* (New York: Stackpole,1936), p. 163; Philippa

Strum, *Louis D. Brandeis: Justice for the People* (Cambridge: Harvard University Press, 1984), pp. 134–35; and "Real Chorus": LDB to Alice Brandeis, February 20, 1910, LC–FF.

57. LDB to Robert La Follette, June 13, 1910, BP, NMF 29-3; to Felix Frankfurter, June 14, 1910, BP, NMF 29-4; to Amos Pinchot, June 14, 1910, BP, NMF 28-3; to Ray Stannard Baker, June 24, 1910, BP, NMF 2904; and to Finley Peter Dunne, June 24, 1910, BP, NMF 1904.

58. Strum, *Brandeis*, pp. 156–57.

59. Ibid., pp. 199–202.

60. Among the matters LDB mentioned to Frankfurter that he thought should be written about were government cancellation of naturalization (LDB to FF, September 16, 1923, FF–LC), limitations on the rights of Japanese immigrants to citizenship and land ownership (November 20, 1923, FF–HLS), workman's compensation laws (February 25, 1924, October 15, 1926, and March 16, 1928, FF–HLS), tax exemptions of charitable organizations (December 21, 1926, FF–HLS), "the departures in practice from the American ideals of liberty & equality" (July 9, 1927, FF–HLS), unemployment (March 29, 1928, FF–HLS), equal taxation of intrastate and interstate commerce (June 15, 1928, FF–HLS), wiretapping (June 15, 1928, FF–HLS), illegal police action (June 15, 1929, FF–HLS), the difference between wholesale and retail prices (February 2, 1931, in Melvin I. Urofsky and David Levy, eds., *"Half Brother, Half Son": The Letters of Louis D. Brandeis to Felix Frankfurter* [Norman: University of Oklahoma Press, 1991], p. 452), excessive fees received by railroad lawyers and bankers (January 6, January 26, and February 2, 1931, Urofsky and Levy, *"Half Brother,"* pp. 449, 451, 453), and salaries paid to officers of banks, utilities, and other large corporations (July 12, 1931, Urofsky and Levy, *"Half Brother,"* p. 496). Other such letters, too numerous to be cited individually, can be found throughout *"Half Brother."*

61. *Near* v. *Minnesota*, 283 U.S. 697 (1931); oral argument: *New York Times*, January 31, 1931.

62. *New York Times*, January 31, 1931.

63. *Times* v. *Sullivan*, 376 U.S. 254 (1964).

64. LDB and Samuel D. Warren, Jr., "The Right to Privacy," *Harvard Law Review* 4 (1890–1891): 193; Roscoe Pound to Sen. William Chilton, included in letters printed in U.S. Congress, Senate, Committee on the Judiciary, *Nomination of Louis D. Brandeis*, 64th Cong., 1st sess., 1916.

65. LDB and Warren, "Right to Privacy," p. 193, quoting Thomas M. Cooley, *Cooley on Torts*, 2d ed. (Chicago: Callaghan, 1875), p. 29, and "Most influential": P. Allan Dionisopoulos and Charles Ducat, *The Right to Privacy* (St. Paul, Minn.: West Publishing Company, 1976), p. 20. For a far less

laudatory appraisal of the article's impact, see James H. Barron, "Warren and Brandeis, '*The Right to Privacy*,' *Harvard Law Review* 4 (1890): 193: Demystifying a Landmark Citation," *Suffolk University Law Review* 13 (1979): 875. William B. Prosser's "Privacy," *California Law Review* 48 (1960): 383, contains a thorough discussion of the article and its impact on state legislation. For a useful explication of the article, as well as a detailed and interesting study of the general and specific events, social forces, and legal dicta reflected in it, see two articles by Dorothy J. Glancy, "The Invention of the Right to Privacy," *Arizona Law Review* 21 (1979): 1, and "Privacy and the Other Miss M," *Northern Illinois University Law Review* 10 (1990): 401. Cf. "Symposium: The Right to Privacy One Hundred Years Later," *Case Western Reserve Law Review* 41 (1991): 643–928.

66. *Casey* v. *United States*, 276 U.S. 413 (1928).

67. Ibid., at 421–25.

68. *Olmstead* v. *United States*, 277 U.S. 438 (1928).

69. *Olmstead* v. *United States*, 277 U.S. 438, 471 (1928) (dissenting), at 474, 475–76.

70. Ibid., at 473–77; "Television Sets in Homes Reproduce Studio Scenes," article from unnamed Schenectady newspaper; "Memorandum" dated February 23, 1928, p. 10, BP–HLS, 48–7.

71. *Olmstead*, at 472, quoting Marshall in *McCulloch* v. *Maryland*, 17 U.S. (4 Wheat.) 316, 409 (1819).

72. *Truax* v. *Corrigan*, 257 U.S. 312, 376 (1921).

73. For a discussion of the relationship Brandeis and Warren saw among individualism, human dignity, and the kind of self-reliance emphasized by Emerson, see Glancy, "Invention of the Right to Privacy," pp. 24–25.

74. *Olmstead*, at 478, 479.

75. *Burdeau* v. *McDowell*, 256 U.S. 465, 476–77 (1921) (dissenting).

76. *Olmstead*, at 485.

77. LDB to FF, June 15, 1928, *Letters*, 5:345, and standards: Fannie Brandeis's notes of a 1931 conversation, BP, Addendum, Box 1.

78. LDB to FF, *Letters*, June 25, July 2, 1926, 5: 226, 228, and nauseating: LDB to FF, *Letters*, November 26, 1920, 4:510.

79. See, e.g., *On Lee* v. *United States*, 343 U.S. 747 (1952); *Griswold* v. *Connecticut*, 381 U.S. 479 (1965); *Katz* v. *United States*, 389 U.S. 347 (1967); *Roe* v. *Wade*, 410 U.S. 113 (1973); *Cruzan* v. *Director*, 497 U.S. 261 (1990); *In re President of Georgetown College*, 331 F.2d 1000 (D.C. Cir. 1964); *In Re T. W.*, 551 So. 2d 1186 (1989); *Stall* v. *Florida*, 470 S. 2d 257 (1990); and *American Academy of Pediatrics* v. *Van De Kamp*, 214 Cal. App. 3d 831 (Ct. App. 1989).

80. See, e.g., the constitutions of the following states: Alaska, Art. 1,

Sec. 22; Arizona, Art. 2, Sec. 8; California, Art. 1, Sec. 1; Florida, Art. 1, Sec. 23; Hawaii, Art. 1, Sec. 6, 7; Illinois, Art. 1, Sec. 6, 12; Louisiana, Art. 1, Sec. 5; Montana, Art. 2, Sec. 10; South Carolina, Art. 1, Sec. 10; and Washington, Art. 1, Sec. 7. In many cases the writers of the constitution's privacy provision credit Brandeis directly. See, e.g., Patricia Dore, "Of Rights Lost and Gained," *Florida State University Law Review* 6 (1978): 652–53. I am grateful to attorney Barney Rosenstein for some of the information in this note.

81. LDB to Alice Brandeis, March 14, 1910, FF-LC.

82. See Conclusion of this book.

83. *Plessy v. Ferguson*, 163 U.S. 537, 559 (1896) (dissenting).

84. See LDB, *Business*, p. xi.

85. See Solomon Goldman, ed., *The Words of Justice Brandeis* (New York: Henry Schuman, 1953), pp. 50–51.

86. Strum, *Brandeis*, pp. 332–34; see letters throughout Urofsky and Levy, *"Half Brother."*

87. *Buchanan v. Warley*, 245 U.S. 60 (1917); *Moore v. Dempsey*, 261 U.S. 86 (1923); *Wan v. United States*, 266 U.S. 1 (1924); *Powell v. Alabama*, 287 U.S. 45 (1932); *Norris v. Alabama*, 294 U.S. 587 (1924); *Hollins v. Oklahoma*, 295 U.S. 394 (1935); and *Hale v. Kentucky*, 303 U.S. 613 (1938).

88. *South Covington v. Kentucky*, 252 U.S. 399 (1920), and *Gong Lum v. Rice*, 275 U.S. 278 (1927); cf. *Corrigan v. Buckley*, 271 U.S. 323 (1926).

89. LDB's letters to FF about racism against Chinese in the United States suggest this may be the case. See, e.g., LDB to FF, September 16, 1927, FF-HLS.

90. *Nixon v. Condon*, 286 U.S. 73 (1932); *Nixon v. Herndon*, 274 U.S. 536 (1927); and *Missouri ex rel. Gaines v. Canada*, 305 U.S. 337 (1938). Cf. *Grovey v. Townsend*, 295 U.S. 45 (1936), and *New Negro Alliance v. Grocery Co.*, 303 U.S. 552 (1938).

91. See Mason, *Brandeis*, p. 91.

92. LDB, "Efficiency and Social Ideals," *The Independent*, November 30, 1914, p. 327, reprinted in *Bigness*, p. 51.

93. Ibid. (emphasis added).

94. A more recent formulation of this idea is in Charles Black, "Further Reflections on the Constitutional Justice of Livelihood," *Columbia Law Review* 86 (1986): 1103–17.

95. LDB, "True Americanism," speech in Faneuil Hall, Boston, July 4, 1915, printed in Solomon Goldman, ed., *Brandeis on Zionism* (Washington, D.C.: Zionist Organization of America, 1942), pp. 3–11.

96. Ibid., p. 5.

97. Ibid., p. 6.

98. Shulman memorandum, FF–HLS, 188–8; LDB to Elizabeth Brandeis Raushenbush, November 19, 1933, *Letters*, 5: 527–28; to FF, August 3, 1933, and August 3, 1934, Urofsky and Levy, *"Half Brother,"* 526, 550; FF to LDB, August 31, 1934, BP, G 9–2; and Nelson Lloyd Dawson, *Louis D. Brandeis, Felix Frankfurter, and the New Deal* (Hamden, Conn.: Archon Books, 1980), pp. 30–31, 72, 91; TVA: Shulman memorandum.

99. LDB referred to the "Civil Conservation Camps." LDB to FF, August 3, 1933, Urofsky and Levy, *"Half Brother,"* p. 526; cf. LDB to Fannie Brandeis, April 20, 1939, *Letters*, 5:616–17.

100. LDB, "True Americanism," p. 6.

101. LDB, "Hours of Labor," p. 32.

102. LDB, "True Americanism," p. 6.

103. LDB, "The Democracy of Business," address to the United States Chamber of Commerce, February 5, 1914, printed in *Bigness*, pp. 137–42, on p. 141. Whether this kind of information constitutes "education" is a nice question, but Brandeis used the word. At another moment, referring to the Department of Labor and Commerce and the Department of the Interior as well as the Department of Agriculture, he used the word "information" to describe the literature disseminated by the government. He went on to call for the establishment of a federal Experimental Station in Railroad Economies that would investigate the best way to achieve railroad efficiency and to provide that information to the railroads. LDB, statement to the Hadley Railroad Securities Commission, March 6, 1911, published as "The Best Solution is a Government Bureau," *Engineering Magazine*, October 1911, pp. 16–18, reprinted in *Bigness*, pp. 192–94, on pp. 193–94.

104. LDB, "True Americanism," pp. 6–7.

105. Ibid., p. 7.

106. Ibid., p. 8.

107. Ibid., p. 9.

108. For a more recent theorist making this point, see Virginia Held, *Rights and Goods* (Chicago: University of Chicago Press, 1989).

109. FF, "Memorandum," BP–HLS, 114–9, p. 19.

110. See chapter 2.

CONCLUSION. THE INDIVIDUAL AND THE DEMOCRATIC STATE

1. "How Far Have We Come on the Road to Industrial Democracy? — an Interview," *La Follette's Weekly Magazine*, May 24, 1913, p. 5, reprinted in LDB, *The Curse of Bigness*, ed. Osmond K. Fraenkel (New York: Viking Press, 1934), p. 45 (hereafter *Bigness*).

2. At least two major strands of thought feed into the American notion of

social contract. One is the theological, exemplified by the Mayflower Compact of 1620; the other comes from English writers such as Thomas Hobbes, *Leviathan*, ed. C. B. Macpherson (Middlesex: Penguin Books, 1968), and John Locke, *Second Treatise of Government*, ed. C. B. Macpherson (Indianapolis: Hacket Publishing Company, 1980). Cf. C. B. Macpherson, *The Political Theory of Possessive Individualism: Hobbes to Locke* (Oxford: Clarendon Press, 1962), and George Mace, *Locke, Hobbes, and The Federalist Papers* (Carbondale: Southern Illinois University Press, 1979). If Isaac Kramnick is correct and Locke was replaced in American ideology with a republican revisionism that emphasized civic humanism rather than liberalism, Brandeis perhaps can be seen as an interesting combination of two trends in American thought. Isaac Kramnick, *Republicanism and Bourgeois Radicalism: Political Ideology in Late Eighteenth-Century England and America* (Ithaca, N.Y.: Cornell University Press, 1990).

3. See the Declaration of Independence; cf. John Phillip Reid, *Constitutional History of the American Revolution: The Authority of Rights* (Madison: University of Wisconsin Press, 1986), and Carl L. Becker, *The Declaration of Independence* (New York: Knopf, 1922). Although Becker's book may be somewhat dated, it makes the important argument that "the Declaration, in its form, in its phraseology, follows closely certain sentences in Locke's second treatise on government" (p. 27).

4. See, e.g., James MacGregor Burns, *The Vineyard of Liberty* (New York: Knopf, 1982), pp. 50–51, 55, 57, 59.

5. Speech: see, e.g., cases discussed in chapter 6; *Dennis* v. *United States*, 341 U.S. 494 (1951); religion: see, e.g., *Reynolds* v. *United States*, 98 U.S. 145 (1879); *Goldman* v. *Weinberger*, 475 U.S. 503 (1986); and *Employment Division* v. *Smith*, 494 U.S. 872 (1990).

6. Thomas Jefferson, *Writings*, ed. Paul Leicester, 10 vols. (New York: G. P. Putnam's Sons, 1892–1899), 7:451.

7. Hobbes, *Leviathan*, part 1, chap. 13, p. 186.

8. See, e.g., LDB to Alvin Saunders Johnson, April 7, 1911, *Letters*, 2:421; to Benjamin Barr Lindsey, April 25, 1912, *Letters*, 2:603–10; to editor of *Survey* (April 1911) in *Letters*, 2:427; to Charles Clifford, July 11, 1912, and July 16, 1912, BP, NMF 51-3.

9. LDB, "Industrial Cooperation," address to the Filene Co-operative Association, Boston, May 1905, published in *Filene Association Echo*, May 1905, reprinted in *Bigness*, pp. 35–37, on p. 35.

10. LDB testimony, U.S. Congress, Senate, Commission on Industrial Relations, S. Doc. 415, 64th Cong., 1st sess., 1914, Serial 6936, pp. 7657–81 (hereafter *Commission*), portions reprinted as "On Industrial Relations" in *Bigness*, pp. 70–95, on p. 72.

11. LDB's actual words referred to "the contrast between our political liberty and our industrial absolutism." See *Commission*, in *Bigness*, p. 72.

12. See chapter 1.

13. *Adair* v. *United States*, 208 U.S. 161 (1908); *Coppage* v. *Kansas*, 236 U.S. 1 (1915); and *Hitchman Coal and Coke Co.* v. *Mitchell*, 245 U.S. 232 (1917).

14. LDB, address delivered to Boston Typothetae, April 21, 1904, printed as "The Employers and Trades Unions," in LDB, *Business—A Profession*, ed. Ernest Poole (Boston: Small, Maynard, 1914), pp. 13–27, on pp. 24, 25 (hereafter *Business*). Cf. Poole, in *Business*, p. lv.

15. Locke, *Second Treatise on Government*, pp. 70–75.

16. *Commission*, in *Bigness*, pp. 72–73.

17. Ibid., p. 73.

18. *Myers* v. *United States*, 272 U.S. 52, 240 (1926) (dissenting); *Schechter* v. *United States*, 295 U.S. 495 (1935); and *Rathbun* v. *United States*, 295 U.S. 602 (1935).

19. "Efficiency and Social Ideals," statement in *The Independent*, November 30, 1914, p. 327, reprinted in *Bigness*, p. 51.

20. See, e.g., his mention of Plato and Aristotle in Solomon Goldman, ed., *The Words of Justice Brandeis* (New York: Henry Schuman, 1953), p. 48.

21. See, e.g., LDB to Adolph Brandeis, November 13, 1905, *Letters*, 1: 371; to Alfred Brandeis, October 12, 1908, BP, M 2–4; and to FF, June 16, 1922, in Melvin I. Urofsky and David Levy, eds., *"Half Brother, Half Son": The Letters of Louis D. Brandeis to Felix Frankfurter* (Norman: University of Oklahoma Press, 1991), p. 103.

22. Alpheus T. Mason, *Brandeis: A Free Man's Life* (New York: Viking, 1946), p. 41.

23. John Dewey, *The Influence of Darwin on Philosophy and Other Essays in Contemporary Thought* (New York: Henry Holt and Company, 1910), p. 274.

24. Will Durant, *The Story of Philosophy* (New York: Simon and Schuster, 1926).

25. LDB to Felix Frankfurter, January 7, 1927, FF-HLS.

26. LDB, "Big Business and Industrial Liberty," address at Ethical Culture Meeting House, Boston, February 10, 1912, reported in the *New York Times*, February 11, 1912, reprinted in *Bigness*, p. 38.

27. LDB, "Organized Labor and Efficiency," address before the Boston Central Labor Union, April 2, 1911; *Survey*, April 22, 1911; *Business*, pp. 38–50.

28. LDB, "Organized Labor and Efficiency," p. 39.

29. Goldman, *Words of Brandeis*, p. 79. Cf. LDB, "True Americanism," speech in Faneuil Hall, Boston, July 4, 1915, printed in Solomon Goldman,

ed., *Brandeis on Zionism* (Washington, D.C.: Zionist Organization of America, 1942), pp. 3–11, on p. 7.

30. Goldman, *Words of Brandeis*, p. 46.

31. See chapter 6. It is not known when Brandeis first read Jefferson. He referred to him at least as early as 1904 (*Boston Globe*, November 16, 1904, reporting LDB speech given that day, BP, Clippings Box 1) and, finally visiting Monticello in 1927, wrote to his brother, "Returned home last evening with deepest conviction of T. J.'s greatness. He was a civilized man" (LDB to Alfred Brandeis, September 22, 1927, BP, M 4–4). Speaking of his proudest creation, savings-bank insurance, Brandeis said that Jefferson "would have had no difficulty in appreciating S.B.I." (LDB to Alice Harriet Grady, September 22, 1927, *Letters*, 5:302).

32. See Poole, in *Business*, p. liii.

33. Ibid.

34. Ibid., p. liv.

35. Ibid.; Goldman, *Words of Brandeis*, p. 58, repeating a conversation with LDB.

36. Mason, *Brandeis*, p. 372.

37. FF, "Memorandum," FF–LC, Box 224, BP–HLS 114–7, 114–8. See Melvin I. Urofsky, "The Brandeis-Frankfurter Conversations," *Supreme Court Review* (1985): 299–339; cf. Philippa Strum, *Louis D. Brandeis: Justice for the People* (Cambridge: Harvard University Press, 1984), pp. 369–71.

38. See Poole, in *Business*, p. lv.

39. LDB, address to National Congress of Charities and Correction, Boston, June 8, 1911, published as "The Road to Social Efficiency," in *Outlook*, June 10, 1911; reprinted in *Business*, pp. 51–64, on p. 53; emphasis added.

40. Shulman memorandum, FF–HLS 188–8.

41. FF, "Memorandum," BP–HLS 114–9, p. 19. LDB, "Hours of Labor," address to the first Annual meeting of the Civil Federation of New England, January 11, 1906, reprinted in *Business*, pp. 28–36; see especially p. 32.

42. LDB, "True Americanism," p. 8, and LDB, "Hours of Labor," p. 31.

43. Arthur M. Schlesinger, Jr., *The Coming of the New Deal* (Boston: Houghton, Mifflin, 1959), pp. 301–14.

44. Ibid. Cf. LDB to Elizabeth Brandeis Raushenbush, October 14, 1939, *Letters*, 5: 625–26.

45. LDB to La Follette, July 29, 1911, BP, NMF 31–1.

46. LDB, "Industrial Cooperation," in *Bigness*, p. 35.

47. Meeting Emerson: James Bradley Thayer to LDB, March 10, 1878, BP, Scrapbook 1; LDB to Alice Goldmark, October 13, 1890, *Letters*, 1: 93, saying that "one of the first good things" Thayer did for him "was to

ask me to his home to meet Emerson;" Mason, *Brandeis*, p. 43; for the quotation from Henry James, see BP, NMF 17–5. LDB does not appear to have read contemporary philosophy much after his early exposure to it. Years later he sent a passage from James to Felix Frankfurter, but it was at the suggestion of Alice Brandeis; see LDB to FF, March 4, 1928, FF–HLS. Other authors: Mason, *Brandeis*, pp. 38–39.

48. Locke, *Second Treatise of Government*, chap. 5 paragraph 3.

49. LDB, "Efficiency and Social Ideals," p. 51; cf. Locke, *Second Treatise of Government*, chap. 2, p. 19, and chap. 6, p. 6.

50. John Stuart Mill, *Principles of Political Economy*, ed. W. J. Ashley (London: Longmans, Green, 1909).

51. John Stuart Mill, *Socialism* (New York: Humboldt, 1891).

52. John Stuart Mill, *The Subjection of Women* (New York: Source Book Press, 1970).

53. Assistant attorney general: LDB to FF, January 8, 1933, in Urofsky and Levy, *"Half Brother, Half Son,"* p. 506; Perkins: LDB to FF, February 23, 1922, FF–LC, Box 28.

54. Meeting: Alfred Lief, *Brandeis: The Personal History of an American Ideal* (New York: Stackpole, 1936), p. 183; contest: LDB to Agnes E. Ryan, September 30, 1915, BP, NMF 47–3; speaking with daughter: Lief, *Brandeis*, p. 339; LDB to Alfred Brandeis, October 22, 1915, BP, M 4–1; experience: LDB to Mrs. F. W. Wile, June 19, 1915, BP, NMF 47–3; cf. LDB to Caroline Hibbard, March 18, 1913, BP, NMF 37–3; encouragement of daughters' careers: Elizabeth Brandeis Raushenbush, interview with author, September 24, 1980, Madison, Wis.

55. This cursory placing of Brandeis in the line of social contract theorists is just that. It is not meant to be comprehensive, nor does it refer to post-Brandeisian theorists such as John Rawls or Ronald Dworkin, with some of whose ideas (e.g., Rawls's theme of liberty as the preeminent social value, Dworkin's differentiation between constitutional "concepts" and "conceptions") Brandeis would no doubt have agreed while finding others completely unacceptable (e.g., Rawls's idea of an agreed-upon diminution of individual liberty and equality, Dworkin's insistence that equality rather than liberty is the core value of the Constitution). See John Rawls, *A Theory of Justice* (Cambridge: Harvard University Press, 1971), and Ronald Dworkin, *Taking Rights Seriously* (Cambridge: Harvard University Press, 1978).

56. Lief, *Brandeis*, p. 209, quoting Hutchins Hapgood in the *New York Globe*, January 8, 1912.

57. Donald Richberg, "The Industrial Liberalism of Mr. Justice Brandeis," in Felix Frankfurter, ed., *Mr. Justice Brandeis* (New Haven, Conn.: Yale University Press, 1932), 130–40, on p. 137.

SELECTED BIBLIOGRAPHY

Numerous secondary sources are listed in the notes, but only primary sources and those secondary sources that were relied on heavily are cited here. The major bibliographic works are Roy M. Mersky, *Louis Dembitz Brandeis, 1856–1941, A Bibliography* (1958; reprint, New Haven, Conn.: Yale Law School, 1987), and Gene Teitelbaum, *Justice Louis D. Brandeis: A Bibliography of Writings and Other Materials on the Justice* (Littleton, Colo.: Fred B. Rothman and Company, 1988).

ARCHIVES

Brandeis, Louis Dembitz, et al. Family Letters. Goldfarb Library, Brandeis University. Waltham, Massachusetts.
———. Papers. Harvard Law School. Cambridge, Massachusetts.
———. Papers. University of Louisville. Louisville, Kentucky.
———. *The Public Papers of Louis Dembitz Brandeis in the Jacob and Bertha Goldfarb Library of Brandeis University*, comp. Abram L. Sachar and William M. Goldsmith. Microfilm. Brandeis University. Waltham, Massachusetts.
Evans, Elizabeth Glendower. Papers. Schlesinger Library, Radcliffe College. Cambridge, Massachusetts.
Frankfurter, Felix. Papers. Harvard Law School. Cambridge, Massachusetts.
———. Papers. Library of Congress. Washington, D.C.

AUTHOR'S INTERVIEWS

Austern, Thomas H. October 22, 1978. Washington, D.C.
Baldwin, Roger. May 19, 1981. Telephone interview.

Freund, Paul A. October 28, 1977. Cambridge, Massachusetts.
Hurst, Willard H. September 24, 1980. Madison, Wisconsin.
Raushenbush, Elizabeth Brandeis. September 23 and 24, 1980. Madison, Wisconsin.
Reisman, David. December 4, 1977. Cambridge, Massachusetts.
Tachau, Mary Kay. June 12, 1980. Louisville, Kentucky.

WORKS BY LOUIS DEMBITZ BRANDEIS

The Brandeis Guide to the Modern World, ed. Alfred Lief. Boston: Little, Brown and Company, 1941.
Brandeis on Zionism, ed. Solomon Goldman. Washington, D.C.: Zionist Organization of America, 1942.
Business — A Profession, ed. Ernest Poole. Boston: Small, Maynard, 1914.
The Curse of Bigness, ed. Osmond K. Fraenkel. New York: Viking Press, 1934.
Other People's Money and How the Bankers Use It. New York: Stokes, 1914.
"The Right to Privacy," with Samuel D. Warren, Jr. *Harvard Law Review* 4 (1890-1891): 193-220.
Scientific Management and the Railroads. New York: *Engineering Magazine*, 1911.
Women in Industry, assisted by Josephine Goldmark. New York: National Consumers' League, n.d.
The Words of Justice Brandeis, ed. Solomon Goldman. New York: Henry Schuman, 1953.

BRIEFS AND TESTIMONY BEFORE LEGISLATIVE BODIES

Brief on Behalf of Traffic Committee of Commercial Organizations of the Atlantic Seaboard. Interstate Commerce Commission. 61st Cong., 3d sess., 1911, S. Doc. 725, Vol. 8, Briefs of Counsel, Docket No. 3400.
Interstate Commerce Commission. *In the Matter of Proposed Advances in Freight Rates by Carriers.* 61st Cong., 3d sess., S. Doc. 725, January 3 and 11, 1911.
U.S. Congress. House. *Hearings before the Commission on Investigation of United States Steel Corp.* 62d Cong., 3d sess., 1912, H. Rep. 1137, pp. 2835-72.
U.S. Congress. Senate. *Financial Transactions of the New York and Hartford Railroad.* 63d Cong., 1914, 2d sess., S. Doc. 543.
————. *Hearings before Committee of Investigation of Interior Department and Bureau of Forestry.* 61st Cong., 3d sess., 1910-1911, S. Doc. 719, vols. 8 and 9.
————. Commission on Industrial Relations. S. Doc. 415, 64th Cong., 1st sess., 1914, Serial 6936, pp. 7657-81.

————. Committee on Interstate Commerce. *Hearings on Control of Corporations, Persons, and Firms Engaged in Interstate Commerce.* 62d Cong., 2d sess., 1911, vol. 1, pt. 16, pp. 1146–1291.

OTHER MAJOR SOURCES

Acheson, Dean. *Morning and Noon.* Boston: Houghton Mifflin, 1965.

Adelstein, Richard P. "Deciding for Bigness: Constitutional Choice and the Growth of Firms." *Constitutional Political Economy* 2 (1991): 7–30.

————. "'Islands of Conscious Power': Louis D. Brandeis and the Modern Corporation." *Business History Review* 63 (Autumn 1989): 614–56.

Baldwin, Roger. "Affirmation of Democracy." *Jewish Frontier* 3 (November 1936): 10.

Bickel, Alexander M., ed. *The Unpublished Opinions of Mr. Justice Brandeis.* Cambridge: Harvard University Press, 1957.

Blasi, Vincent. "The First Amendment and the Ideal of Civil Courage: The Brandeis Opinion in *Whitney v. California.*" *William and Mary Law Review* 29 (Summer 1988): 653–97.

Brandeis, Frederika Dembitz. *Reminiscences.* Privately printed, 1944.

Cover, Robert M. "The Left, the Right and the First Amendment: 1918–1928." *Maryland Law Review* 40 (1981): 349–79.

Dawson, Nelson Lloyd. *Louis D. Brandeis, Felix Frankfurter, and the New Deal.* Hamden, Conn.: Archon Books, 1980.

de Haas, Jacob. *Louis D. Brandeis: A Biographical Sketch.* New York: Bloch Publishing Company, 1929.

Dewey, John. *Characters and Events: Popular Essays in Social and Political Philosophy,* ed. Joseph Ratner. 2 vols. New York: Henry Holt and Company, 1929.

————. *The Ethics of Democracy.* Ann Arbor: Andrews and Company, 1888.

————. *How We Think, A Restatement of the Relation of Reflective Thinking to the Educative Process.* Boston: D. C. Heath and Company, 1933.

————. *The Influence of Darwin on Philosophy and Other Essays in Contemporary Thought.* New York: Henry Holt and Company, 1910.

————. *Psychology.* New York: Harper and Brothers, 1890.

————. *The Quest for Certainty: A Study of the Relation of Knowledge and Action.* New York: Minton, Balch, 1929.

————. *Reconstruction in Philosophy.* New York: Henry Holt and Company, 1920.

————. *Studies in Logical Theory.* Chicago: University of Chicago Press, 1903.

————, and J. A. McLellan. *Applied Psychology.* Boston: Educational Publishing Company, 1889.

————, and James H. Tufts. *Ethics*. New York: Henry Holt, 1910.

Erickson, Nancy S. "Muller v. Oregon Considered: The Origins of a Sex-Based Doctrine of Liberty of Contract." *Labor History* 30 (1989): 228–50.

Filene, Edward A. "Louis D. Brandeis As We Know Him." *Boston Post*, July 14, 1915.

Flexner, Bernard. *Mr. Justice Brandeis and the University of Louisville*. Louisville, Ky.: University of Louisville Press, 1938.

Frankfurter, Felix, ed. *Mr. Justice Brandeis*. New Haven, Conn.: Yale University Press, 1932.

————, assisted by Josephine Goldmark. *The Case for the Shorter Work Day*. New York: National Consumers' League, 1915.

Freund, Paul A. "Justice Brandeis: A Law Clerk's Remembrance." *American Jewish History* 68 (1978): 7–18.

————. "Mr. Justice Brandeis." *Harvard Law Review* 55 (1941): 195–96.

————. "Mr. Justice Brandeis: A Centennial Memoir." *Harvard Law Review* 70 (1957): 769–92.

Gal, Allon. *Brandeis of Boston*. Cambridge: Harvard University Press, 1980.

Goldmark, Josephine. *Fatigue and Efficiency*. New York: Russell Sage Foundation, 1912.

————. *Impatient Crusader: Florence Kelley's Life Story*. Urbana: University of Illinois Press, 1953.

————. *Pilgrims of '48*. New Haven, Conn.: Yale University Press, 1930.

Graber, Mark A. *Transforming Free Speech: The Ambiguous Legacy of Civil Libertarianism*. Berkeley: University of California Press, 1991.

Gunther, Gerald. "Learned Hand and the Origins of Modern First Amendment Doctrine: Some Fragments of History." *Stanford Law Review* 27 (1975): 719–73.

Haber, Samuel. *Efficiency and Uplift: Scientific Management in the Progressive Era 1890–1920*. Chicago: University of Chicago Press, 1964.

Hamilton, Walton N. "The Jurist's Art." *Columbia Law Review* 33 (1931): 1073–93.

Hapgood, Norman. *The Changing Years*. New York: Farrar and Rinehart, 1930.

Holmes, Oliver Wendell. *Collected Legal Papers*. 1921. Reprint. New York: Peter Smith, 1952.

————. *The Common Law*. Boston: Little, Brown, 1881.

Horwitz, Morton J. *The Transformation of American Law, 1780–1860*. Cambridge: Harvard University Press, 1977.

Kallen, Horace. *The Faith of Louis D. Brandeis, Zionist*. New York: Hadassah, n.d.

Konefsky, Samuel J. *The Legacy of Holmes and Brandeis.* New York: Macmillan, 1956.

Kraines, Oscar. "Brandeis' Philosophy of Scientific Management." *Western Political Quarterly* 13 (March 1960): 191–201.

La Dame, Mary. *The Filene Store: A Study of Employees' Relation to Management in a Retail Store.* New York: Russell Sage Foundation, 1930.

Lehav, Pnina. "Holmes and Brandeis: Libertarian and Republican Justifications for Free Speech." *Journal of Law and Politics* 4 (1988): 451–82.

Landis, James. "Mr. Justice Brandeis and the Harvard Law School." *Harvard Law Review* 55 (1941): 184–90.

Levy, David W. "The Lawyer as Judge: Brandeis's View of the Legal Profession." *Oklahoma Law Review* 22 (1969): 374–95.

Lief, Alfred. *Brandeis: The Personal History of an American Ideal.* New York: Stackpole, 1936.

Locke, John. *Second Treatise of Government,* ed. C. B. Macpherson. Indianapolis, Ind.: Hacket Publishing Company, 1980.

McClennen, Edward F. "Louis D. Brandeis as a Lawyer." *Massachusetts Law Quarterly* 33 (1948): 1–28.

McCraw, Thomas K. *Prophets of Regulation.* Cambridge: Harvard University Press, 1984.

Mason, Alpheus T. *Brandeis: A Free Man's Life.* New York: Viking, 1946.

———. *Brandeis. Lawyer and Judge in the Modern State.* Princeton, N.J.: Princeton University Press, 1938.

———. *The Brandeis Way.* Princeton, N.J.: Princeton University Press, 1938.

———. *Bureaucracy Convicts Itself: The Ballinger-Pinchot Controversy of 1910.* New York: Viking Press, 1941.

———, and Henry Lee Staples. *The Fall of a Railroad Empire: Brandeis and the New Haven Merger Battle.* Syracuse, N.Y.: Syracuse University Press, 1947.

Mill, John Stuart. *Considerations on Representative Government.* New York: Liberal Arts Press, 1958.

———. *On Liberty,* ed. Alburey Castell. Arlington Heights, Ill.: Harlan Davidson, 1947.

———. *Principles of Political Economy,* ed. W. J. Ashley. London: Longmans, Green, 1909.

New Palestine 32 (November 14, 1941), entire issue.

Shapiro, Yonathan. *Leadership of the American Zionist Organization, 1897–1930.* Urbana: University of Illinois Press, 1971.

Staples, Henry Lee, and Alpheus T. Mason. *The Fall of a Railroad Empire.* Syracuse, N.Y.: Syracuse University Press, 1947.

Strum, Philippa. *Louis D. Brandeis: Justice for the People.* 1984. Reprint. New York: Schocken, 1988.

Todd, Alden L. *Justice on Trial.* New York: McGraw Hill, 1964.

Urofsky, Melvin I. *American Zionism from Herzl to the Holocaust.* Garden City, N.Y.: Doubleday, 1975.

————. *A Mind of One Piece: Brandeis and American Reform.* New York: Scribner, 1971.

————, and David W. Levy, eds. *"Half Brother, Half Son": The Letters of Louis D. Brandeis to Felix Frankfurter.* Norman: University of Oklahoma Press, 1991.

————, and David W. Levy, eds. *Letters of Louis D. Brandeis.* 5 vols. Albany: State University of New York Press, 1971–1978.

Zimmern, Alfred. *The Greek Commonwealth.* 1912. Reprint. Oxford: Clarendon Press, 1931.

CASES CITED

Abrams v. *United States*, 250 U.S. 616 (1919).

Adair v. *United States*, 208 U.S. 161 (1908).

Adams v. *Tanner*, 244 U.S. 590, 597 (1917).

Adamson v. *California*, 332 U.S. 46 (1947).

Adkins v. *Children's Hospital*, 261 U.S. 525 (1923).

Allgeyer v. *Louisiana*, 165 U.S. 578 (1897).

American Academy of Pediatrics v. *Van De Kamp*, 214 Cal. App. 3d 831 (Ct. App. 1989).

Argersinger v. *Hamlin*, 407 U.S. 25 (1972).

Ashwander v. *T.V.A*, 297 U.S. 288 (1936).

Atherton Mills v. *Johnston*, 295 U.S. 13 (1922).

Bailey v. *Drexel Furniture Co.*, 259 U.S. 20 (1922).

Baker v. *Carr*, 364 U.S. 186 (1962).

Bartels v. *Iowa*, 262 U.S. 404 (1923).

Bedford Cut Stone v. *Journeyman Cutter's Association*, 274 U.S. 37 (1927).

Black & White Taxi Co. v. *Brown & Yellow Taxi Co.*, 276 U.S. 518 (1928).

Brandenburg v. *Ohio*, 395 U.S. 444 (1969).

Buchanan v. *Warley*, 245 U.S. 60 (1917).

Bullock v. *Florida*, 254 U.S. 513 (1921).

Bunting v. *Oregon*, 243 U.S. 426 (1917).

Burdeau v. *McDowell*, 256 U.S. 465 (1921).

Cantwell v. *Connecticut*, 310 U.S. 296 (1940).

Carter v. *Carter Coal Co.*, 298 U.S. 238 (1936).

Casey v. *United States*, 276 U.S. 413 (1928).

Cohens v. *Virginia*, 19 U.S. (6 Wheat.) 264 (1821).

Colegrove v. *Green*, 328 U.S. 549 (1946).

Commonwealth v. *Davis*, 162 Mass. 510 (1895).

Coppage v. *Kansas*, 236 U.S. 1 (1915).

Corrigan v. *Buckley*, 271 U.S. 323 (1926).

Cruzan v. *Director*, 497 U.S. 261 (1990).

Debs v. *United States*, 249 U.S. 211 (1919).

DeJonge v. *Oregon*, 299 U.S. 353 (1937).

Dennis v. *United States*, 341 U.S. 494 (1951).

Di Santo v. *Pennsylvania*, 273 U.S. 34 (1927).

Duplex Printing Co. v. *Deering*, 254 U.S. 443 (1921).

Employment Division v. *Smith*, 494 U.S. 872 (1990).

Erie Railroad v. *Tompkins*, 340 U.S. 64 (1938).

Farmers' Loan & Trust v. *Northern Pacific Railroad*, 60 Fed. 803 (1894).

Fox v. *Washington*, 236 U.S. 273 (1915).

Frohwerk v. *United States*, 249 U.S. 204 (1919).

Frontiero v. *Richardson*, 411 U.S. 677 (1973).

Frost v. *Corporations Comm.*, 278 U.S. 515 (1929).

Gideon v. *Wainwright*, 372 U.S. 335 (1963).

Gilbert v. *Minnesota*, 254 U.S. 325 (1920).

Gitlow v. *New York*, 268 U.S. 652 (1925).

Goldman v. *Weinberger*, 475 U.S. 503 (1986).

Gong Lum v. *Rice*, 275 U.S. 278 (1927).

Griswold v. *Connecticut*, 381 U.S. 479 (1965).

Grovey v. *Townsend*, 295 U.S. 45 (1936).

Hale v. *Kentucky*, 303 U.S. 613 (1938).

Hammer v. *Dagenhart*, 247 U.S. 251 (1918).

Hitchman Coal and Coke Co. v. *Mitchell*, 245 U.S. 229 (1917).

Holden v. *Hardy*, 169 U.S. 366 (1898).

Hollins v. *Oklahoma*, 295 U.S. 394 (1935).

Immigration and Naturalization Service v. *Elias Zacharias* (no. 90–1342, January 22, 1992).

In re President of Georgetown College, 331 F.2d 1000 (D.C. Cir. 1964).

In re T. W., 551 So. 2d 1186 (1989).

Jay Burns Baking Co. v. *Bryan*, 264 U.S. 504 (1924).

Katz v. *United States*, 389 U.S. 347 (1967).

Liggett v. *Baldridge*, 271 U.S. 105 (1928).

Liggett v. *Lee*, 288 U.S. 517 (1933).

Lochner v. *New York*, 198 U.S. 45 (1905).

Louisville v. *Radford*, 295 U.S. 555 (1935).

McCulloch v. *Maryland*, 17 U.S. (4 Wheat.) 316 (1819).

Mapp v. *Ohio*, 367 U.S. 643 (1961).

Meyer v. *Nebraska*, 262 U.S. 390 (1923).

Milwaukee Publishing Co. v. *Burleson*, 255 U.S. 407 (1921).

Missouri ex rel. Gaines v. *Canada*, 305 U.S. 337 (1938).

Moore v. *Dempsey*, 261 U.S. 86 (1923).

Morehead v. *New York ex rel. Tipaldo*, 298 U.S. 587 (1936).

Muller v. *Oregon*, 208 U.S. 412 (1908).

Myers v. *United States*, 272 U.S. 52 (1926).

NAACP v. *Alabama*, 357 U.S. 449 (1958).

National Surety Co. v. *Corielli*, 289 U.S. 426 (1933).

Near v. *Minnesota*, 283 U.S. 697 (1931).

New Negro Alliance v. *Grocery Co.*, 303 U.S. 552 (1938).

New State Ice Co. v. *Liebmann*, 285 U.S. 262 (1932).

Nixon v. *Condon*, 286 U.S. 73 (1932).

Nixon v. *Herndon*, 274 U.S. 536 (1927).

Norris v. *Alabama*, 294 U.S. 587 (1924).

Olmstead v. *United States*, 277 U.S. 438 (1928).

On Lee v. *United States*, 343 U.S. 747 (1952).

Panama Refining Co. v. *Ryan*, 293 U.S. 388 (1935).

Patterson v. *Colorado*, 205 U.S. 454 (1907).

Pennsylvania Coal Co. v. *Mahon*, 260 U.S. 393 (1922).

People v. *Williams*, 189 N.Y. 131 (1907).

Pierce v. *United States*, 252 U.S. 239 (1920).

Plessy v. *Ferguson*, 163 U.S. 537 (1896).

Powell v. *Alabama*, 287 U.S. 45 (1932).

Powell v. *Pennsylvania*, 127 U.S. 678 (1888).

Quaker City Cab Co. v. *Pennsylvania*, 277 U.S. 289 (1928).

Railroad Retirement Board v. *Alton R.R. Co.*, 295 U.S. 330 (1935).

Rathbun v. *United States*, 295 U.S. 602 (1935).

Reed v. *Reed*, 404 U.S. 71 (1971).

Reynolds v. *United States*, 98 U.S. 145 (1879).

Ritchie v. *People*, 155 Ill. 98 (1895).

Ritchie v. *Wyman*, 244 Ill. 509 (1910).

Roe v. *Wade*, 410 U.S. 113 (1973).

Ruthenberg v. *Michigan*, 273 U.S. 782 (1927).

St. Louis & O'Fallon Railway v. *United States*, 279 U.S. 461 (1929).

Santa Clara County v. *Southern Pacific Railroad Co.*, 118 U.S. 394 (1886).

Schaefer v. *United States*, 251 U.S. 466 (1920).

Schechter v. *U.S.*, 295 U.S. 495 (1935).

Schenck v. *United States*, 249 U.S. 47 (1919).

South Covington v. *Kentucky*, 252 U.S. 399 (1920).

Southwestern Bell Telephone Co. v. *Public Service Commission*, 262 U.S. 276 (1923).

Stall v. *Florida*, 470 S. 2d 257 (1990).

INDEX